DAMN YANKEES!

Walter Lynwood Fleming Lectures in Southern History
Louisiana State University

GEORGE C. RABLE

DAMN YANKEES!

DEMONIZATION & DEFIANCE IN THE CONFEDERATE SOUTH

Louisiana State University Press Baton Rouge

Published by Louisiana State University Press

Manufactured in the United States of America
First printing

Designer: Barbara Neely Bourgoyne
Typeface: Quadraat
Printer and binder: Maple Press

Library of Congress Cataloging-in-Publication Data are available at the Library of Congress.

ISBN 978-0-8071-6058-9 (cloth: alk. paper) — ISBN 978-0-8071-6059-6 (pdf) —
ISBN 978-0-8071-6060-2 (epub) — ISBN 978-0-8071-6061-9 (mobi)

The paper in this book meets the guidelines for permanence
and durability of the Committee on Production Guidelines for
Book Longevity of the Council on Library Resources. ♾

To William J. Cooper, Jr.,
Scholar, teacher, mentor, friend

Contents

DAMN YANKEES!

INTRODUCTION

We must ~~not~~ be enemies

"We are enemies as much as if we were hostile states," the Georgian informed his Senate colleagues. Lame-duck president James Buchanan's last annual message had been received by Congress the day before; in a little over two weeks, the state of South Carolina would leave the Union. Alfred Iverson Sr. had held a variety of state and federal offices for over three decades, had just celebrated his sixty-second birthday, and in less than two months would withdraw from the Senate. Far from being a leading political light, he delivered a speech that in most respects was hardly notable. He meandered back and forth between discussing Buchanan's message, defending secession, and prophesying the future, yet Iverson spoke what some would have acknowledged to be painful truths. "Disguise the fact as you will," he pointedly remarked, "there is an enmity between the northern and southern people that is deep and enduring and you never can eradicate it." Iverson talked of "revolution" and even "war" but more importantly of hatred: "I believe that northern people hate the South worse than ever the English people hated France; and . . . there is no love lost upon the part of the South."[1] There was surely a good deal of hyperbole in these remarks, and it is doubtful that most northerners and southerners despised each other quite in the ways Iverson described. At least not yet.

In a way, his remarks were premature even as the sectional crisis of the 1850s approached an apparent climax. States were preparing to secede, but whether disunion meant war was by no means clear to many Americans. Nor was the growing sectional enmity irreversible. Addressing his "fellow countrymen," Abraham Lincoln in his inaugural address would famously plead: "We are not enemies, but friends. We must not be enemies."[2] Of course it would take the new president some time to realize the extent and depth of disunion sentiment in the seceding states. He would never quite learn to speak the language of hatred, yet war itself requires no little hatred. There must be enemies, and those enemies must be defined, denounced, and defeated. This process in turn influences a war's policies and conduct; it helps determine the duration of the contest; and it most assuredly helps shape the conflict's termination and subsequent settlement.

Whatever the psychological complexities of hatred, whether directed at groups or individuals, loathing, disgust, and revulsion all enter into play. Blind rage may take over. Wartime propaganda typically portrays "the enemy" as somehow outside the bounds of civilization or even humanity. At the same time, real and imagined enemies converge into powerful images.[3] If they have not already done so in the period leading up to war, soldiers and civilians learn to despise the enemy so that they can hope for, long for, pray for, and bring about his defeat (and perhaps destruction).

Subtlety and ambiguity vanish. The enemy embodies evil at least for the purpose of ginning up and maintaining a war fever, and raw emotion readily supplants cool reason.[4] The lines between good and bad, between legitimate and illegitimate, become ever sharper, especially as a war drags on. This is true even though in their origins, course, and culmination, ideas about the enemy are shifting and evolving, though seldom nuanced. "When our own nation is at war with any other, we detest them under the character of cruel, perfidious, unjust and violent," wrote the philosopher David Hume. "But [we] always esteem ourselves and allies equitable, moderate, and merciful."[5] Whether or not enemies are deemed subhuman, emotional distance between our side and theirs is essential. Demonizing a group is ironically much easier than singling out individuals. Better the homogenous mass than the particular person; better to generalize than to specify.[6] After reading Confederate letters found following the evacuation of Fort Henry in Tennessee, a *New York Times* correspondent well described such thinking: "The magnitude of their [Confederates'] love [for their families] is only equaled by one single thing, and that is their contempt—yea, their utter loathing—for the Yankees. In these letters the Northerners are all Yankees; they are nasty Yankees; they are dirty Yankees; cowardly Yankees; infernal Yankees; d——d Yankees—in short, every kind of Yankees that the dictionary of abuse, and Billingsgate affords a cognomen for."[7]

Yet defining the enemy entails more than passion and hatred; it involves the brain as well as the viscera. We often speak of a "war of words," but we might just as easily consider the "words of war." Language matters because descriptions of the enemy carry serious and sometimes deadly consequences for all concerned. In wars generally, and especially in civil wars, the words deployed against the other side help cement or establish national identity.[8] By the nineteenth century, the word *propaganda* in its modern senses had not yet come into widespread use, but the art was clearly being practiced. With some exaggeration but much truth, George Orwell observed that "one of the most horrible features of war is that all war propaganda, all the screaming and lies and hatred, comes inevitably from people who are not fighting."[9] He no doubt had editors, correspondents, and politicians in mind. Speeches and official messages are important, but on a weekly or daily basis, newspapers presented the narrative, the incidents, and most importantly the words that struck a chord, that shaped opinion, and that ultimately fostered hatred and resistance. But what Orwell's point misses is that soldiers too—and this is certainly true of Civil War soldiers regardless of rank—expressed strikingly similar views of the enemy. Appeals to fear along with broad-brush attacks against the foe stirred the passions and buttressed morale.[10]

Epithets—whether nouns or adjectives—became the weapons in this verbal war. "The truthful historian," one North Carolina editor claimed in the summer of 1861, "will write down the Yankee Nation, as ineffable asses and miserable cowards, thoroughbred brutes and blackguards." Not to be outdone, a Little Rock, Arkansas, newspaper excoriated Jim Lane's Kansas Jayhawkers as "hell hounds of Puritanic nigger worshippers." This style dictated piling word upon word, insult upon insult. Three years into the war, the *Richmond Dispatch* railed against "Yankeedom," this "vast assemblage of pimps, prostitutes, gamblers, infidels, and sharpers." Whether the words actually applied was largely beside the point. Northerners seemed capable of any crime, and any respectable Confederate could reel off a long list of their offenses with ease.[11]

Northerners and southerners had become distinct and separate peoples, or at least such claims had been bruited about for several decades before the war began. Sectional extremists had exaggerated sectional differences, and the war in turn put a premium on creating an ever wider chasm. "The Northern and Southern people are entirely different," Georgian Gertrude Thomas remarked. "They are moraly and socialy as well as politicaly the antipodes of each other. This war makes the line of demarcation broader." Emphasizing a North-South divide—regardless of shared characteristics and historical heritage—became critical for sustaining a war that was increasingly described as two civilizations locked in mortal combat.[12] By their very nature, civil wars arouse especially intense hostility. The violence becomes less impersonal in struggles between people who in fact have much in common, and the results can be bloodier and longer lasting, with bitter enmity continuing to shape the postwar world. "We separated because of incompatibility of temper," Mary Boykin Chesnut wrote in the expanded version of her wartime diary. "We are divorced, North and South, because we hated each other so."[13]

For their part, the Yankees certainly excoriated and often hated the Rebels. Attacks on the southern character and reports of atrocities became commonplace in the northern press. Yet somehow they never grew quite as intense as Confederate attempts to define and vilify their enemies. And although a comparative study of Union and Confederate demonization would be valuable, the approach here will be admittedly one-sided. Nor will this study pay much attention to internal divisions among Confederates or the supposed strengths and weaknesses of Confederate nationalism. This is not to say that the question of nationalism is irrelevant. After all, the often quoted and variously attributed definition of a nation as "a group of people united by a mistaken view about the past and a hatred of their neighbors" certainly applies to the Confederacy.[14] Nationalism feeds on not only shared values but shared enmities. Therefore the focus here will be largely on what might be termed a standard or orthodox denunciation of the Yankee enemy, based on broad themes found in the newspapers, speeches, and private musings of committed Confederates.[15]

What is most striking is how pervasive the anti-Yankee invective became—regardless of age, wealth, geography, or even ethnicity. Writing from Quitman, Texas, shortly after the surrender of Vicksburg, W. J. Deupree, a surgeon in General Stand Watie's Cherokee regiment, conjured up stock images of what was likely to follow: "Woes, arrests, wretchedness & misery of every hue. Rapes, Rapine by the Feds & our negroes & every insult & disgrace that ever was offered a people we will have to bear. . . . All the horrors of negro insurrection, murder & every crime that ever was perpetrated on earth will soon be the fate of the Lone Star State."[16] Such views (often stated in remarkably similar language) were expressed across the Confederacy and throughout the war. Not only did politicians, preachers, and editors help create and spread frightful images of the foe, but soldiers and civilians alike—privately and publicly—echoed these sentiments.

This study draws on the comments of nearly two hundred soldiers. Inevitably given the nature of the surviving literary evidence, there are over- and under-represented groups.[17] The only way to deal with this problem is to cast a wide net. Readers will find a number of famous generals quoted but also a good mix of obscure privates and many company-grade officers.[18] Some of these men enlisted early in the war, some later. Their backgrounds ranged from extremely privileged to quite humble. A goodly number came from slaveholding families, though as historian Joseph Glatthaar has shown, sheer percentages underestimate Confederate soldiers' commitment to defending the peculiar institution.[19]

But rather than simply examining soldier opinion, *Damn Yankees!* devotes considerable attention to civilians, everyone from politicians, preachers, and polemicists to women living on farms and plantations. Confederate president Jefferson Davis, various governors, and other political leaders naturally had their say, and anti-Yankee polemics became an important element of wartime propaganda. In addition to more than two dozen political figures, a dozen or so leading ministers, and similar numbers of essayists and intellectuals, I have culled material from nearly 140 other civilians. Many of these are women from planter families, though also included are wives and daughters of professionals and small slaveholders.

Even a cursory glance at the notes will reveal the central role of newspapers in the rhetorical war against the Yankees. Comments on the enemy appeared frequently not only in editorials and letters to the editor but in news articles and even small pieces on unrelated subjects. I have consulted sixty-four newspapers and nearly a dozen periodicals. For business reasons if for no other, editors had to be sensitive to opinion in their communities, and abundant evidence from soldiers and civilians alike showed that the appetite for newspapers remained strong despite paper shortages and circulation problems. Taken altogether, these disparate sources reveal much about how Yankees were defined, defamed, and decried.

In the course of the war, Confederates developed various critiques of their northern enemies that strained not only credulity but the limits of language itself. Their zeal knew few bounds. This vituperation flourished and survived regardless of what was happening on the battlefield, its staying power as remarkable as its hyperbole. Yankee demons haunted Confederate imaginations, compounding and intensifying the real suffering and damage caused by flesh-and-blood Yankees. Ironically, the overheated rhetoric itself undoubtedly lengthened the war (and southern suffering) by making so many Confederates so reluctant to give up the fight or indeed make any concessions to their seemingly barbarous foes.

Verbal onslaughts served to dehumanize the enemy. As philosopher David Livingstone Smith has written, describing other human beings as less than human "acts as a psychological lubricant, dissolving our inhibitions and inflaming our destructive passions."[20] The process had actually begun before the war as southern intellectuals, politicians, and editors had created powerful and all-purpose images of the "Yankee." A search for the essence of the northern character had produced a literature long on argument and bombast. A vivid picture of a money-grubbing, puritanical, fanatical, and infidel people emerged, and in some discussions, the Yankees almost seemed to be a separate race. How much such ideas influenced the mass of southerners is hard to say, but the notion of a distinctive Yankee character carried weight in the polemical battles of the antebellum era. During the war, this all laid the groundwork for demonstrating how Yankee characteristics manifested themselves in Yankee behavior. Whether it was cowardice, vulgarity, or general depravity, the northerners repeatedly proved to be unworthy foes. Mercenary, low-class, and evil-looking, black-hearted Yankees reportedly filled the northern ranks, though many editorialists (and some soldiers) claimed that the Federals had largely to rely on foreign-born men driven into battle by alcohol and bounties.

Not surprisingly, such fiends would be destructive, thieving, and cold-hearted. Bluecoats polluted southern soil by their very presence, invading the privacy of southern homes, treating soldier and civilian with equal contempt and cruelty. They were barbarous and destructive, Goths and Vandals, inhuman brutes reveling in murder and rape. They were abolition fanatics determined to strike at the very heart of the southern social order through emancipation and miscegenation. Along with their African American allies (or "deluded" slaves as Confederate might have said), the Yankees appeared hell-bent on exterminating southern white people. Therefore hatred and revenge became the inevitable and appropriate Confederate response. After all, subjugation—with its attendant horrors vividly described by politicians and propagandists and parroted by soldiers and civilians—was simply unthinkable. In the end, this demonization of the Yankee enemy in all its variety and contradictions undoubtedly lengthened the war, shaped the course of Reconstruction, and left an enduring legacy.

CHAPTER 1

The Universal Yankee Nation

"As a driving, penetrating, indefatigable, business people, the Americans have a name literally all over the world; they are emphatically the 'universal Yankee nation.'" Thus in an 1838 essay on steam navigation, London's *Quarterly Review* had attempted to sum up "brother Jonathan's" national character.[1] By this time the phrase "universal Yankee nation" had become a commonplace in European commentary on American affairs. It evoked a certain admiration but also sly criticism, and in the United States, the phrase became something of a badge of honor. In the southern states by the 1840s, however, the words carried a distinct note of sarcasm or even a growing sense that the "so-called universal Yankee nation" had become a disgrace to civilization. By the beginning of the Civil War, newspaper editors used the phrase to encapsulate northerners' mercenary qualities, to excoriate men who worshiped profit and served the Devil. These prototypical Yankees paid little heed to God or man. They excelled in lying, wallowed in corruption; only their cruelty exceeded their cowardice.[2] Such powerful images (often conveyed by overblown rhetoric) surely laid the groundwork for a war carried on at ever-mounting cost and with ever greater cruelty. Demonization of the foe by both sides partook of self-fulfilling prophecy and became self-reinforcing, as each action of the enemy lent itself to the darkest of interpretations.

"Yankee," a word of uncertain origin at first applied to New Englanders, had come to include northerners in general. Early on it had signified not only money-grubbing and sharp practice but also a rustic crudity. Even during the American Revolution, one Confederate writer maintained, these Yankees had cared more for profits than principles. Such hypocrites had been heavily involved in the African slave trade, but their descendants had become bigoted, superstitious, and intolerant abolitionists. And ironically, those northerners who had migrated south had turned into the cruelest of slave masters.[3] To present the enemy as both unprincipled and fanatical at the same time showed little regard for consistency, but that was not the purpose here, and ultimately Confederates could choose which qualities of their opponents to emphasize and when to emphasize them.

Southerners often viewed Yankees as rootless vagabonds in both an intellectual and geographical sense, men with little respect for tradition or place. Ironically some northerners would have agreed that theirs was a society in constant flux, lacking a firm political, moral, or religious foundation.[4] Picking up on this theme, southern intellectuals sought to build a case for their region's distinctive virtues and even lay the groundwork for a southern nation.[5] By the 1840s, writers such as William Gilmore Simms and Nathaniel Beverley Tucker sharply criticized northern manners and mores. They resented outsiders' condescension and contempt toward the South even as they trumpeted a southern literary nationalism. Their dreams of a South shorn of Yankee influence, the growing partisanship of southern periodicals, and a touchy defensiveness in an era of bitter sectional politics all helped create staple images of a defective "Yankee" civilization. Of course, the most privileged southerners had attended Yankee schools, and the reading public had eagerly consumed Yankee periodicals. At home, some had been taught by Yankee teachers. Others had vacationed at Yankee watering holes. When it came to Yankees, the best-educated and most widely traveled southerners claimed a broad expertise.[6]

Whether their critiques of northern civilization had actually penetrated the consciousness of the typical southerner is difficult to say. After all, many southern writers felt unappreciated by their own people and sadly lamented their marginal influence, not to mention their fellow citizens' lack of enthusiasm for cultural autonomy and disunion. Yet the intellectuals' sense of victimhood had a much wider application. In their diatribes against northern culture, writers portrayed Yankees as would-be oppressors, and southerners as the persecuted. If not exactly nationalism, the idea of southerners as an embattled people about to be overwhelmed by a northern majority fueled calls for intellectual and eventually political independence.[7] The notion of southerners as a badly outnumbered minority—with a sprinkling of references to the beleaguered patriots of the American Revolution—would also become a staple of Confederate propaganda and its unremitting appeals to fight on regardless of the odds.

The archetypal "Yankee" in turn became the perfect villain in this narrative of cultural conflict and nascent tyranny. "It is the only name or word in the English, or any other language, living or dead, that can be applied with scope and force," wrote one Confederate chaplain. It is doubtful whether many southerners thought much about John C. Calhoun, numerical majorities, the concurrent voice, or other such political underpinnings of the philosophical case against the Yankees, but Chaplain Nicholas Davis knew how to tell a vivid story, such as the undoubtedly apocryphal tale of the Yankee "clock peddler who stole the land-lady's counterpane off her own bed, and then sold it to her." With no fear of exaggeration, he noted how the word "Yankee" applied to "their every act of lying and stealing from the days of Washington till the present hour, in all their political, legislative, executive, commercial, civil, moral, literary, sacred, profane, theological, and diabolical history." And just to make sure readers grasped the point, he recited a long list of adjectives capturing the northern character in all its infamy: "meddlesome, impudent, insolent, pompous, boastful, unkind, ungrateful, unjust, knavish, false, deceitful, cowardly, swindling, thieving, robbing, brutal and murderous."[8]

With considerably more economy of words, a Baptist newspaper predicted that the war would "give to the pages of history another word, expressive of a still deeper dye of depravity than Europe ever dreamed of. It is Yankeeism."[9] To plumb the depth of such wickedness became the task of politicians and propagandists, but initially at least the groundwork had been laid by antebellum descriptions of northern character. Some high-minded critiques traced the American sectional conflict back to the earlier English contest between a Saxon North and a Norman South, though the later clash between Puritans and Roundheads during the English Civil War received much closer attention.[10] A straight line of descent presumably ran between those hypocritical knaves who had put Charles I's head on the chopping block and those vile miscreants who would invade the Confederacy. "Our enemies are a traditionless, rootless race," Confederate president Jefferson Davis asserted. "From the time of Cromwell to the present moment they have been disturbers of the peace." As Davis and other Confederate leaders pointed out, the story had been the same in England, Holland, and the United States. "History is only repeating itself in this country," a Richmond editor added. "The brutal, cruel, greedy, licentious, hypocritical and sacrilegious Roundheads are alive against their descendants." A Texas woman even cast Abraham Lincoln as a latter-day Oliver Cromwell.[11]

All this seemed historically straightforward (and strained), but some commentators added a racial element to the mix. "The Yankee is the same now that he was at the time of Cromwell," remarked a Virginian who was visiting Louisiana early in the war. "It is the same now that it was more than two hundred years ago—the Saxon against the Norman, the Puritan & Cavalier, and this time Mason & Dixons line divides two Races as different as the Irish & the English, the Gaul & the German." Labeling the Yankees a separate race in a most race-conscious society made sectional differences both wider and irreconcilable. There was no more convenient wedge to make northerners and southerners appear to be separate and mutually hostile peoples. Whatever the complexities of colonial settlement, describing northerners as somehow racially distinctive made their supposedly fanatical and despotic character stand out. Proslavery ideologue George Fitzhugh added Huguenots and Jacobites to the southern mix and even declared the Puritans a "slave race." According to an Arkansas Confederate, "We have no affinity with the slimy, hypocritical, bigoted fanatical race that landed at Plymouth Rock."[12] Would the war against the Yankee literally become a "race war"? That frightening phrase had long been a staple of proslavery polemics, and predictions of such a conflagration would appear throughout the war and well beyond.

However that might be, some would add that the war also marked a continuation of the battles between Roundhead and Cavalier, but the conflict was often portrayed much more broadly. Polemicists kept pressing home the point that northerners and southerners had little or nothing in common. They might speak the same language, but their ways of life and values were antithetical, and as this emphasis on fundamental cultural differences developed, the contrast had to be nearly absolute. Ruddy-complected southerners enjoyed the outdoor life of an agricultural people while pale, shriveled Yankees huddled together in cities.[13]

Once this idea of the Yankees as an ignoble race developed, Confederate writers poured forth endless streams of abuse. Northerners were loathsome, detestable people, "the vilest race on the face of earth," claimed one editor. The war itself might be the proverbial blessing in disguise because it filled "every Southern bosom" with "loathing for this abominable race." Was bigotry, vulgarity, spite, envy, or cowardice the Yankees' besetting sin? It was hard to choose among so many. Running through a list of "peoples," George Fitzhugh could not find a single one that came close to matching the Yankees for rapacity and cruelty.[14] How important this racial component was for boosting Confederate morale is impossible to say, but clearly the idea of the enemy as an inferior race with traits that would ultimately cause their downfall surely made soldier and civilian alike more confident.[15]

These assumptions made it easy to dismiss any northern newspaper account—especially of a Confederate defeat—as a tissue of falsehoods. After all, everyone knew that the Yankees were inveterate liars. "It has undoubtedly become generally true of the Yankee race, that with the exception of the Chinese, they have the least reverence for truth of any people on the face of the earth," claimed one editor. Pointing this out, however, failed to fully capture the nature of a people whose religion, morals, commerce, and indeed entire view of life had become hopelessly corrupt, a remarkable deterioration that had turned the Yankees into a degenerate race.[16] And even those broad-brush attacks hardly went far enough for the harshest critics, who maintained that the Yankees simply lacked humanity. One Confederate soldier compared them to "ferocious monkeys," and the significance of such a statement was ominous.[17] In a long disquisition on northern (more specifically "Puritan") character that appeared only a short time after the firing on Sumter, an editor presented the looming conflict as a "war of passions between hating and hated races. It is a war of fanaticism and subjugation on the part of the North; of scorn and contemptuous hatred on the part of the South."[18] Comparing the Yankees to animals and harping on their "racial" characteristics appeared tailor-made to fire southern hearts and minds. Such appeals prepared Confederates to face an unworthy foe and undoubtedly bred a certain swagger.

Claims for southern superiority logically followed denunciations of northern inferiority. Aside from the usual hyperbole and defensiveness, some writers again harkened back to English history, notably to the Cavaliers. Heirs of a fine tradition, southerners were simply a superior race of gentlemen, especially when compared to the northern abolitionists, "sprung from the scum of England, of Scotland and of Ireland, bred in bigotry and intolerance." These last two qualities of course appeared in abundance in much of the anti-Yankee literature, some of it set at a high intellectual pitch but most of it containing a mix of inflammatory words and *ad hominem* arguments. Part of the appeal was clearly antidemocratic and in some ways aristocratic, but more often the emphasis was on southerners' superior spirit, courage, and military prowess.[19]

Once Confederates started railing against Yankee atrocities (a process that began before the Yankees had actually committed any atrocities), the contrast between what a Virginia woman termed the "peculiar dispositions" on each side grew ever sharper: "how poorly does the thieving, burning, murdering Yankee compare with the generous, chivalrous Southerner." Soldiers and civilians alike referred to an "ignoble" enemy and lauded their fellow citizens as a "noble race." Summing up this way of thinking and going one step further, Mississippian Kate Foster boasted: "The meanest of our men are ten times better and more a gentleman than the best of the Yankees."[20]

Overtones of millennialism—a facet of the wartime defense of slavery—entered into this discussion. Besides excoriating the enemy, thoughtful Confederates talked of a special destiny for their people, though even the intellectuals did not fully develop this idea. That southerners would in the end prove to be a superior "race" almost went without saying. Adopting a gentler tone, Mississippi physician William Henry Holcombe argued that the Yankee and Confederate "each has a separate mission to fill and glorious destiny to accomplish."[21]

Race and history became hopelessly entangled, but even for staunch Confederates, the Cavalier myth proved hard to swallow. Details kept getting in the way of the sweeping and simplified accounts that filled articles and essays. William A. Hall could not decide whether "ignorance or passion" best explained the apparently widespread belief that the Puritan vs. Cavalier conflict continued during the present war. He doubted there had ever been any great number of Cavaliers on the American continent, and such dubious history hardly advanced the Confederate cause.[22] Admittedly much of this discussion appeared either in literary magazines or long newspaper editorials that may have been of limited interest or influence. Contradictions and complications may also have lessened the effects of a seemingly stark contrast between northern Puritan and southern Cavalier.

In point of fact, the "Cavalier" element was always secondary, and whatever the limits of its popular appeal, denunciations of Yankee Puritans were far more ubiquitous. The largest-circulation newspaper in Richmond, the *Daily Dispatch*, carried at least 225 references to Puritanism during the war, printed several long editorials on the question, and led the way in emphasizing the Puritan origins of Yankeeism. The story did not exactly begin at Plymouth Rock (the Pilgrims were sometimes absolved of carrying the germ of discord and conflict), but it was clear that the early Puritan settlers could not live at peace with anyone—whether Indian or European. Bickering, division, and treachery began with the first migration of long-faced hypocrites determined to crush out liberty of conscience. Such blanket condemnations appeared in editorials, articles, pamphlets, and even song:

> How peace and blest was America's soil,
> Till betrayed by the guile of the Puritan demon

All the worst Yankee characteristics had first appeared in the New World among Satan's spawn: seventeenth-century New Englanders. Even Robert E. Lee, according to British military observer Arthur James Lyon Fremantle, "spoke of the Puritans with intense disgust" and denounced "the pestiferous crew of the Mayflower."[23]

Confederates could therefore trace the "irrepressible conflict" not just to the antebellum period but back into the seventeenth century, if not earlier. There had not been any "brotherhood" between the "Cromwellian fanatics" and southerners in the first place, so talk of a "fratricidal war" was highly misleading, declared the *New Orleans Picayune*. How could there ever have been any common ground with such a people? Their sins were legion: self-righteousness, covetousness, envy, pride, conceit, bigotry, arrogance, presumptuousness, cowardice. The list went on endlessly. The Yankees' pretended piety, civilization, and philanthropy for enslaved Africans all bespoke a deep-dyed hypocrisy that ran through their entire history.[24]

For those seeking a more shorthand condemnation, "witch-burning Puritans" achieved great currency among Confederates, despite the fact that the condemned witches in America had been hanged. A combination of "hypocrisy, self-righteousness, bigotry, intolerance, cruelty and cowardice," declared a Georgia editor, led their Yankee descendants to "war on the weak, on women and children, on unarmed men, and in numbers ten to one, or even as cowardly as a hundred to one." One antebellum southern arithmetic book had included a story problem about the Puritan persecution and execution of witches.[25]

Witchcraft scares offered the most vivid examples of religious prejudice that so characterized northern civilization, but they were not the only ones. Had not the Puritans persecuted the saintly Roger Williams? They had been equally intolerant of Catholics, Quakers, Baptists, and Methodists; in more recent memory, a mob had burned a Charlestown, Massachusetts, convent. A history of narrow-minded interference with other people's lives had unfolded, from Connecticut's infamous "blue laws" through the Maine anti-liquor law. This same spirit would animate Yankee tyrants dragging ministers out of churches to take an oath of allegiance. Their Puritan ancestors had sought to set up a theocracy; might the same fate now await a conquered South? After all, the invasion had begun even before the war, a South Carolina pamphleteer pointed out, when Yankee schoolmasters had come south "bringing with them their nasal twang, their false morality, their proscriptive religion, and their fanatical opinions." It was, then, hardly surprising when Confederate newspapers eagerly reprinted—often on their front pages—Ohio Democrat Samuel S. Cox's long discourse on "Puritanism in politics."[26] Here were all the makings of a holy war between the Yankee aggressors and their Confederate foes.

What popular novelist Augusta Evans termed a "plague of Puritan locusts" had taken over the northern states and threatened to sweep over the southern states. "After a desperate struggle of eight generations," William Naylor McDonald observed, the spirit of Puritanism had "finally succeeded in vitiating the wholesome public sentiment of the North, and converting a nation of intelligent persons into a half-crazed mass of malignant fiends." Despotic by nature, Yankees might declare themselves friends of liberty but never hesitated to ride roughshod over others' freedom. "Of all the tyrants known to history, the Puritan is the most implacable," declared a Georgia newspaper correspondent. "More cruel than the Spaniard, more treacherous than the Italian, more blood-thirsty than the Turk, there is no wrong or humiliation, however atrocious, that his malignant ingenuity would not devise, and in which his savage nature would not find a diabolical pleasure."[27]

The word "Puritan" acquired an elastic meaning in Confederate discourse. Some saw the Yankee Puritans as modern Pharisees, enemies to the teachings of Christ, who turned religion into a gloomy, legalistic exercise. Others thought latter-day Puritanism largely ignored law and certainly shunned orthodoxy, loosely interpreting the Bible and eventually lapsing into Unitarianism and worse. The Puritans began, George Fitzhugh argued, "by persecuting people who would not conform to their faith, and are ending by having no faith at all." They now stood in the guise of abolitionist Republicans, scoffing at biblical authority and scorning the Constitution. Throwing off all forms of order, the Yankees by turn embraced "superstition," "rationalism," and "infidelity."[28] This last claim by a Mississippi editor illustrated how scattershot the critique of Yankee Puritanism had become. But such inconsistencies mattered little, because the point was that Yankees were not only persecutors of men but enemies of God.

To declare your enemy to be God's enemy is commonplace in wartime and a way to link religious and political life. By painting the adversary in the darkest possible hues, propagandists can help turn the conflict into a holy crusade. The enemy becomes quite literally a "devil," yet this was not just a question of behavior, but a matter of belief. Confederates often asserted that the Yankees in fact believed in nothing. One newspaper cited as evidence the sale of church property to pay back taxes in the infidel North. Who but a heathen would tax religious practice? Despite Lincoln's proclamations for days of fasting, humiliation, and prayer or days of thanksgiving, the *Charleston Mercury* insisted, the "savage" Yankees in truth shunned the Almighty. "There is faith about nothing—speculation about all things," claimed an article in *DeBow's Review*.[29] Confederates who seemed hardly bothered by the inconsistency of condemning the Yankees as both religious bigots and modern infidels could readily deploy either argument or both to suit their tastes.

Denunciations of Puritanism were quickly followed by tirades against a people who had seemingly abandoned faith itself. The Yankees, the common charge went, warred against both God and his word. Disputes over the scriptures had long been a staple in debates about slavery, and so this accusation was neither fresh nor original, but it served as a mainstay of Confederate propaganda. In East Tennessee, the pious Eliza Fain feared that the invading Federals "would soon take our Holy Bible and mutilate it until the word of God would become the traditions of men." She refused to believe that "Christian mothers North laid their sons with the same loyalty of feeling upon their country['s] altar that we mothers of the South have done. I feel it can hardly be possible." She knew that the Bible sanctioned slavery, and many other southerners had long been appalled by northern appeals to a so-called "higher law" of morality. A poet dismissed Yankees as a people

> Whose warrant is the grasping hand
> Of creeds without a Christ

Another versifier was even harsher in skewering the enemy's false religion:

> They preach the gospel of Murder
> And pray for Lust's Kingdom to come.

Even Confederates who had once respected the piety of their northern brethren sadly noted how the war had brought out the Yankees' true colors.[30]

Confederate preachers warned against relying too heavily upon an "arm of flesh" (including such heroes as Stonewall Jackson and Robert E. Lee), but then that was exactly what the Yankees would do. Indeed northerners had placed their faith entirely in men and machines. "They believe in brute material force," declared the *Charleston Mercury*, "and use religion, virtue, and morals, as they do their shin-plasters—as mere conveniences to carry on their work of fraud, violence, and blood." Even the northern clergy taught the most heretical doctrines to please their benighted people. Confederates never tired of pointing out how the United States Constitution failed to mention the Almighty, their hope being that the Lord's wrath would quickly be poured out on such infidels.[31]

Yet amazingly, the Yankees pretended to be among the most pious and virtuous of people even as their overweening self-righteousness would hardly fool the world, much less vigilant Confederates. Northerners condescendingly viewed their benighted southern brethren from the heights of conceit. A prisoner on Johnson's Island in Lake Erie imagined that the bluecoat who called roll "daily thanks God he is better than other men, more particularly Southern men, and who firmly believes the true road to heaven itself is only a magnificent seraglio filled with thick-lipped African houris." Yankee women only pretended to be virtuous and their menfolk only pretended to be honest, Edmund Rhett pointedly informed an English visitor.[32]

Northern professions of religious devotion ironically reflected religious decline. Again Confederates appealed to history. "We have no means of ascertaining the condition of the churches of the North," a Baptist editor wrote with no little self-righteousness. "But we know the declension in evangelical piety has kept pace with the spread of fanaticism. Where abolition reigns, religion droops, languishes and dies." No longer did northerners worship the living God, but instead bowed before the false idols of flag and Union. Even as South Carolina was seceding, a Mississippi politician blasted the "red Republicanism, infidelity, anti-Christian ideas; the intemperance and violence and indecorum of the Northern clergy, and anarchy of opinions upon all questions of social interest."[33]

For Confederate critics of northern religion, the key word in that statement was "infidelity." This encompassed everything from what a letter to a Georgia newspaper termed "inveterate Unitarianism" to "bacchanals on the birthday of Tom Paine." The northern states had become infected with all manner of heresy, and lists of Yankee "isms" became standard fare in screeds against northern religious apostasy. Mormonism, spiritualism, and Millerism were prime examples, but so were universalism, deism, and mesmerism. Little wonder that the Yankees often expressed such contempt for orthodox ministers and congregations in the southern states when the northern people had become, in the words of a Virginia minister, a "seething mass of diverse and conflicting theories on the subject of religion imported

"Worship of the North," engraving, Adalbert John Volck.

from all parts of the world, augmented by the perpetual influence of emigration from the dregs of European society."[34]

The introduction of foreign heresies such as French atheism and German transcendentalism had taken a terrible toll among the Yankees. The exact connections remained tantalizingly vague, but Confederates had no trouble identifying northern infidels. Theodore Parker and Henry Ward Beecher became favorite whipping boys. Even at the beginning of the war, the northern religious press—including organs that southerners would once have considered theologically sound—had launched bloodthirsty attacks on the nascent Confederacy. By the middle of the war, a Georgia editor scorned the United States as a "Nation of Infidels and Savages." Presumably southern churches would triumph over such dark forces and become a shining light to the world, though some descriptions of the struggle carried a more somber, apocalyptic tone. In any event, pious Confederates spoke of a holy war to vindicate God's word.[35]

And, they might have added, a war to defeat the forces of infidelity and fanaticism. Those two words—often linked together—carried much weight in the Confederate critique of northern society. These twin abominations, a Tennessean declared, had driven the Yankees "into the wildest isms ever known amongst a civilized enlightened people." This line of argument held sway before the war, gained much currency at the beginning of the war, and persisted throughout the war. "Infidelity pervades one portion of the Northern population and fanaticism another," declared a Richmond editor shortly before Ulysses S. Grant's overland campaign began in the spring of 1864. In fact, the more desperate the Confederate military situation grew, the more perfervid the language became. Later, with Petersburg besieged, this same editor hammered home the point: "Fanaticism, its impelling motive, has ended in such an increase of infidelity and frightful corruption of private character as the world has rarely seen. A new chapter, a new volume, full of black and frightful horrors, will have to be added to the works on Moral Epidemics."[36]

"Epidemic" was just the right word because Confederate polemicists treated fanaticism as a contagion that had swept across the North. Sometimes the disease was described as "malignant," at other times interpreted as a sign of "insanity." An article in the *Southern Literary Messenger* even claimed that mental disorders were far more prevalent in the free states. The Yankees had accepted military rule by the Lincoln administration, had embraced emancipation, and had called for subjugating the southern states—all signs of madness by Confederate standards. This left no room for negotiation or compromise with a people who had abandoned rationality to wage a relentless war against southerners. In this view, the Yankees were plunging headlong toward national suicide. Aside from the folly of the war itself, such fanaticism had fatally corrupted northern society. The greed of northern capitalists, the demoralization of city life, and the breakdown of families all proved how the Yankees were sowing the seeds of their own destruction.[37]

Accordingly, the "Black Republicans" had enthroned a despotism the day Abraham Lincoln was placed in the office once occupied by George Washington. To argue that an infidel fanaticism had driven the Yankees toward tyranny and lunacy bespoke both conviction and wishful thinking, especially when Confederate military prospects dimmed. Surely southerners could never be reunited with a people who carried the most crack-brained ideas to their logical extremes. Perhaps northern conservatives would yet rise up against these crazed revolutionaries, but like the chimera of aid from Europe, that hope proved vain. Ironically, as some disillusioned Confederates admitted, there was no shortage of fanaticism on their side when the southern cause grew hopeless.[38]

Unfortunately, the Yankees embraced almost every variety of fanaticism. Power-hungry, greedy, ambitious, they appeared to embody all the worst qualities of an Oliver Cromwell, a Robespierre, and a Russian czar. "Without ballast or restraint, liberty has necessarily degenerated into license," the *Charleston Mercury* warned. "License is subject to no laws, and hence is without the control or direction of a limiting power. The shifting will of the mobocracy, guided by interest or passion alone, becomes their law." A letter to an Atlanta newspaper diagnosed the North as suffering from both "Red Republicanism" and "Black Republicanism." To cite but two examples, rabid Yankees had once persecuted the harmless Masons and temperance zealots had attempted to remove wine from the Eucharist.[39]

Ultimately such extreme and ever-changing ideas had led to war. And now the battle was joined, claimed one North Carolina editor, with "fanaticism and unjust power . . . on one side—God and our native land on the other." At Cedar Mountain, Virginia, a Louisiana chaplain looked over a battlefield "drenched with the blood of the victims of fanaticism, tyranny, and injustice." Such enemies would go to any length to achieve their evil designs, and as usual Confederates did not worry about avoiding hyperbole. A Richmond editor seemingly found the perfect comparison: "If any Turk or heretic of modern times has conducted a warfare on principles more antagonistical to the Gospel than the present Puritan crusade, we do not know where to look for his record."[40]

These strong words might have described a formidable if not unstoppable enemy. Presumably the mighty Yankee armies would become juggernauts driven by blind hatred for southerners and their institutions. As the war dragged on—and the powerful and evocative images of the utterly evil Yankee undoubtedly made the war last longer—such descriptions of a wild enemy hell-bent on subjugating the southern states crept into Confederate accounts of the fighting. Yet as in many other instances, there appeared to be few worries about presenting a consistent picture of the enemy. After all, northern fanaticism might just as easily prove to be a fatal weakness.

During the war's first year, the hope had been that the Yankees would burn themselves out and could not long continue the struggle. In early 1862, right before the Federals' capture of Forts Henry and Donelson in Tennessee, an Alabama editor predicted that northern "fanaticism is reaching the climax of its extravagance, and its declension will be as rapid as its rise." The Yankees might spill much of their own blood but would soon learn they could not prevail.[41]

Even before the first shot had been fired at Fort Sumter, the always fire-breathing *Charleston Mercury* had declared that true southern men would never bow to Yankee despotism, but this assertion added another and perhaps more ominous element to the usual descriptions of northern fanaticism. "No tyranny has ever existed whose power to do evil was so great—whose disposition to do good so small," the editor maintained. "A popular tyranny of *fanatics* and low minded politicians—a tyranny so much the worse, because it is many headed—a popular tyranny, even when composed of less foul elements than the present, is more degrading than the tyranny of a monarch. It never dies." Especially for more reactionary Confederate thinkers, northern democracy was corrupt at its very core. Not only was it infidel and materialistic, it embodied the worst excesses of the French Revolution. "Jacobin" became an all-purpose epithet throughout the war and indeed throughout the Reconstruction period. The overtones were frightening and the purpose of such rhetoric was to generate its own kind of fanaticism, a fanaticism that would manifest itself in a greater, longer, and ever unreasoning commitment to the Confederate war effort. And in point of fact, the Yankees were even worse than the Jacobins, but like their French counterparts had declared a war on God in the name of "the people."[42]

Decades ago, Americans had foolishly embraced a "leveling democracy," the most ardent critics of northern society maintained. Southern intellectuals had long expressed reservations about democracy, and at the beginning of the war such opinions became both more open and more frequent in periodicals such as *DeBow's Review* and the *Southern Literary Messenger*. This high-brow material flattered the pretensions of planter aristocrats who prided themselves on being bulwarks of conservative order. Here the distinctions between republicanism and democracy became all-important. South Carolina governor Francis Pickens believed that a "consolidated democracy" would degenerate into anarchy and eventually into military despotism. Nothing was in place to check the excesses of northern democracy, and that was exactly the problem.[43]

Expressing an antidemocratic animus in learned essays that would never attract the attention, much less the ire, of the masses who had to fill the ranks of the southern armies was both cathartic and safe. Yet these reactionary sentiments revealed a great deal about the nature of Confederate political thought. Slavery had supposedly served as a counterweight to fanatical northern democracy, and a few Confederates frankly confessed that universal manhood suffrage had been a mistake. So too the rise of political parties had created vast patronage machines that corrupted the polity and threatened property rights. One pamphleteer candidly if somewhat confusingly praised Confederates as "hereditary, organic Republicans, let your enemies understand, my countrymen, that you are towards them and their barbarian Democracy, an aristocracy in arms." In this way, southerners would stand against radical democracy and defend the classical unity of interests between capital and labor.[44]

These polemical forays were not only antidemocratic, they were hopelessly abstract. This was especially true of vague warnings against "agrarianism," a menace that southern intellectuals conjured up without ever giving it a precise meaning that would resonate beyond their own circles. The whole idea hinted at economic or political leveling, a "licentious and destructive" doctrine, claimed one essayist. In any case the triumph of agrarianism would surely bring on disorder and anarchy, if not mob rule.[45] Alabama attorney William Falconer pointed to the "restless immaturity of opinion" and an "impatience of restraint" that had long plagued Americans. Falconer and others routinely deplored the rise of a rootless northern society with no fixed ideas about law or government. "Agrarianism" signified a Yankee embrace of any "ism" that came along, however foolish or dangerous. Confederate vice president Alexander H. Stephens well summed up the matter: "The utmost licentiousness of the French Jacobins, in their most unbridled fury and phrenzy, did not exhibit greater extravagance and recklessness in total disregard of law and order, and everything essential to good government, than these people at the North have exhibited in this wild, unnatural, irrational and fanatical crusade against us."[46]

"Abduction of the Yankee Goddess of Liberty: The Prince of Darkness (Abraham Lincoln) Bears Her Away to His Infernal Regions," *Southern Punch*, November 14, 1863.

References to the French Revolution appeared throughout the war, and the clergy echoed standard attacks on northern "liberty and equality." The idol-worshiping Yankees had "virtually dethroned the God of the Bible," Episcopal bishop Stephen Elliott declared on one fast day. According to Presbyterian Benjamin Morgan Palmer, atheistic abolitionists transformed "liberty, equality, and fraternity" into "bondage, confiscation, and massacre." Even though democratically elected, Abraham Lincoln would create a despotism beyond the imaginings of the worst tyrants in human history. Others feared that the Union government would obliterate the states and launch a reign of terror. The most radical Republican faction (again the term "Jacobin" came into play) might even set up "guillotines"—a term generally but not always used metaphorically.[47]

The search for historical comparisons proceeded far afield. Was the new Lincoln administration worse than Austrian autocrats or Russian czars? When it came to tyranny and despotism—and sometimes both terms were thrown in for good measure—the Union government seemingly exceeded all others in villainy. "Give us Mexican, give us Spanish, Portuguese, Russian, Chinese," declared one Georgia editor who sounded like he was running out of countries. "Any government under the heavens is preferable to the

United States of America." Many of these comparisons appeared during the war's first year, and at one point Baltimore was even labeled the "Warsaw of America." In short, no other government could match the ruthless tyranny of the once glorious American Union.[48] In essence this meant that Confederates—if one believed such statements—would in fact be fighting against what appeared to be the wickedest despotism in human history.

On the very day of Lincoln's inauguration, Confederates were already limbering up their rhetorical guns. The coward had snuck into Washington, a city now bristling with bayonets, but expectations for the new president were contradictory, and Confederates also worried that he would become the worst of the tyrants' breed. In South Carolina, young Emma Holmes dismissed the inaugural address as "stupid, ambiguous, vulgar and insolent." At the same time, she termed it a "virtual declaration of war." The very idea, not to mention the reality, of a "Black Republican" president intensified Confederate fears, generating both paranoia and fury. Consequently, public statements and private sentiments sounded wilder and more conspiratorial. Lincoln and his party hated southerners and especially slaveholders; southern homes would soon be laid waste amidst the terror of slave insurrections; the Yankees were hell-bent on destroying the southern economy and subjugating the southern people.[49]

What to make of Lincoln sent fearful and enraged Confederates off in many directions at once, their disparate rants becoming a cacophony of denunciations. As northern military preparations proceeded apace, more than one editor referred to him as the "Baboon Despot." This combination of ridicule and horror bespoke confusion and perhaps even a bit of fear about a man who would be derided as both a simple fool and a crafty usurper. Was Lincoln devoid of all convictions, as some claimed? More than a month before a significant battle had been fought, General P. G. T. Beauregard offered a stirring call to arms against this "unprincipled tyrant" and invader who would sanction almost any act of violence or outrage against innocent southerners.[50]

All the Yankee talk of "liberty" amounted to nothing more than empty words. As a leading war correspondent put it, "Nominally, Mr. Lincoln is a republican President—really, he is a despot, the violator of his country's laws, the usurper of its rights and liberties, and the base and beastly oppressor of the people. The honored seat of the peerless Washington has become the throne of a fanatical and ignorant barbarian, who has banished all law and destroyed every right." On March 4, 1862, the pious Virginian Lucy Buck noted "the anniversary of the inauguration of the arch-fiend Lincoln." Not only had the northern president become a tyrant, tyranny had been his goal all along.[51]

This narrative of the North's descent into a dark night of political oppression aligned well with traditional states' rights arguments. The Lincoln administration would trample constitutional protections, ride roughshod over the states, and create a "consolidated" despotism. One could hear echoes of John C. Calhoun, though these arguments became especially prominent in the Upper South states that had not seceded until after the firing on Fort Sumter.[52] Sometimes this meant denying that slavery or economic differences had anything to do with the conflict and simply declaring that the war was a contest for liberty and freedom. Properly understood, that is. The northern idea of liberty, a Georgia editor asserted, "consists of luxurious ease, barbaric and uncouth display, and easy plunder." Speeches and editorials defended secession with caustic barbs against Yankees who had rallied around the despot Lincoln.[53] Most of the points at first remained fairly abstract, sweeping generalizations that seldom got down to cases. But that all came in good time, and Confederates would soon be able to rattle off a list of Lincoln's crimes—real and imagined. By making the president into the personification of many Yankee vices, Confederates would put a face on the incipient tyranny.

For the time being, what might be simply termed "despotism by definition" drove the verbal salvoes against Yankeedom. In a lengthy address to his fellow Kentuckians, John C. Breckinridge repeatedly invoked fears of tyranny without going into particulars. Increasingly, warnings came of "military despotism" under which northerners' freedoms would be the first to disappear. How could one even think, Jefferson Davis asked in the fall of 1861, of reunion with a government that made war without congressional consent and violated civil liberties with impunity? There had been rumors of proposals for reconstruction as the Confederate government was being formed, but as the true nature of the northern people and their leaders became clearer, surely that was out of the question. The fiery Edmund Ruffin wrote that the United States had turned into an "unlimited despotism" ruled by "the basest scoundrels and low fools, that ever directed the policy of a great nation." In the once sacred Union, the peoples' rights had become extinct.[54]

The prime exhibit in the case was Lincoln's suspension of habeas corpus and so-called "arbitrary arrests." Even southern men and women, Governor Joseph E. Brown of Georgia claimed, had been snared in this dragnet. Midnight arrests by a brutal soldiery, and denial of bail, rounded out a picture of unchecked dictatorial power. Then too, the suppression of several northern newspapers guaranteed that any criticism of these outrages would be muted. Inevitably, Confederates—including Jefferson Davis—referred to northern prisons as "Bastilles." The swift progress of tyranny in the northern states stood without parallel in human history; executions must soon follow. And to make matters worse, thousands of deluded Yankees cheered on the tyrannical Lincoln.[55]

The inexplicable acquiescence of the northern people in ever more outrageous violations of their liberties grew into an important theme in Confederate propaganda. The most blatant attacks on individual freedom had created hardly a murmur. A deadly silence and the absence of sustained opposition proved that Yankees would not even defend their own rights, much less anyone else's. They seemed almost "anxious," a prominent Virginian noted in his diary, "to lay their liberties at the foot of the ignorant despot who sways their destinies." One could only wonder how long such pusillanimity would prevail in the northern states.[56]

But here was another fundamental inconsistency in Confederate thinking. The misreading of public sentiment had become habitual on both sides of the Mason-Dixon Line during the antebellum period, and it continued during the war. Even as some Confederates asserted—without much evidence—that northerners meekly submitted to Lincoln, others seized on and exaggerated any signs of dissension in the northern states. The arrests along with the suppression of newspapers certainly offered hopeful evidence of divisions among their enemies. Perhaps Lincoln and his minions had reason to fear a backlash, and partisan strife would certainly be a good sign. Some Yankees must eventually awaken to the danger, and apparent tranquility in the North was perhaps deceiving, a calm before an impending storm of internal convulsion or even revolution. As Confederate armies kept throwing back the invaders, recrimination and backbiting would bedevil their foes. And eventually—and here the wish was certainly the proverbial father to the thought—there would be an uprising against Lincoln. Early on, Confederates even speculated about the possible assassination of this American Caesar.[57]

As for the northern people, they could neither enjoy nor preserve their own freedom, and they appeared determined to subjugate the southern people. Their invading armies offered nothing but the chains of despotism. So whether one deplored Yankee acquiescence or hoped for Yankee dissension hardly mattered, as either viewpoint buttressed redoubled efforts to win southern independence. Warnings that battlefield defeats would lead to northern politicians' striking the death knell of southern liberties became a rallying cry for the faint-hearted when Confederate fortunes languished. Writing to his sons, a Georgia lieutenant explained, "But then it is better that your Father should leave and become a soldier than that you should become slaves and serfs, losing all hopes of becoming great and good men." Especially by the middle of the war, soldiers and civilians, editors and politicians, all warned that giving up the fight would mean living under the worst tyranny in human history.[58]

Indeed history would eventually record the dark and bloody deeds of the would-be dictator Lincoln. Searching for historical analogies and at times running out of suitable comparisons, some Confederates simply ranted against the Yankees and their president. The attacks grew ever more rabid and at times incoherent. That longtime voice of Virginia Democrats, the *Richmond Enquirer*, blasted Lincoln as a "coward assassin, and flagrant criminal against civilization and his race." The even wider-circulating *Richmond Dispatch* reported Lincoln leaving the White House in a carriage accompanied by "fierce looking guards" and cavalry "in the style of Eastern despots."[59]

Before the inauguration, General Winfield Scott had ordered troops to Washington because the new president required what a Georgia editor termed an "army of mercenaries" for protection. The old hero of the Mexican War had become a mere sycophant for an oppressive regime. What made matters worse was that Scott was a Virginian who had now turned his back not only on his state but on the southern people. "Renegade" and "traitor" were but two of the choice words used to excoriate this apostate.

For the time being, hanging (or burning) Scott and Lincoln in effigy would have to do until Confederate troops marched on Washington and captured the two miscreants.[60]

In some ways, the wide-ranging criticisms of Winfield Scott exemplified the broader assaults on northern civilization. The general's "long connection with Yankees and Yankeedom has corrupted his nature," a Richmond editor speculated. "He now stands as one of them by adoption, a violator of his allegiance to his native State and betrayer of his country. He has become a Yankee—could we say more to his disgrace?" To some Confederates, Scott had never been a southerner, and he now embodied the treachery and hatred that had characterized so many northerners during the past decade and more of sectional strife. Moreover, from the earliest stages of his life he had shown a kind of self-seeking that had defined the Yankee character. He had fought for himself rather than for his country, or at least that was one popular criticism. The general's military record in the Mexican War had benefited from the careful planning by others more than anything else. Unlike true southerners, Scott had shown little devotion even to his own family, having reportedly neglected an impoverished sister living in Mississippi. Indeed any sense of larger loyalty appeared utterly lacking in the man. Not surprisingly, Confederates compared him to Benedict Arnold, though even then some wondered if this pathetic creature could measure up as a classic traitor.[61]

A general whom southerners had once admired they now dismissed as a selfish egotist, a rapidly failing dotard who cared most about life's creature comforts. Even the poor man's obesity and gout became a subject for ridicule. The Yankees had purchased Scott's loyalty, and some critics suggested he had only remained general-in-chief—despite poor health and clashes with General George B. McClellan—to draw a salary.[62] The Confederate victory at the first battle of Manassas had only added to Scott's infamy. The general had proven himself to be a moral imbecile, induced by political pressure to send an unprepared army into battle. His responsibility for the slaughter was undeniable, and shame would forever attach to his name. A North Carolina newspaper editor labeled Scott a "wholesale murderer" and "miserable coward."[63] Early in the war, Confederates especially favored the latter canard in describing their enemies, though that kind of thinking could and often did lead to a kind of blind optimism. Exaggerated views of the Yankees' physical and moral weaknesses in turn prevented many Confederates from realistically evaluating their own military resources and prospects.

As the first battles were being fought, many Confederates believed they at last saw the true nature of their Yankee opponents. The broadside attacks on Lincoln and Scott were but one example of Confederates deploying a rhetorical arsenal that brought any number of Yankee characteristics into their range of fire. Such braggart descendants of Puritan bigots were hardly a worthy foe. Whether they were dismissed as fanatics or infidels (or both for those not terribly worried about a contradictory characterization), the Yankees were clearly an ignoble people, if not actually a degenerate race. The uncouth Lincoln and the turncoat Scott perfectly represented the Yankee nation. Intellectuals might emphasize the dangers of revolution, Jacobinism, and even democracy, but more broadly speaking, staunch Confederates saw the Yankees as capable of almost any imaginable and indeed many unimaginable crimes. The war itself would undoubtedly reveal not only the Yankees' barbarism but other weaknesses. The essential defects of the Yankees' character—including such an elemental fault as cowardice—would surely prove their undoing.

CHAPTER 2

Defining and Defaming the Enemy

A little over a month after the Battle of Gettysburg, Walter Taylor, a staff officer in the Army of Northern Virginia, declared that his "contempt" for the Yankees' fighting ability was growing "every day." Dismissing them as a "miserable cowardly race," he prayed that Confederate soldiers would not "for a moment contemplate the bare possibility of being conquered by such a people." But of course, General Robert E. Lee's army had just been forced to retreat after fighting a three-day bloodbath against such unworthy foes. A year later a South Carolina editor still maintained that the Yankees—despite often overwhelming numbers—ran away at the first shot and "in the depth of their craven hearts" could "have no more hope of conquering the Confederacy than of scaling the mountains on the moon."[1] Yet by this time fewer and fewer Confederates spoke so confidently about Yankee cowardice, at least in the arrogant manner of the war's first year. As the soldiers themselves might have put it, that sort of boasting was "all played out." Now Confederates more often railed against a destructive enemy carrying a war without mercy to the southern home front. They accused the Yankees of most any imaginable crime from warring against women and children to plotting the extermination of the southern people.

Confederate views of the enemy shared certain constant themes but also shifted as morale rose and fell. During the war's early phases, the weaknesses of Yankee character received the greatest attention. There was not yet an obsession with the wickedness that would lead northern soldiers to commit atrocities, but instead Confederates pointed to flaws that would hamstring their opponents' armies. As in the broader critique of northern civilization, a persistent historical dimension received much attention. Even before the war began, a Washington correspondent for a Richmond newspaper recounted how Yankee courage had often faltered during the American Revolution. And now the pattern simply continued. The surrender of Fort Sumter revealed what one writer called the "cowardice and impotency" that had prevented the Federal navy from relieving Major Robert Anderson's garrison. Confederates soon crowed over their enemies' hasty retreat after a blundering attack at Big Bethel, Virginia. The "cowardly scamps," one newspaper reported, could hardly throw away their equipment and skedaddle fast enough.[2]

Even a single intrepid Confederate picket managed to bag two "cowardly Lincolnites" near Manassas Junction, Virginia. This incident served as a prelude to the first great Rebel victory—or for the purposes of the argument being advanced here—the disgraceful Yankee defeat in the war's first great battle. Confederates naturally reveled in their triumph at Manassas, but many accounts also described how rapidly their foes had fled from the battlefield. The northern hosts had "fought precisely as we have since expected," the *Charleston Mercury* exulted. "This race of sharpers . . . have less fight in them than any white race now on the globe." The *Mercury* always excelled at such broadsides, but even the usually cautious Jefferson Davis celebrated the Yankees' headlong flight after the battle and compared them to a "covey of partridges." Soon the Confederate victory at Wilson's Creek in Missouri added to the accumulating evidence that Union troops would scatter at the first opportunity. And they would now surely quail even more as Confederate forces threatened to besiege Washington.[3]

This early success merely confirmed an assumption that the northern people were cowardly *by nature*, but according to Richmond editor John M. Daniel it was a quality carefully cultivated. Yankees supposedly learned early on that fighting did not pay and instead found "cunning and sharpness and cheating" much more profitable. Daniel's dismissal of northern courage was penned before any major fighting had taken place, but early battles appeared to confirm these assumptions. The enemy proved more gutless than he could have imagined, claimed one of Jeb Stuart's staff officers. Some base fellows had reportedly donned breastplates and other types of body armor. One Georgia woman even hoped to be in Savannah when the Yankees attacked so she could watch them run. Superior northern numbers counted for little when the result was always the same—bluecoats fleeing from the field of combat. Why then should Confederates fear such a foe? Little wonder that expectations for the "liberation" of Maryland or even the capture of Washington ran high.[4] So from the first months of the war, public expectations in the Confederacy veered sharply from military realities.

Confederates readily discovered Yankee cowardice wherever they looked, at least during the war's first year. Their hopes for European intervention and an early end to the fighting rose when Captain Charles Wilkes stopped the British mail steamer *Trent* and seized Confederate commissioners James M. Mason and John Slidell. But Lincoln and Secretary of State William H. Seward cleverly defused the crisis by releasing the diplomats while claiming that the traditional American position on the rights of neutral vessels had been recognized by the British. The Confederate press offered a radically different assessment. To cite but a few of many examples, several Georgia newspapers viewed the outcome of the *Trent* affair as an abject surrender by a spineless administration. After authorizing and defending what were obviously highhanded if not illegal actions, claimed a Milledgeville editor, Union Secretary of the Navy Gideon Welles ended up "sneaking out like a whipped spaniel, with tail curled under his legs." This disgraceful episode exposed the Lincoln government's true character. The *Athens Southern Banner* was dismissively contemptuous, claiming that the Yankees had proven themselves to be a "nation of cowards or a nation of fools." Not to be outshone when it came to blackguarding the enemy, a Georgia enlisted man thought it would be necessary to "call on the Hottentots & wild Africans to produce an instance of equal cowardice & self-stultification."[5]

Much of the commentary on the early battles and the *Trent* debacle had revealed a dangerous overconfidence. A Confederate army could easily defeat the Yankees even if outnumbered three to one, a figure regularly bruited about during the war's first year. Some ardent patriots claimed that one Confederate could actually whip ten Yankees; even into the war's third year, one of Robert E. Lee's generals cited this same ratio but only applied it to the "lowest scum of the Yankee foreign population." With Confederate fortunes still riding high at the beginning of 1862, an Alabama editor recommended that Confederate soldiers resort to the bayonet because the Federals "have shown they are absolutely incapable of meeting a charge of cold iron."[6]

The Union capture of Forts Henry and Donelson did not exactly end such fantasies, but now at least some Confederates conceded two elemental facts: early victories had bred unrealistic expectations for a short war; and the Yankees would stand up to their foes. "Our people must also disabuse themselves of any erroneous impressions as to the inability of our enemy to cope with us upon a fair field," a Georgia lieutenant wrote to his father. "Puritan stock will fight." One editor who had long railed about the "fanatical, cruel, intolerant devilish" character of the Yankees admitted they were "hardy and courageous." Not willing to go quite so far, some Confederates conceded that the most lily-livered Yankees fought in the eastern theater; the western bluecoats were much tougher. Others raised the possibility that southern imputations of cowardice actually made northerners more determined to vindicate their own character.[7]

Even if the Federals relied on sheer numbers bolstered by dragooning foreigners and black men into their ranks—as Confederate propagandists often charged—southern braggadocio on the whole question of courage had worn thin. Nurse Kate Cumming, who dealt with the war's carnage firsthand, claimed that by the fall of 1863 the fighting had "opened our eyes to the disagreeable fact, that one of our men is not equal to five of the enemy." Based on conversations with wounded Confederates, she decided that the Federals had "exhibited a bravery and determination worthy of a better cause." Very early in the war, a thoughtful colonel had even suggested that "two or three sound whippings" might be required to remedy overblown estimates of southern courage.[8]

On this whole question, a shift in opinion took place as the war grew bloodier. More and more Confederates were willing to admit that the Yankees would fight hard and even applied the term "coward" to southerners who murmured against their leaders and lost hope. Descriptions of Yankee "cowardice" increasingly had less to say about their physical than their moral weakness. General John Pope's infamous 1862 orders threatening to seize Rebel property and string up Rebel guerrillas provoked outrage, including charges of moral cowardice. This all anticipated a standard condemnation of hard war policies and practices. Everything from the bombardment of cities, to the destruction of homes, to raids into the countryside all provoked diatribes against dastardly Yankees. Only the most craven men would resort to starving out their enemies. Newspapers and generals alike denounced the vandal hordes who preferred harassing the innocent and defenseless to facing soldiers on a battlefield.[9]

When confronting armed men rather than unarmed civilians, the "marauders" (another favorite term for northern troops) might still beat a hasty retreat. Even late in the war a few Confederate soldiers were claiming that the Yankee cavalry—if not the infantry—showed little stomach for battle. In early 1865, young Grace Brown Elmore wrote of wishing to be a man so she could strike a blow at the "cowardly wretches" who were pillaging South Carolina. By warring on women and children, such men (if they should even be called "men") displayed an especially barbaric form of cowardice.[10] The late-war revival of these charges of cowardice reflected a certain desperation, as people such as Grace Elmore could hardly believe that the enemy had arrived on their doorsteps. Who could have imagined such an unworthy foe would enjoy such success?

The fading belief that Yankees would not fight hardly stopped Confederates from searching for and speculating about their enemies' weak points. After all, depictions of northern cowardice had formed but a small part of a broader critique of Yankee character. In seeking to explain why the bluecoats so often cowered on the day of battle, southerners not surprisingly pointed to their foes' mercenary qualities. The Yankee obsession with the almighty dollar had long been a literary cliché, and less than a week after Fort Sumter, a Georgia newspaper printed a joke about a northern soldier pointing a gun at a southern soldier. The Confederate should have been a dead man, but instead pulled out his pocketbook and simply purchased his enemy's weapon. Everyone supposedly knew that a Yankee would walk a mile to save five cents. All this signified a fundamental difference in heart and soul: the northern people waged war to enrich greedy contractors, while idealistic southerners fought to defend their liberties.[11]

If swindling was the Yankees' "natural trade," as one aspiring poet claimed, such cupidity masked a more basic flaw. The apparent prosperity of the North was nothing but a sham, or as one newspaper correspondent claimed, "railways, ships, machine shops, manufacturing establishments . . . themselves produce nothing or little." Such an absurd statement echoed some antebellum assessments of industrial civilization and reflected hopes that the entire house of cards would collapse under the pressures of war. Southern writers had long ridiculed Yankee inventiveness that reputedly excelled only in scams such as quack medicines.[12] Building on these dubious assumptions, Confederates cheered any signs that the northern economy was languishing. During the war's first year, it was widely reported in the southern press that northern commerce had dried up and a desperate government had suspended specie payments, driving the financial system to the verge of collapse. The Yankees would spend millions upon millions in a vain effort to subjugate the Confederacy, and as economic problems multiplied, even they would come to realize that fighting simply did not pay.[13]

That was literally the bottom line for the prototypical Yankee, and all these statements suggested the irony of a people known for sharp business practices ruining their own economy. According to Edmund Ruffin's calculations, the war was costing the U.S. government two million dollars a day, and therefore northern credit must soon evaporate. As one soldier stationed near Yorktown, Virginia, simply put it at the end of 1861, "The Yankees are spending so much and accomplishing so little they cannot stand it much longer." Increasingly, Confederate commentary focused on the ever-rising northern public debt. In his inaugural address on February 22, 1862, Jefferson Davis predicted that "our foes must sink" under a "load of debt" that had reached "fearful dimensions." The problem was that such statements rested on conflicting assumptions, doubtful evidence, and wishful thinking. Was northern indebtedness really a fatal weakness, or would it make the money-mad Yankees fight all the harder to subjugate the southern states so they could confiscate property and make their vanquished foes assume this economic burden? Alternately, it was hoped, the Union's financial woes would provoke more antiwar sentiment, especially in the western states. Or perhaps, the British would take advantage of the inevitable crash to absorb the United States into their empire once again.[14] The disparate nature of such predictions proved their flimsy basis but also reflected an ability of the most purblind Confederates to twist facts to suit their hopes. Indeed a certain flexibility in argument, which became an absolute specialty of newspaper editors, served to reinforce basic assumptions about Yankee weaknesses long after they should have been disproven.

The most sanguine Confederates flatly predicted their enemies' bankruptcy. Even here definitions were broad, and "bankruptcy" signified moral as well as economic ruin, a stunning development that might provoke a war between the United States and England. Newspaper scribblers and other polemicists oddly enough linked this impending financial debacle to the Yankees' already well-publicized cowardice. If all of this seemed scattershot and far-fetched, it was. More realistic voices claimed that the Confederacy could not be saved simply by northern folly, but realism often proved to be in short supply.[15]

Nowhere was this truer than in Confederate assessments of northern fighting men. In this instance, the stereotype of the Yankee as money grubber assumed at least two distinct forms. First, the typical northern soldier—the single-minded, one-dimensional economic man—was fighting for his pay. Rations and cash became his raison d'être. As the always flamboyant Rebel general John Bankhead Magruder stated in an address to troops on the Virginia Peninsula, "Our enemy, dead to the spirit of liberty, can only fight while their coffers are unexhausted. Commerce is their king. Their god is gold. They glory in their shame." Such claims soon appeared in Confederate propaganda abroad, playing into British and French assumptions about dollar-mad Americans.[16] Before a major battle had been fought, Vice President Alexander H. Stephens dismissed northern soldiers as "hirelings and mercenaries," and the *Charleston Mercury* even applied these epithets to the commander of the Fort Sumter garrison, Major Robert Anderson.[17] In essence, Yankee soldiers became men without a real or at least without a legitimate cause.[18] This in turn explained why they acted so cowardly. Those who fought for the basest of motives—and notably for mere pay—naturally could not measure up to noble-hearted Confederates.[19]

A second point in this critique cropped up with even greater frequency. Not only did the typical northern soldier fight for "mercenary" reasons, but the Yankees turned to foreign-born mercenaries to fill their armies. One Texas cavalryman combined both arguments by dismissing the "Irish and Dutch" dead found on the field at Shiloh as "foreigners who fight for good rations and pay."[20] Although three of four Union soldiers were native-born,[21] anyone perusing the Confederate press might conclude that the northern troops were largely German or Irish. At the first battle of Manassas, claimed George Fitzhugh, the "motley hosts of the North" had consisted of "men speaking every language of Europe." They may have fought but "knew not and cared not for what." Such men had presumably been dragooned into the Union army, desperate to eke out a living. Strictly speaking, the United States did not even field a "Yankee" army but rather a "European" army.[22]

The obvious precedent was the American Revolution, and many Confederates dubbed enemy soldiers "Hessians." A Georgia editor warned against the "polluting tread" of "Abolition Wide Awakes" (referring to the Republican clubs of the 1860 presidential campaign) and "Federal Hessians." Naturally, Abraham Lincoln would play the role of George III in this historical reenactment, and such simple references would have resonated with a much wider audience than learned essays about the Puritan roots of Yankee civilization. First Manassas reinforced such comparisons when a Richmond headline screamed, "Flight of the Hessians." Such blasts against a mercenary enemy persisted for the rest of the war, though some Confederates maintained that the "real" Yankees were a more brutal and fanatical foe than any foreign troops or immigrant cannon fodder.[23]

Especially after Lincoln began recruiting African American soldiers, Confederates harped on the Union army's polyglot character. When a South Carolina newspaper noted how the U.S. government grabbed up men of "every shade and class and color," these words connoted both ridicule and alarm. There was bitter contempt but also the humiliation of having to confront and perhaps be defeated by such a rabble in arms. As the spring 1864 campaign was about to begin in Virginia, a Confederate officer told his wife that the Union Ninth Corps was nothing but a "horde of Negroes, Dutchmen & substitutes."[24] Such imagery obviously struck a chord with a people obsessed with racial distinctions, but it also reinforced the belief that the Yankees were an especially degraded if not mongrel race.

Northern armies had gathered up the lowest forms of humanity, many Confederates declared. Georgia Methodist bishop James O. Andrew sneered at "the scum and offscourings of foreign lands generally as well as the scum of the Northern States picked up from their prisons and the purlieus of their towns." A Richmond editor wrote of penitentiaries thrown open with "jail birds and murderers marshaled into a legion for the work of pillage, rapine and massacre." The Union government had reportedly sent agents to Europe recruiting yet more desperate characters for the northern armies. Later in the war, the Federals ended prisoner exchanges, supposedly because they could easily round up more foreign mercenaries. Confederate governors and other politicians loved to contrast these dregs of society with the fine men who filled the Rebel ranks. Descriptions of Yankee regiments composed largely of felons, foreigners, and Negroes became commonplace in Confederate propaganda.[25]

Yet these mercenary, plundering invaders—despite all the ridicule heaped upon them in Confederate newspapers—threatened to sweep across the Southland. One songwriter referred to the "lice of Egypt," though solders in both armies had already become more than familiar with that particular form of vermin. Images of Yankees swarming the countryside and invading homes would surely sound the tocsin even for war-weary Confederate soldiers and civilians. Addressing their troops on the eve of battle, Confederate generals warned of northern armies filled with vengeful foreigners hell-bent on pillage and rape. Stonewall Jackson's mapmaker Jedediah Hotchkiss considered German troops to be the worst specimens. Such men had imbibed radical ideas in Europe (denunciations of "red republicans" referred to refugees from the revolutions of 1848), though the more wishful thinkers speculated that such fanatics might eventually turn against their Yankee masters.[26]

In point of fact, Confederates often asserted, few "true" Yankees had enlisted in the northern armies. There appeared to be great "reluctance" among what the *New Orleans Picayune* termed the "natural born Americans of the North" to butcher "other Americans in the South for the crime of resisting robbery and asserting the rights of self-government." Or perhaps the better class of Yankees were more than willing to send "hirelings" into the southern states but would recoil at actually joining such brutes on a battlefield and putting their own precious skins at risk. What might be termed sociological speculation widened and grew more far-fetched. Should the U.S. government ever resort to conscription, the real Yankees would balk and bring the war to a close. Some Rebel soldiers claimed that most of the Union dead on any battlefield were foreign-born. Plantation mistress Catherine Edmondston explained disparities between Union and

Confederate casualty figures by asserting that the Yankees ignored the "Irish, Germans & Negroes" and only counted native-born white men. After the Fredericksburg bloodbath, one Confederate soldier predicted that "from this time on, I think we will play havoc with the real genuine blue bellied Yankees themselves."[27] Confederates expressed contempt for what they considered the ragtag enemy armies filled with men gathered up from various lands and races, but then ironically attributed similar views to their foes.

Indeed, Confederates almost took pity on the ignorant dupes who presumably made up the bulk of the northern armies. "It seems to me the Yankees do not care how many of their men die," Virginian Mary Stribling remarked. "It is nothing when they have only the dregs of society and those foreigners whose lives are not valuable to the Yankees." The popular image of General Ulysses S. Grant as a butcher in part rested on Confederate claims that he had recklessly sacrificed his "European hirelings" during the Overland Campaign. For cold-blooded northerners, it came down to a matter of expediency: their foreign-born troops were the most expendable. This was notably true of Irish Catholics, and it gave old-line Democratic editors in the Confederacy an opportunity to trumpet anew the Know Nothing violence of the 1850s as a striking example of Yankee bigotry.[28]

Confederates even relished seizing the high moral ground against northern ethnic and religious prejudice. Past experience, including riots and attacks on convents, should have taught Catholics that the Yankee Puritans could not be trusted. How long would it be before they again turned to persecuting immigrant Catholics? The southern press naturally reported any signs of religious tensions among their enemies, especially emphasizing how abolitionists had long despised both slavery and Catholics. Newspapers cited the old battles going back to Cromwell's England and the urban riots of more recent years as part of a great conflict now continuing as northern troops desecrated and destroyed Catholic churches in the South. Praising the purported "loyalty" of southern Catholics, Confederates proclaimed themselves models of religious tolerance—a virtue that some traced back to Cavalier roots.[29]

Broadmindedness, however, did not extend to welcoming northern immigrants. The fire-eaters had tried and failed to place a constitutional ban on admitting free states into the Confederacy, but George Fitzhugh specifically pointed to the danger of introducing a "foreign element" into the new nation. In Marion, Alabama, Cornelia Lockett overheard many "imprecations on every living Yankee." Born in the North, she had married a southerner and Confederate officer no less but could never "overcome the feeling that persons do not look upon one [meaning herself] as anything but a Yankee." Perhaps once a Yankee, always a Yankee best summed up these attitudes. South Carolina governor Francis Pickens suggested that legislators add "into our Constitution a principle refusing to allow any man to vote, except those who were citizens at the time of our adoption of the present Confederate Constitution, or unless hereafter born in some one of the Confederate States." If the language was convoluted the meaning was clear: disfranchisement of future northern immigrants. Florida governor John Milton recommended that "no Yankee of doubtful character" be permitted to edit a newspaper.[30]

Support for disfranchising Yankee immigrants and other restrictive measures reflected a certain paradox. The Confederate drive for economic and cultural independence rested in part on a desire to quarantine the southern states against northern fanaticism. Yet if the nationalist project were successful—as most Confederates assumed it would be—the southern states would prove attractive to outsiders. The most sanguine expected a migratory flood once the war ended. Some feared that the degraded manufacturing classes of New England would flock to the South; others suggested keeping out the genuine Yankees while welcoming European immigrants.[31]

To have no real laboring class other than slaves and to remain an agricultural people, as some ideologues urged, meant keeping out a host of undesirables. Would "swarms of Yankees" suddenly infest the South like a great plague of locusts? They might arrive with what one editor called "their nasal whine, their vile notions, their viler manners, all at heart our enemies, but wearing the hypocritic mask of friendship." The characters of northerners and southerners were so at odds that the two "peoples" could never live together in peace, and that assumption fueled an editorial drumbeat for tough naturalization laws. More conservative voices hoped that such measures might even limit the influence of demagogues appealing to the easily manipulated masses. Any migration from a free state seemed frightening, especially when newspapers raised the specter of money-grubbing, Puritanical abolitionists casting their covetous eyes southward. As one Atlanta editor declared, "we want no more association with them [i.e., Yankees] this side of eternity," though he must not have thought there would be much chance of meeting any Yankees in heaven.[32]

The various components of anti-northern dogma filled these discussions along with an undercurrent of antidemocratic bias, but questions of class also appeared. Some Confederates reveled in finding new and colorful ways to condemn their enemies. The words simply poured forth: "rabble," "riffraff," "scum," all showing both disgust and contempt. The Yankees appeared to be creatures of a low order, and this became a convenient way both to denigrate the enemy and exalt the southern soldier. "The crowd we are to fight," declared one Georgia editor before any real fighting had taken place, consists of "roughs, thieves, [and] pickpockets." A Richmond editor added "unscrupulous liars . . . inveterate swindlers, coarse and brutish vulgarians" along with "swaggerers and poltroons" to this veritable rogue's gallery.[33]

In parlance familiar to white and black southerners alike, the Yankees were simply "white trash." One Confederate soldier considered Federals from the western states—he specifically mentioned Ohio—"scum, spawned of prairie mud, these world's wonders of brutality." Did not the northern government eagerly recruit paupers and criminals? Confederates readily dismissed Union soldiers as the "off-scouring" of humanity.[34]

Expressing a Jeffersonian disdain for city life that had also entered into the proslavery argument, Confederates routinely portrayed enemy soldiers as urban roughnecks. The Yankees were sending the most desperate characters into their armies. Straight from what the *Charleston Mercury* called "the stews of New York, Philadelphia, and Boston," these "ruffians" raised the age-old cry of "beauty and booty" as they prepared to despoil the South. Not to be outdone in rhetorical overkill, the *Richmond Dispatch* predicted that the bodies of these "thieving, idle, abandoned, dissolute, God-forsaken, hell-deserving and gallows-tending" Yankees would soon manure southern soil.[35]

The northern government had gathered up denizens of the barrooms and gutters; reports about drunken generals and rowdy enlisted men only confirmed old assumptions about the degradation of the northern masses and the inherent vices of a free-labor society. The stock characters of proslavery polemics all put in more than cameo appearances in Confederate propaganda. Would drunken and licentious brutes from New York's notorious Five Points set a new standard for inhumanity in war?[36] All this may appear wildly overstated, but anyone reading the southern press or even perusing private correspondence would have concluded that all the demons of hell were being loosed upon innocent southerners. And it was these reports and descriptions that shaped how flesh-and-blood Rebels would deal with flesh-and-blood Yankees. Confederate newspapers poured out reams of anti-Yankee polemics, and such diatribes not only shaped public opinion but influenced the war's course. Given the dark assessments of enemy character, the fight simply had to go on because the Yankees embodied nearly every contemptible characteristic in the human imagination.

To describe northern soldiers as "black-hearted" showed that outward appearance was not deceiving, the genuine Yankees being an evil creature through and through. One correspondent, whose writings appeared in many newspapers, derided the northern recruits as "human vermin" driven into the military by hunger and desperation. Forced by the war to conduct their courtship by correspondence, two young Georgians wrote of "vile" Yankees, "cowardly invaders," or simply "madmen." Women facing the problems that came with military occupation naturally hated to look upon a northern soldier, and some claimed their enemies really appeared different from other human beings.[37]

Their evil-looking faces bore all the marks of a fiendish character. To have such men walking the streets of southern towns, or even worse, entering southern homes and churches, became intolerable. For women, a hurried crossing to the other side of the street or a discreet veil could only partly assuage the pain and humiliation. Hard features and cruel expressions made the Yankees seem barely human. Many civilians and especially children had heard so many bloodcurdling tales that mere mention of the word "Yankee" proved frightening and disconcerting. "Such an abominable looking set they are," Ellen Renshaw House wrote from East Tennessee, her fury no doubt compounded by living among so many native Unionists. "None look like gentlemen," she sniffed. Another East Tennessee Rebel agreed there was "something repulsive in a Yankee's look. Not like the bold candor, handsome and brave heart of Southern heroes."[38]

Appearance and even odor supposedly reflected the invaders' base character. "I cannot bear to be nearer than three or four pews," a disgusted Mississippi woman wrote of the Yankees who trooped into her church. "They are such dirty creatures." And to think of these men entering a sacred place, that only redoubled the insult and increased Confederate ire. More aristocratic southerners added "common" to their depictions of filthy Yankees who occupied towns and cities. The mere presence of these men elicited strong reactions that often dripped with class prejudice. Damning them came naturally to southerners accustomed to social deference and unused to mingling with "common" whites. Observing some passing Union troops, a prisoner in St. Louis dismissed the entire lot as "dirty, filthy, low-lived pimps, thieves, and cut-throats."[39]

Confederates occasionally expressed surprise when Yankees acted like gentlemen but more often reported that their crude behavior matched their unkempt appearance. As the war swept back and forth through Winchester, Virginia, Mary Greenhow Lee had more contact with northern soldiers than she could ever have imagined (or certainly desired). On one occasion, she noted how a motley contingent who had recently been paid, immediately got drunk, tried to shake hands with the southern girls, and when rebuffed swore at them. Intoxicated and vulgar summed up the behavior of northern soldiers as far as many Confederates were concerned. According to General Lafayette McLaws, the Yankee pickets across the Rappahannock River from Fredericksburg, Virginia, did little but utter long strings of profanity. Some local Unionists admitted that "their feelings have changed to utter loathing for the depraved wretches, totally devoid as they are of all delicacy and decency and refinement." Not surprisingly, such debauched fellows scrawled obscenities on fences and buildings, and even inside churches.[40]

This hardly meant, as one Confederate soldier admitted, that southern troops while in camp or on the march did not curse and blaspheme. Yet he rationalized such momentary and emotional outbursts as opposed to the "foul and polluted phrases which gratuitously, like streams of filth, proceed out of the mouths of our adversaries." Worse still, the Yankees did not hesitate to cut loose in front of ladies, and the officers hardly attempted to curb the foul-mouthed enlisted men. "Their throats were open sepulchers," the pious Mary Mallard wrote as some of William T. Sherman's men swarmed around her Georgia home. With Columbia, South Carolina, in flames, young Emma LeConte recorded the scenes in her diary. Bluecoats stormed through the town, "swearing—blaspheming—singing ribald songs and using such obscene language that we were forced to go indoors." She added a final bitter note: "This is the way in which the 'cultured' Yankee nation wars upon women and children! Failing with our men in the field, *this* is the way they must conquer!"[41] All might be seemingly lost, her town in flames, and her own home threatened, but LeConte would maintain her sense of cultural superiority and perhaps still nurse the illusion that such dreadful, godless creatures could not possibly triumph in the end.

Profane language further marked the depths of Yankee depravity. In abandoned Federal camps along the Rappahannock River, Confederates discovered scores of obscene books. But then as George Fitzhugh had pointed out in the midst of the secession crisis, northern literary taste had long run to the "vulgar, infidel, sinful, and base." Reports of enemy letters left behind on battlefields after Confederate victories inevitably termed them crude and indecent. Southern soldiers explained to their families that the correspondence was too disgusting to quote or send home. More shocking still, even Yankee women wrote vulgar letters to their menfolk. Giving readers a bit of titillation, one newspaper reported that these missives were "indescribably vile, containing confession, of illicit intercourse, filthy and obscene anecdotes, told in coarse language." However repulsive Confederates claimed to find these letters, the *Richmond Whig* recommended the documents be retained, "bound in book form, in the Congressional Library" as "irrefutable proof" of the Yankees' "moral depravity."[42]

Abraham Lincoln—the natural leader of an utterly corrupt and degraded people—had dispatched these degenerate legions. To Confederates, he perfectly fit the vulgar Yankee mold, and some commentators connected the president's humble birth to his low character. A Richmond editor ran through a long list of adjectives to describe a man at once despotic and despicable: "shrewd, energetic, shallow, cunning, selfish, egotistical, hard hearted, vulgar, hypocritical, and fanatical." And entering the White House, a rival editor pointed out, would come "slang, rowdyism, brutality, and all moral filth; . . . the tag and rag of Western grog-shops and Yankee factories." Even before the inauguration, a South Carolina fire-eater's wife complained about how Lincoln "bandies jokes" with just about anyone and "kisses bold women from promiscuous crowds." Where this last bit of intelligence came from, she did not say, and it did not matter. Every report of some scandal back in Illinois or smutty stories repeated during a cabinet meeting became fodder for the southern press. That this rail-splitter from the western prairie would be crude and unprincipled almost went without saying. A long and wretched "dramatic poem" portrayed Lincoln as a "royal ape" talking to himself and drunkenly leering at young girls. Wild tales of Lincoln's "Negro blood" rounded out this picture of a man who had sunk—in Confederate eyes—to the lowest rung on the social ladder.[43]

Lincoln had already ruined Washington society, and his minions promised more of the same in the southern states. The operative word became "pollute," and Yankee soldiers became part of this general contagion. Soldiers and civilians alike talked as if the very feet of their enemies would taint anything they touched; Confederates often referred to the Yankees' "filthy tread." Their footsteps despoiled the most sacred grounds of southern memory, and Confederates strained their imaginations and vocabularies to convey their outrage.[44]

Early in the war, a North Carolina editor hoped that brave Tar Heels would soon drive out "Abe's mercenaries" from the U.S. Capitol "where they have quartered their vile carcasses of pollution and filth." But instead the enemy's invading hosts would eventually contaminate the very soil of the Southland. It was almost as if Confederates were warning against some impending environmental disaster. Virginians especially fretted about dangers posed to their state's "sacred soil." Public meetings and calls for more troops all summoned Confederates to throw back the Yankees' polluting advance.[45]

The language was often wildly evocative. "Had we manfully resisted the first aggression," the mayor of Savannah advised his father as Georgia was seceding, "we might have stifled the serpent in its den, and not now have been suffering from the poisonous brood which with hissing tongue and noxious breath are crawling everywhere and polluting the otherwise wholesome air of this once pure and happy country." Alarms about invading Yankees took many forms. Abolitionists were part of this plague, but they were mixed in with soldier mobs sacking cities and, of course, despoiling the streets. Indeed, the Yankees' very presence would defile churches. Such prospects appeared both frightening and imminent as Confederate officers rallied their forces to repel the foe.[46]

And worst of all, reprehensible Yankees would assail the sacred circle of home and family. And defending the hearth—a common enough cry in any war—became especially powerful in a society with a widely scattered population and few large cities. The threat to isolated women and children in rural areas nearly stripped of menfolk seemed palpable. One South Carolinian waxed poetic:

> The demon Goth pollute our halls
> With fire and lust and hate

A Georgia editor summoned his fellow citizens to "protect your homes from the pollution of these Northern negro worshippers." To dismiss such statements as newspaper bombast would be a mistake. The prospect of Union soldiers daring to enter those private places most dear to southerners proved especially horrifying for civilians even as it worried and enraged Confederate soldiers. In early 1865, Virginian Lou Fleet spoke for thousands of others in noting how the cry "the Yankees are coming" could send her heart sinking "below zero." She had been packing a box for her dear brother in the army and could "just imagine their hateful hands dipping in the pickle we had just fixed."[47]

Her brother Fred likely assessed the threat in a much different way because throughout the war, Confederate propagandists predicted that enemy soldiers would also "pollute" mothers, sisters, wives, and daughters. Where were the red-blooded southern men who would protect innocent women from lustful Federals? The implicit threat of rape lingered here because with many of the men off fighting, not only had the home circle been broken and violated, but families in many areas had been left defenseless. What these people would suffer under longer-term Yankee occupation became a favorite theme of officers addressing their troops before a battle, or newspaper editors seeking to rouse resistance to the invaders. A Georgian on the Virginia Peninsula defined the proper response: ""The acme of a Southern soldier's ambition consists in the fervent hope that he be afforded the earliest practicable chance of crossing bayonets with the mercenaries of a despotic tyrant who has without a cause forced upon him the alternative of resistance to servilism and drive him in confusion and dismay from the sacred soil of the sunny South!"[48]

Many Confederates believed or at least hoped that such bold statements would inspire equally bold deeds. A combination of sheer bravado and wishful thinking added a dangerous and almost serene arrogance to many tirades against the northern enemy. This was especially true for civilians far removed from the battlefields. "I would rather see Richmond shelled a thousand times than have a Yankee pollute the soil by his tread," Maggie Tucker wrote as General George B. McClellan's army inched toward the Confederate capital. Others noted the utter shame of being killed by such brutes, and even at the end of the war some Confederates could hardly believe that what a South Carolina woman called the "vilest of the vile, the dregs of earth" would prevail.[49] How could southern soldiers fail to defeat such an enemy? How could God allow such devils to succeed? The very character of the Yankees must surely in the end thwart their barbarous designs.

CHAPTER 3

The Barbarous Yankees

His purpose was to instill fear of a yet distant and somewhat amorphous enemy in order to drive the state of Kentucky out of the Union. Alabamian Stephen F. Hale would do his best, and though trained as a lawyer, this graduate of Transylvania University would put aside logical appeals for visceral ones. Should the secession movement fail, he warned Kentucky governor Beriah Magoffin, "the dark pall of barbarism must soon gather over our sunny land, and the scenes of West India emancipation, with its attendant horrors and crimes . . . be re-enacted in their own land upon a more gigantic scale."[1] Everyone could have expected Hale to play on racial anxieties, but the "pall of barbarism" struck a complementary and equally ominous chord. Months before the Civil War began and months before the Yankees had committed a single "barbarous" act, Hale was anticipating the worst. He was not alone. Rants against northern savagery would become pervasive during the war, but even in the midst of the secession crisis and at the very beginning of the contest, secessionists were already labeling the Yankees barbarians.

Many of these early blasts against the Yankees grew out of long-held convictions about the character of northern society, but Confederates soon fleshed out a horrific picture of invading hordes. General descriptions gave way to often vividly painted word portraits of a relentless and remorseless enemy. The key here is perception and emotion rather than reason or ideology.[2] The question became not so much the policies and actions of the northern government and northern armies but how those policies and actions were interpreted and presented. Rhetoric might partly reflect reality but at the same time deal in caricature and exaggeration. The result was a frightening picture of a cruel and merciless adversary. Yankee generals egged on by both politicians and the northern public would let loose a brutal soldiery on the southern people. Thieving, destructive, and unmerciful Yankees would conduct a war that would shame the most benighted savage. Confederate propagandists built on their cultural assumptions about infidel and degraded northerners to emphasize and exaggerate their enemies' crimes.

Only days after the firing on Fort Sumter, a Richmond editor fumed about the "barbarians who compose the lower orders of the Northern cities," but in his view the more respectable Yankees were even worse. He portrayed the "wealthy classes" as "reptiles who have emerged from the same Stygian mud in which the more demonstrative and unclean mob are now wallowing." Presenting an expansive notion of barbarism, some Confederates cited the most unexceptional acts of warfare to predict the Yankees would soon reach new depths of depravity. In their fevered imaginations, it seemed like the earth was about to enter into a new dark age. This titanic struggle would mean a contest conducted without rules, with standards of civilized conduct simply tossed aside; it would be a war without mercy waged by a cruel and vindictive people. In point of fact, some Confederates argued, Yankees would prove to be far worse than the barbarian hordes that for centuries had formed such a blot on human history.[3]

Yet definitions of barbarism have always been elastic, wildly varying over space, time, and culture. "Everyone gives the title of barbarism to everything that is not according to his usage," the French essayist Montaigne had sharply observed. But not surprisingly, most Confederates showed little appreciation for cultural relativism if they even recognized the concept. To label (and libel) enemies as barbarians, savages, semihuman, or even subhuman had long been common in wars of all kinds. Even conflicts between "brothers" or closely related people (the American Revolution being a prime example) had produced much demonizing of the enemy, and in any case it was all too easy to see wartime foes as inherently treacherous.[4]

In war, people plumb the depths of their opponents' evil characteristics and define their adversaries' essential nature in ways that explain why their enemies are worth fighting. Aside from ethnic and racial epithets, historical references worked well to show how the Yankees had descended to a level of brutality comparable to some horrific example from another era.

Confederates often referred to them as "Goths," "Huns," or "Vandals," with occasional "Visigoths" or "merciless Danes" thrown in for variety. Sometimes Confederates tried to explain how such labels applied to their enemies but usually just assumed they fit the case. A sonnet published in the *Charleston Mercury* somehow brought Yankees, Huns, and Vandals together for an "hourly" crucifixion of Christ. Preachers and churches compared Yankee crimes to those of various savage peoples who had rampaged for both blood and spoils across the pages of human history. Even during the war's first year, one editor was trumpeting Yankee outrages that "would have disgraced the Goths and Vandals."[5]

Historical references to the decline and fall of the Roman Empire had long been a staple of American political discourse, but Confederate polemicists ranged much further afield. Perhaps the Yankees had "sunk to a level with the Barbary States," as one Virginian suggested. Maybe savage Arabs or cruel Hottentots were more comparable. Turks, Tartars, and Mongols might be worth mentioning as well.[6] Neither plausibility nor precision mattered in such statements. What counted was the ability to stir outrage against the foe and presumably support for the Confederate war effort. Early on, some journalists cited the Sepoy rebellion in India as a model for Yankee brutality. Eventually some even called the Federals "Sepoys" or compared atrocities in Missouri, for example, to the outrages committed by the Indian mutineers against the British. Abandoning such specific, human comparisons, a few Confederates simply claimed their enemies behaved like demons or devils.[7]

If the Yankees had in fact turned into cruel Sepoys or tools of Satan, one might readily conclude they were barely human—if human at all. The word *dehumanization* first appeared in the early nineteenth century, but the idea had been around much longer. Ancient texts had compared people to various animals, and Enlightenment concepts such as the Great Chain of Being, not to mention the pseudoscientific racism so popular in antebellum America, made it possible to consign entire swaths of humanity to the bestial realm. In June 1861, a North Carolina minister spoke of the "polluting touch of the Northern vandals, from whom every spark of humanity appears to have departed." Nor were such sentiments simply for public consumption. In the summer of 1863, with Confederate fortunes riding high right before Gettysburg, an official in the Confederate War Department wrote in his diary:

"The Earth contains no race [i.e., the Yankees] so lost to every sentiment of manliness, honor, faith, or humanity, at once so servile and so tyrannical, so mean and so cruel, such willing slaves, and so bent on destroying the independence and existence of their enemy."[8]

To the most ardent Confederates, the world had entered into a dark age of Yankee barbarism. Northern armies had stayed the progress of humanity toward a more restrained brand of warfare and were reverting to the savagery of the Middle Ages. Even Goths and other uncivilized people, a Texas chaplain wrote, "exhibited more of kindness and nobleness of nature" than General William S. Rosecrans's forces advancing through Tennessee, but then the Southern Baptist Convention had made a similar statement about Yankees more generally only a month after the firing on Fort Sumter. The wicked nature of the northern armies and their commanders appeared all encompassing, involving everything from the most revolting crimes to the pettiest acts of vengeance.[9]

The Yankees behaved as savages not out of some momentary burst of passion or because war itself is cruel but because brutality was simply part of their nature. Confederates maintained that barbaric acts revealed the essence of northern character. According to the president of the Georgia Senate, Federals ignored "all the claims of humanity" and exhibited "a contempt even of the canons of civilization" that was "almost without a parallel in the annals of our race." In a rather ironic twist given Confederate complaints about a fiendish enemy showing an utter disregard for the southern people, such statements in turn barely acknowledged the Yankees' own humanity.[10] Confederates often condemned their adversaries as people without a conscience who felt no remorse over the worst crimes. Standards of justice and morality meant nothing to men whose wanton acts of cruelty struck at the very heart of civilized life.[11]

Confederates buttressed their case with a multitude of atrocity stories widely reported and reprinted in the newspapers. Civil wars always generate deep anger that make attempts to control violence and protect civilians more difficult. Intense hatred and brutality go hand in hand as charges and countercharges bring calls for retaliation. Such cycles of recrimination become hard to break and so help lengthen wars and poison the peace. And of course what counts as an "atrocity" is very much in the proverbial eye of the beholder. Naval blockades had long generated diplomatic and legal controversy, but Confederates defined the mere interdiction of supplies as especially malevolent. More serious charges soon appeared, though they often included a tantalizing mix of fact and rumor. Reports that Yankees left their dead unburied on battlefields—especially after First Bull Run and Fredericksburg—clearly reaffirmed what many southerners already believed about their erstwhile enemies. So did rumors that the Federals were using poisoned ammunition, had handcuffs at the ready for Confederate prisoners, or encouraged what amounted to assassination by sharpshooters.[12]

As the war continued and intensified, so did Confederate complaints. Showing no regard for innocent life, the Yankees shelled towns and cities; and a Lynchburg editor raged over the "modern Goths and Vandals" attacking Fredericksburg, a place associated with the sacred memory of George Washington. What another editor termed a "barbarous horde of Bedouin Arabs" had then sacked the town as General Ambrose Burnside's Army of the Potomac degenerated into a "mob of thieves and outlaws." The subsequent battle of Fredericksburg brought an appropriately bloody retribution for these crimes.[13] To the most ardent Confederates, the dead of Fredericksburg were clearly the victims—innocent and not so innocent—of the Yankees' own cruel and brutal mode of warfare.

That campaign had produced a goodly number of refugees, and when so many families had to flee their homes all across the South, it appeared as if the world were entering into a new dark age. "What we may all expect," screamed a headline in a Milledgeville, Georgia, newspaper after William T. Sherman's army expelled civilians from Atlanta. Was there any outrage—large or small—the Yankees would not commit? Smaller incidents sometimes generated a great deal of indignation. Near Front Royal, Virginia, soldiers gleefully slaughtered chickens in a Baptist church and tore apart school desks.[14]

Anecdotes and accusations steadily accumulated, receiving much public and private attention in every imaginable venue. Newspaper editorials detailed various enormities in expansive and imaginative language. Talk of invasion, destruction, arrests, and even extermination became commonplace in Confederate screeds. Besides praying for Rebel victories, preachers held forth against godless foes warring on the aged and the young, men and women alike. Politicians' stump speeches overflowed with anti-Yankee invective; pamphleteers recounted everything from abusing prisoners to counterfeiting Confederate currency. Writing home, soldiers blasted their northern opponents for all manner of barbarities.[15] What is perhaps most remarkable is the range and consistency in all of these sources, and this shows how demonization of the Yankee enemy resonated with a vast array of people throughout the Confederate South.

Sheer repetition of even the more improbable incidents no doubt brought greater conviction. Secretary of State Judah P. Benjamin—hardly a naïve flag-waver—wrote in a diplomatic dispatch to John Slidell that "no crime is too revolting for this vile race." After running through a long list of Yankee misdeeds, Benjamin defined enemy intentions in the starkest and most extreme terms: "I entertain no doubt whatever that hundreds of thousands of people at the North would be frantic with fiendish delight if informed of the universal massacre of the Southern people, including women and children, in one night. They would then only have to exterminate the blacks (which they are fast doing now), and they would become owners of the property which they covet, and for which they are fighting."[16]

Benjamin recognized the propaganda value of atrocity stories, as did other politicians. Governor Henry Watkins Allen ordered "reports of Yankee outrages" compiled so that the "world may know . . . what Louisiana has suffered." In part, he sought to create a historical record for future generations, but more importantly the hair-raising descriptions would presumably stir a patriotic revival in his beleaguered state. The people needed to realize that Yankees would not only destroy plantations, they would plunder libraries and most anything else, leaving paths of destruction that spared neither Unionists nor slaves. The fiends would rob men, women, children, and even the dead. God himself, declared one Episcopal clergyman, would record these horrific crimes "in the book of remembrance" and would eventually requite them with blood. All wars produce atrocities and atrocity stories, and for participants the emphasis is almost always on placing the guilt on one side. These tales not only portrayed Yankees as unrelenting brutes but Confederates as innocent victims. After detailing outrages that ranged from deliberately infecting prisoners with contagious diseases to stripping infants of their clothing, the Confederate Congress concluded that "the atrocities are too incredible for narration."[17] Just as southern virtues were too many to enumerate.

Claiming to be shocked by enemy behavior even during the war's first year, Jefferson Davis stressed Yankee barbarism to win sympathy for the Confederate cause abroad and sustain patriotic sacrifice at home. In November 1861, he accused the enemy of shelling "undefended villages without giving notice to women and children." He feigned surprise about this and other deviltries while claiming that the Yankees stood outside the bounds of humanity. In later addresses and like other politicians and editors, Davis rattled off long lists of enemy misdeeds. The language was often inflammatory, and in messages to the Confederate Congress he recounted particular episodes such as the bombardment of Charleston or excoriated the most obnoxious Union generals. And he emphasized how the victims were often the young, the aged, and the unarmed.[18]

Davis and others maintained that the Yankees' crimes had not only revealed their true character but had been followed by renewed evidence of southern patriotism and self-sacrifice. All across the Confederacy, generals issued orders summoning men to resist the invading hordes. With a great gift for bombast, John Bankhead Magruder struck some typical notes: "Our barbarous foe already gloats over the prospect of your desolated homes, and your helpless women sacrificed to his unbridled licentiousness." As the war dragged on, it was not only fear of future torment but also the memory of past depredations that inspired troops to keep up the fight. Here was the connection between accounts of enemy atrocities and soldier motivation. In Jackson County, Georgia, a meeting of women saw a clear linkage: to "prevent such barbarism from coming upon us, our brave soldiers are now rushing out by thousands, deaf to the roaring of the cannon, and blind to the mangled bodies of those who fall victim to the cruelty of the enemy."[19]

Such perfervid statements are easily discounted, but the most dedicated soldiers echoed the rhetoric of the editors, politicians, and other civilians. In one of the last letters he wrote to his wife before being mortally wounded at the Battle of Cedar Creek, Dodson Ramseur railed against the "miserable Yankees" who had "placed themselves outside of the pale of civilization" by their fiendish destruction in the Shenandoah Valley. A quartermaster in General George Pickett's division could hardly find the words to express his disgust for these "miscreants, barbarians, thieves and scoundrels, disgraces of humanity" and could only hope that "the avenging anger of a righteous and just God will ultimately blot them out of existence or make them a prey to their own miserable and fiendish hearts." Cries for vengeance only intensified as the war dragged into its second, third, fourth years. Historian Kenneth Noe has argued that repelling a barbarous invader motivated many later-enlisting Confederates. Early in 1865, a resolution adopted in a South Carolina brigade announced that the men's determination to keep fighting had only been strengthened by the enemy's "outrages and cruelty." Although offensives directed at the civilian population such as William T. Sherman's marches through Georgia and the Carolinas further fueled public rage against the Yankees, a deep loathing for the enemy had been apparent from the very beginning of the war.[20]

The result was more fighting and more bloodshed as Confederates maintained that the northerners' demonic nature made peace and reconciliation inconceivable, a point repeatedly emphasized even as Confederate fortunes plummeted. After reading about General David Hunter's rampage through the Shenandoah Valley, Catherine Edmondston decided that such crimes had so "embittered the war . . . that Peace seems scarcely possible." One could hardly consider the United States any longer a Christian nation, and indeed Yankee depredations had (or at least should have) squelched all talk of compromise and reunion. Northerners might claim they were simply fighting for the old Union, but their behavior proved otherwise. How could any loyal Confederate contemplate "reconstruction" with such a people? Early in the war a North Carolina private pointedly remarked how the ruins and lone chimneys in Kinston, North Carolina, "show how the Yankees are trying to reconstruct the Union." In a striking editorial entitled "War as Beneficial Evil," the *Daily South Carolinian* even argued that wartime hatred had become providential. Upon a complete separation from the U.S. government and northern society "depends not merely our sole mode of escape from the sure contamination which must result from any association with the most corrupt race that ever defiled the earth, but also the sole mode of preserving true liberty, genuine virtue and pure religion upon this continent." Ironically therefore, beleaguered Confederates "ought to rejoice at every new barbarity which the enemy perpetrates, every repeated violation of the laws of war which brings down upon him the contempt of the world, and every additional proof which he gives that he is growing more reckless in his carnival of crime."[21] This all signified a certain desperation, though a desperation masked by wishful thinking and sheer delusion.

Destruction—both real and imagined—became the surest sign of Yankee barbarism, with references to Goths or Vandals or invading hordes that emphasized this particular brand of villainy. One widely circulated story reported that some three years before the war, William H. Seward had crafted a policy calling for the "total destruction of all existing things in the Southern States," a scheme that went beyond physical wreckage to include the social cataclysm of emancipation.[22] Rumors of dark plots and deep-laid conspiracies had long been pervasive in antebellum America, and the Confederates sought to fit each new example of Yankee misbehavior into some larger design. Thus events both large and small, incidents both major and minor all became part of an overall narrative of enemy perfidy and savagery.

By 1863 if not before, ruin and wreckage had seemingly marked the paths of northern armies. According to the *Charleston Mercury*, the "track of the destroyer" had "laid waste" to much of Virginia, Tennessee, the Carolina coast, most of Florida, and parts of Mississippi, Louisiana, Arkansas, and Missouri. The exaggeration here was breathtaking and dramatic even by wartime standards, but more was involved here than merely the scope of the devastation. All this damage was not simply an unfortunate side effect of war. The raising of Union troops in western Virginia, Governor John Letcher charged, formed part of a deliberate design to "desolate the firesides" and provoke "bloodshed and massacre." All this created an iniquitous policy carried out by northern generals. "From first to last," claimed a major writing from Lee's headquarters in the midst of the Overland Campaign, "Grant has shown great skill and prudence combined with remorseless persistency and brutality. He is a scientific Goth resembling Alaric, destroying the country as he goes, and delivering the people over to starvation." In the view of Jefferson Davis and many others, the northern politicians, generals, and soldiers deliberately violated the rules of "civilized warfare."[23] However oxymoronic that phrase might be, it expressed a firm conviction that Yankee destructiveness knew few limits but also reflected a diabolically crafted plan.

Even the southern food supply became fair—or Confederates would have said unfair—game for northern marauders. Recounting how enemy armies had deliberately ravaged homes, gardens, fields, and mills that provided sustenance for innocent civilians, War Department ordnance chief Josiah Gorgas plaintively asked, "Has war ever been carried on like this before, among civilized people?" Soldiers and their families complained of bluecoats snatching bread from the mouths of women and children, and such statements proved all of a piece with the more general outrage over destructive northern armies. One Virginia woman compared a score or so Union soldiers to a "pack of wolves in the smoke house." As these men gleefully cut off the heads of her mother's chickens, she could only hope "to see the guillotine take their heads off in just such rapid style." When Yankees burned homes and barns, provisions also went up in flames, with families reduced to beggary. In early 1863, one Georgia editor charged that the northern government had "turned its war for the nigger into one of general devastation and destruction." The Yankees could boast of having "General Starvation" and famine on their side in a war against the defenseless. The mother of a prominent Confederate general claimed that the Yankees who arrived in St. Augustine, Florida, were showing a "determination to starve the poor women and children into submission."[24] Again all such crimes were no mere side effects of a bloody war; they reflected the intentions of a remorseless enemy.

By carrying out a policy of destruction, and especially by burning homes and displacing families, the Yankees descended to new depths of inhumanity. Obviously these tactics were at least partially effective, and the plaintiveness of the civilian protests reflected that success. Watching Federals take pleasure in ravaging the countryside made their presence all that more frightening whether Confederates admitted it or not. What nurse Kate Cumming termed the "insatiate Moloch" war found many victims among women and children left homeless by the invading armies. Whether in official statements, editorials, or even songs, Confederate propagandists trumpeted the sufferings of helpless civilians driven from towns and cities.[25]

The home folks often had little to subsist on because Yankees were remarkably thorough in their destructive raids. Solders would grab most anything, according to one Mississippian, and especially sought to wreck farm equipment in a "diabolical determination" to starve out their enemies. A Louisianan reported that the Teche country had become "a complete desolation and a solitude." One midwar estimate placed damage inflicted by northern troops in various parts of the Confederacy at $15 million, but most accounts stressed the nature and scope of the destruction more than its quantity or cost. Long denunciations of Yankee depredations emphasized their supposedly unprecedented, relentless, and inhuman character. When the famous fire-eater Edmund Ruffin railed against northern policies of "plunder" and "extermination" along with "cruelty and atrocity" in Virginia carried out "on the most extended scale of operations ever known in civilized regions, or attempted by a people claiming to be Christian," he was hardly alone.[26]

Newspapers reported (and people repeated) many stories—both true and highly embroidered—of Yankee depredations. Whether such wanton acts reflected northern policy and purpose depended upon the particular line of criticism. Were the Yankees cleverly fiendish, or uncontrollably barbaric? Part of the Confederate outrage focused on their enemies' evil schemes, but unpredictability and capriciousness might also explain random plundering. The apparent carnival of destruction, claimed one Tennessee planter, "would better suit an army of Savages than of a Christian people." A host of examples drove home this point. According to Captain William L. Nugent, Albany, Mississippi, had gone up in flames simply because some "Dutch rascal wanted to warm his toes" and had set a house ablaze to avoid having to gather wood. In Confederate telling, the sack of Fredericksburg before, during, and after the battle became little more than complete pandemonium and pointless damage that spared neither homes nor churches. Jedediah Hotchkiss thought there was "scarce one thing that makes life pleasant and comfortable that the Vandals have left behind or have not destroyed."[27]

Even as they supposedly committed outrage upon outrage, the Yankees claimed to be engaged in a holy crusade for freedom when in fact they had declared war against the Almighty. Here the Confederate critique of Yankee behavior broadened into a wide-ranging attack on northern society whose declension had proceeded steadily and inexorably. Echoing antebellum sectional broadsides, polemicists outlined the steps in this devil's progress. Not only had the Yankees embraced radical religious doctrines if not infidelity itself, they carried out their destructive policies in the name of religion. The blood-curdling rhetoric of various Christian groups in the northern states encouraged the soldiers in their assaults against civilized values. Claims to a superior philanthropy and theology all preceded sending armies of mercenaries and ruffians to ravage and kill. With great shows of piety, hymn-singing troops devastated the southern countryside, and their worship amounted to little more than blasphemy against the Lord's holy ordinances. The Yankees' official thanksgiving proclamations barely masked their hypocrisy. Referring back to Reverend Henry Ward Beecher's notorious dispatch of rifles to bleeding Kansas in the 1850s, Confederates accused their enemies of preaching a "gospel of murder."[28]

For sure, the Yankees had preached and practiced a gospel of destruction, and one that extended to the most sacred places. Early in the war, Federal troops uttering all manner of horrid oaths reportedly destroyed a fine Episcopal church in Centreville, Virginia, mutilating the pulpit Bible and scrawling obscenities on the altar. Besides citing specific incidents, newspapers broadly charged the Yankees with defiling churches. In Louisiana, an official report accused Federals troops of showing less respect for religious property than had the French Jacobins.[29]

"The Yankees are afraid of prayer," declared one editor of a religious newspaper. And well they might be, for as many Confederates pointed out, the fiends apparently took pleasure in destruction. "These people delight to destroy the weak, and those who can make no defense; it just suits them," remarked Robert E. Lee as the Federals shelled Fredericksburg. Raiding parties entered homes and reveled in busting up furniture, chopping up pianos, and tearing up libraries. One Confederate speculated that even Yankee prisoners likely dreamed of "burning dwellings and devastated fields, of pillage and rapine."[30]

Their actions, thoughts, and fantasies contrasted sharply with those of the Confederates who claimed to be fighting for the noblest of motives. On entering Kentucky in the fall of 1862, General Braxton Bragg drew a clear distinction: "We come not as conquerors or as despoilers, but to restore to you the liberties of which you have been deprived by a cruel and relentless foe." Confederate armies, according to the standard narrative line, embodied the very flower of youth whose pure hearts and lofty patriotism should inspire a war-weary and outnumbered people to yet greater sacrifices. Pointing to how the Army of Northern Virginia had respected civilian property during the Gettysburg campaign and speaking for many others, Jefferson Davis asserted that soldiers' "forbearance" sprang from "their own self-respect, which forbade their degenerating from Christian warriors into plundering ruffians, assailing the property, lives, and honor of helpless noncombatants. If their conduct, when thus contrasted with the inhuman practices of our foe, fail to command the respect and sympathy of civilized nations in our day, it cannot fail to be recognized by their less deceived posterity."[31] This last statement at least hinted at the possibility of defeat but still promised ultimate historical vindication. Some Confederates might no longer be able to assert that the forces of barbarism would certainly fail, but they still expressed great faith that the judgment of future generations would fall heavily on their enemies.

In the short term at least, such statements served important political purposes, and leading Confederates recognized the usefulness of trumpeting and exaggerating enemy savagery. In a lengthy 1862 proclamation, Virginia governor John Letcher condemned the "hirelings who have pillaged our land, desecrated our churches, polluted our fair fields, sacked our towns, and insulted the innocent and helpless." Federal officers had "sent their myrmidons into churches and dragged our ministers from the sacred desk for a mere omission to put up a petition to the Almighty for their execrated President." Innocent men and women had been thrown into dank prisons. Channeling grievances echoing from the era of the American Revolution, Letcher complained about the quartering of Federal troops in private homes. Warming to his subject, the governor cited still more fearful and, what he considered, unprecedented crimes: "When has it been known that wives and pure and spotless maidens have been violated by soldiers without an effort on the part of their officers to pursue the perpetrators with the vengeance of the law?" Nor did Union troops apparently hesitate to fire on clearly marked hospitals. And in occupied areas, Federal commanders persecuted and even executed Confederate civilians. At the local level, citizens offered similar descriptions of northern outrages. Responding to stinging military defeats early in 1862, a "War Meeting" in Carroll County, Mississippi, touched on nearly every politically potent theme: "Our homes are threatened with instant invasion by vandal hordes, our families with pollution, our property with destruction, and civil liberty with extermination. We contend with an enemy who spares neither age, sex, nor condition; whose fearful pathway is marked by desolation."[32]

Secretary of War James A. Seddon maintained that the Federals' "atrocious system of warfare" had "never been practiced by any people professing civilization and Christianity" but predicted that all the destruction would "awaken the abhorrence of Christendom, as it has aroused among our people glowing indignation and thirst for vengeance." Seddon wrote these comments to Lee less than a month before Gettysburg, and they suggested equal measures of indignation and confidence. Some officers talked of Almighty God's avenging arm or of Confederate victories causing rivers to run red with Yankee blood. As even war-weary soldiers explained to their families, the fight against these predatory invaders must go on. If his wife could only fathom the Yankees' evil designs, a North Carolina officer wrote early in the conflict, "you would say keep this war as far from our own soil as possible."[33]

But most of the fighting would be on southern soil, and as the war grew more destructive, the mental and psychological anguish mounted. After Lincoln was reelected in 1864, a Virginia editor, having witnessed the devastation of the Shenandoah Valley, warned: "The unbridled licentiousness of the past four years is to be continued for the next four, with all the ingenious adjuncts which the minds of our Barbarian Enemies can devise." Like the politicians, the most ardent Confederates hoped that the destruction they had already witnessed and ever-darkening future prospects would rally their less dedicated neighbors. "Women of the South," nurse Kate Cumming pled, "let us remember we have a foe as relentless as Tamerlane or Atilla, who, if we are to believe his own threats, has resolved to lay our towns in ashes, lay waste our fields, and make our fair land a blackened mass of ruins if we will not submit to his domination."[34]

Confederate propagandists emphasized "barbarism" and "destruction" in explicating both Yankee policy and behavior, but soldiers and civilians, and of course editors and politicians, also decried northern troops as mere thieves and plunderers. "Booty" had become their watchword, indeed their main goal and guiding principle. In the summer of 1861, an address to a Georgia rifle company drew the inevitable contrast: "The Northern hordes come upon you for pillage and for plunder. . . . You fight for God and liberty." In strikingly similar language ("power and plunder" versus "liberty and independence"), Georgia governor Joe Brown limned the stark differences in both motive and character that made subjugation to the northern enemy unthinkable.[35]

Sneaking about and stealing everything in sight somehow suited the Yankee temperament—certainly better than facing brave Confederates on an open battlefield. What one Rebel cavalry officer termed the "rich prospect of plunder" was the real reason the invaders kept up the fight. And this was thievery carried out on a grand scale and maybe even according to a grand design, some Confederates concluded. Northern businessmen, declared the *Richmond Dispatch*, literally speculated in blood; the war best served the interests of corrupt contractors. This in turn led to accusations that the Union government intended to colonize the South for the benefit of moneyed interests. Merchants, manufacturers, but most of all politicians, expected to reap the profits of human misery. This explained (albeit not all that logically) why the pillaging was so thorough: each act of thievery helped advance a systematic policy.[36]

Reckless destruction came at a high price because the war cost the northern government more than a million dollars each day, though even on this score there was a devilish Yankee method to the seeming Yankee madness. After the war, the northern government would confiscate southerners' property and impose onerous taxes to pay off a staggering public debt. Edmund Ruffin compared all this to Oliver Cromwell's treatment of Ireland. In the meantime, Yankee armies would subsist off the southern countryside, seizing everything from cotton bales to the smallest household items. According to Confederate accounts, Yankees would steal most anything. They came looking for whiskey, or grabbed food off dinner tables, and in Tennessee snatched up hens sitting on eggs.[37]

Conciliating such brigands would not work. During the Red River campaign, a Louisiana woman politely offered one of General Nathaniel P. Banks's commanders a drink of water from a silver goblet, but after slaking his thirst the rascal examined the cup, slipped it into his pocket, and rode off. Federal soldiers even purloined ladies' dresses for their womenfolk back home. Nor were the old and feeble spared by the northern vandals;

reports of grave-robbing circulated in the press. Such tales proved—at least to the satisfaction of loyal Confederates—that Yankee thieving knew few bounds, and worse atrocities would surely follow should the northern armies prevail.[38]

Besides being thorough and unremitting, the thieving was shameless. "Yankee preachers," claimed Governor Henry Watkins Allen, "boastfully exhibit on their shelves rare and costly books stolen from the libraries of Southern gentlemen. Yankee women are daily seen in the streets of Yankee cities and towns, bedecked in stolen silks and bespangled with jewels of which their husbands and paramours have robbed the persons of our country-women. Yankee boys drink from stolen silver cups, while Yankee babies cut their teeth on stolen silver spoons!" His Alabama counterpart Thomas H. Watts complained about works of art and even small knickknacks spirited off from southern homes and now adorning northern parlors.[39]

But what else could be expected given the makeup of Union armies? Confederates believed or at least accused their enemies of filling regiments with burglars and other criminals, thieving having literally become a qualification for service. A Georgia editor sneered that whatever the Yankees' failings on the battlefield, they absolutely excelled at thievery. They had learned this trade from a tender age, and so rather than developing the moral courage of the soldier they displayed the brute courage of the highwayman.[40]

Soldier behavior may have reflected the enemy's broader national character, but Confederates often shifted from describing the Yankees as an undifferentiated mass of barbarians to focusing on specific generals who had repeatedly behaved in an uncivilized way. When in May 1862 General John Basil Turchin allowed his soldiers to sack Athens, Alabama, denunciations of this Russian-born officer as "Lincoln's Cossack" inevitably followed. Some Confederates mildly observed that Lincoln and his generals were simply not gentlemen, but more often they echoed the words of a South Carolina pamphleteer who reeled off a long list of Yankee commanders bound to share in the "eternal shame and disgrace of their [soldiers'] innumerable savage enormities, their wholesale burglaries, their arsons, their rapes, and their murders."[41]

By Confederate lights, no northern general more deserved obloquy, or for that matter the lowest place in hell, than Benjamin F. Butler. In an early 1863 speech, after a passing reference to the "stealing of our silver forks and spoons," Jefferson Davis summed up the case for the prosecution: "In New Orleans Butler has exerted himself to earn the execrations of the civilised world, and now returns with his dishonors thick upon him to receive the plaudits of the only people on earth who do not blush to think he wears the human form. He has stolen millions of dollars in New Orleans from private citizens. . . . It is in keeping, however, with the character of the people that seeks dominion over you, claim to be your masters, to try to reduce you to subjection—give up to a brutal soldiery your towns to sack, your homes to pillage and incite servile insurrection." And of course Butler had earned the sobriquet "Beast" after his infamous order threatening to treat any defiant Rebel female in New Orleans as "a woman of the town plying her avocation." A Chattanooga editor claimed that Butler's name had become "the synonym the world over of everything that is brutal and cowardly and indecent." A young Alabama officer thought Butler would go down in history alongside Roman emperors Caligula and Nero. Confederates ran out of epithets and historical comparisons when it came to Butler even as they tried to make him out as a representative northern man embodying all the worst traits of Yankeedom. Invoking the name of Beast Butler should only inspire southerners to fight harder and more successfully.[42]

Butler may have stood at the top, but Confederates of all stripes readily compiled diverse lists of Yankee generals for all manner of condemnation. In Missouri, General Henry W. Halleck had proven just as barbaric as the late Nathaniel Lyon (mortally wounded at the Battle of Wilson's Creek). Or there was the much hated John Pope, whose notorious orders threatening confiscation and executions had so roused Lee and other Virginians to heights of indignation. Jefferson Davis declared Pope and his officers to be "robbers and murderers." Those ravagers of the Shenandoah Valley, Robert Milroy and David Hunter, had earned their own special place in any cast of Yankee malefactors. Eventually William T. Sherman would overshadow all other northern villains in Confederate annals, though even in late 1864, South Carolinian Grace Brown Elmore only deemed him one of several Yankee miscreants who included, oddly enough, William S. Rosecrans and

Ambrose Burnside.[43] Putting a human face to more generic denunciations of Yankees had the advantage of giving a patriotic Confederate particular villains to execrate. Such bogeymen undoubtedly served their purpose in Confederate propaganda, and comments on their crimes readily spread from newspaper reports to soldier and civilian conversations.

More shameful still was the apparent Yankee endorsement of their most barbaric commanders. Confederates kept pointing out how the northern public applauded and the government promoted generals whose brutal acts had made their names a byword among civilized nations. The most outrageous conduct had undoubtedly received tacit if not explicit sanction at the highest levels of the U.S. government, thus serving as harbingers of the future should the Yankees be allowed to continue on their course of invasion and occupation.[44]

"What cruel brutes the Yankees are," a Georgia congressman wrote to his wife at the end of 1864. "You doubtless remember hearing me say some time since—last year perhaps—that the Yankees would become more and more brutal and savage as the war progressed and this opinion is being confirmed almost daily." Such statements even harkened back to condemnations of northern Puritanism. Here the emphasis was on a New England cold-heartedness revealed not only in the bluecoats' unfeeling behavior toward Confederates but even in family letters left scattered on southern battlefields. More often, Confederates described the Yankees as simply hateful and vicious in their treatment of southern civilians.[45]

If much of this seems contradictory, it no doubt was, but then consistency hardly mattered much when it came to painting broad-brush portraits of the enemy in the midst of a raging war. Early dismissal of cowardly Yankees as unworthy foes gave way to linking their inherent cowardice to their cruelty, and especially to their abuse of the aged and defenseless. Even the most victorious generals reportedly showed little magnanimity toward their defeated opponents. Ironically, many northerners tried to conceal their brand of warfare behind claims to superior religious virtue. However, they would hardly fool alert Confederates who readily saw through such pretense and realized that the enemy was not only relentless but merciless. The obvious conclusion: compromise with such a people was impossible and any "reconstruction" of the Union inconceivable. This meant that Confederate troops must fight all that much harder to protect their fledgling nation from the proverbial fate worse than death. Taking the argument one step further, General (and former Episcopal bishop) Leonidas Polk advised his men that the North surely waged a "war against heaven, as well as a war against earth."[46]

From the beginning, denunciations of Yankee barbarism proved to be, if not exactly self-fulfilling prophecies, at least bedrock assumptions buttressing the Confederate case for separate nationhood. Combined with the actual behavior of northern armies and generals, this all fed into a picture of noble Confederates engaged in a war to the death against a savage foe. But it was not only the countryside, or the towns, or the cities, or physical property that would face devastation from merciless invaders. The Yankees had literally declared war on the southern people and this in turn became a major theme in the propaganda battle. Northern soldiers would invade the most private recesses of southern life, sparing neither women nor children. They would not even stop at rape or murder but would attempt to exterminate the southern people and strike at the very foundations of the southern racial order.

CHAPTER 4

The Inhuman War, or the War against Humanity

At a public meeting in Wilkinson County, Georgia, a doctor who had just enlisted in the Wilkinson Rifles accepted a flag sewn by some local women. In a fervid address filled with talk of God and country, he pledged his company to "dispute every inch of ground before our altars and fire-sides shall be desecrated by the foul footsteps of the Puritanic hordes of the North."[1] These words were hardly unusual; they in fact embraced familiar themes of wartime invective, including a standard and contradictory picture of the Yankees as both religious bigots and barbaric invaders, not to mention their always polluting footsteps. But the threat of desecrating southern "fire-sides" suggested something more ominous. Enemy soldiers would enter the sacred precincts of domestic life, threatening both property and persons. What would be the fate of innocent mothers, wives, and daughters at the hands of such brutes? Would the bluecoats not only pillage but also rape and murder? In a broader sense, did the Union armies really intend to "exterminate" the southern people, another word often used when discussing northern intentions? And then what about slavery and slaves? Were the Union abolition armies hell-bent on destroying the southern social and racial order? There loomed the specter of miscegenation and worse, all compounded as the enemy turned to what had once been unthinkable: the use of black men to fight white men.

That Georgia doctor had anticipated the worst, but he was not alone. Only a little over a month after Fort Sumter, Virginian Judith McGuire wrote: "It makes my blood boil when I remember that our private rooms, our chambers, our very sanctums, are thrown open to a ruthless soldiery." Imagine rough hands rummaging through women's clothing, pawing delicate dresses and chemises, and then picture how women would be forced to witness such scenes. The soldiers tossed about children's clothes, deaf to any protests from the mothers. Smashing furniture and pianos, even tearing up Bibles, these northern demons held nothing sacred.[2]

Still mourning the death of a beloved brother and Unionist father, twenty-year-old Sarah Morgan had to flee from the family home in August 1862 when the war finally reached Baton Rouge, Louisiana. From her older sister Miriam, she later learned what had befallen the place. Yankee troops had emptied out the library, shattered china, and taken axes to the sideboards. "Her [Miriam's] desk lay open with all letters and notes well thumbed and scattered around, while [Cousin] Will's last letter to her was open on the floor, with the Yankee stamp of dirty fingers. Mother's portrait half-cut from its frame stood on the floor." Word was that it had not been enlisted men but officers who had ransacked the house. Upstairs a mahogany armoire had been looted, and various letters marked "private" were "strewn over the floor." Sarah's own desk "was broken open. Over it was spread all my letters, and private papers, a diary I kept when twelve years old, and sundry tokens of dried roses, etc., which must have been *very* funny, they all being labeled with the donor's name, and the occasion. Fool! how I writhe when I think of all they saw; the invitations to buggy rides, concerts, 'Compliments of,' etc.—!" The wretched soldiers cavorted about bedecked in ladies' dresses and bonnets. After they left, the women found clothes "used for the vilest purposes, and spread in every corner—at least those few that were not stolen."[3]

Nothing remained private, and hardly anything could be safeguarded from prying Yankee eyes and grasping Yankee hands. Soldiers looked into everything: presses, cupboards, trunks, closets, pantries, wardrobes. Sometimes they cursed or pounded on a piano as an accompaniment to a thorough and destructive search. A North Carolina woman described "torrents" of Union soldiers pillaging everything from bacon to bedclothes. Worse still, they not only scattered legal documents but read private letters—often aloud for the amusement of their comrades. Even women who did not witness such scenes or face much of a direct threat lay their pens down and fell silent. Near the end of the war, inveterate diarist Catherine Edmondston put away her writing for a time because the thought of her "private papers . . . in Yankee hands, of hearing them read in vile Yankee drawl amidst peals of vulgar Yankee laughter, or worse still, of knowing them heralded abroad in Yankee sensational newspapers, restrained me!"[4]

Would such contemptible acts be followed by even worse? That was the largely unspoken (and occasionally spoken) question on many people's minds. Fear of assault or rape or even murder grew with each rumor or newspaper report. Such crimes did take place, but worries also multiplied in fevered imaginations, all fueled by Confederate propagandists who charged the Yankees with literally warring on women and children. The dastardly foe would obviously prefer harassing women to testing their mettle against soldiers, or at least that became one line of argument. Merciless northern troops cared little for starving families. To further drive home these points, Confederates almost invariably cast the female victims of such brutality as harmless, young, and beautiful.[5] This all stood in stark contrast with many Yankee descriptions of southern women as venomous, prematurely old, and slatternly, but sorting out fact from fiction here is beside the point. The purpose was to present female Confederates as innocent and indeed helpless. Real life confrontations between "secesh females" and Union soldiers surely raised doubts about the "helpless" part of the description, but that hardly stopped Jefferson Davis from using the word repeatedly in calls for a reinvigorated Confederate fighting spirit.[6]

Aside from the many general statements about Yankee misdeeds, Confederate civilians and newspaper correspondents recounted more specific incidents of insulting behavior. Soldiers camping in the yards of farms and plantations shocked female modesty with what an official report in Louisiana termed "indelicate exhibitions of camp life." In Missouri, German troops berated respectable ladies as "damned secesh bitches." Cursing and profanity made Yankees appear like devils as they searched homes and grabbed food. Drunken officers and even generals reportedly cavorted with slave paramours within earshot if not within sight of plantation mistresses and their daughters.[7]

And there were threats of worse to come. Some northerners liked to playfully (or not so playfully) announce that they were looking for wives. "Are all you ladies married?" an Ohio colonel asked some Virginians. "I suppose you find some difficulty in getting Rebel husbands. We'll send some Yankees here to marry you and that's the way to build up the Union again." In all seriousness, a Florida planter serving in the Confederate army insisted his wife promise that whatever might happen, she would never wed a Yankee. According to outraged Confederates, Union soldiers coveted southern land and lusted after southern women. Aside from the usual denunciations of "Beast Butler," there came reports that the old cry of "beauty and booty" had spurred northern enlistments.[8]

Such loose talk—not to mention its official sanction—might well incite rape, and of course in the endless denunciations of Butler, that charge appeared repeatedly. Subject to all manner of rumors and newspaper accounts, women naturally expected the worst, yet even if Federals stopped short of ravishment, they behaved badly enough. At a fine house in Holly Springs, Mississippi, Yankees poked their heads into young ladies' bedrooms and then chided them for sleeping late. After a soldier "caught hold" of one woman's dress, she threatened to "scratch his eyes out." On a nearby plantation, some Kansas troops tore earrings, breastpins, and rings off several ladies. Soldiers ran their hands over women's bodies supposedly looking for contraband; a report from Baltimore claimed that Federal officers sometimes disguised themselves as women to conduct such illicit searches. One bold rascal out for a walk tried to kiss a Virginia woman, but she drew a pistol and shot him. Such stories spread among neighbors, in family letters, and especially in newspapers. Much information came second- and thirdhand with significant omissions and embellishments, but Confederates found most any tale of Yankee wickedness believable. In Prince George County, Virginia, a group of Federals reportedly forced a mother and daughter to strip naked and then made the former play a piano.[9] Indeed, details made these accounts more credible but also added to their horror. There had to be a delicate balance struck between frightening civilians and stirring resistance to the enemy, and many accounts of Yankee outrages likely sparked as much fear as resistance.

In any event, was the depraved behavior described in Confederate accounts but a prelude to rape? Sometimes it was, and that crime had long been associated with war and in some cases had become a weapon of war. In official propaganda, bestial enemy soldiers often appear intent on raping innocent women, and Confederates played up both the threat and reality of sexual assault. A sketchy report in a Richmond newspaper was typical: "We have heard of an outrage perpetrated upon one of the most respectable married ladies of Fairfax, in the presence of her children, which has no parallel except among the atrocities of the Sepoys and Druses."[10] Not surprisingly such accounts seldom named the victim, and many were quite vague and general. For their part, politicians condemned Yankees brutality against women without getting down to cases.[11] Euphemisms such as a "fate worse than death" often appeared in the press or in correspondence. In their diaries and letters, women wrote only of revolting crimes, and even the voluble Catherine Edmondston talked in the most general terms and shrank from being more specific.[12] In a fiery appeal to potential recruits, a Texas colonel declared that the Yankees intended to "pollute our wives and daughters with a degradation deeper than a thousand deaths." A Virginian reported that such "monsters have been hunting married females from house to house, for the gratification of their brutal lusts."[13]

Though often describing such crimes in broad-brush terms, newspapers occasionally offered fuller accounts of the most heinous incidents. Some reports had a set piece quality with young and respectable females falling victim to crazed fiends. Aside from condemning the Yankees as demonic ravishers, the longer articles included details guaranteed to infuriate Confederate soldiers. Some women had been attacked with their children present; in another instance, five soldiers gang-raped a Tennessee woman. Other accounts added that soldiers held pistols to women's heads or even cursed the Savior while assaulting their victims. Some articles merely recited brief information, but others sought to explain the larger significance of these attacks. After recounting an especially brutal rape of two Virginians in front of their parents, the *Charleston Mercury* inevitably pointed out how this crime "perfectly illustrates the Yankee character."[14]

But even these assaults were hardly the crowning outrage for many Confederates. In Mississippi and Tennessee, reports told of slaves raping white women while Yankee soldiers either did nothing to stop them or looked on approvingly. A few northern soldiers apparently saw such acts as just retribution for the crime of slavery. After denying that he had invented such a story to arouse Confederates' fighting spirit, a correspondent for a

Mobile newspaper suggested that southern men "think of a negro, your slave, gratifying his hellish lust upon one of your countrywomen! think of her future degradation through life; fancy her cry for rescue form his fiendish embrace, while those wearing the form of men stood gazing upon her, unabashed by the presence of outraged innocence, inciting the negro to his diabolical work."[15]

Generals and politicians readily conjured such images in addressing Confederate troops. Bristling at Butler's infamous woman order, General P. G. T. Beauregard asked his men, "Shall our mothers, our wives, our daughters, and our sisters be thus outraged by the ruffianly soldiers of the North, to whom is given the right to treat at their pleasure the ladies of the South as common harlots?" Others spoke more euphemistically about the abuse of women and children. In letters sure to raise alarm at home, soldiers warned their wives that the vile Yankees were ravishing women. Very early in the war, a Georgian grandiloquently talked of dying for his country "in defence of innocent girls and women from the fangs of the lecherous northern hirelings." And it did not take long before many Confederates were claiming that their worst fears about the Yankees had been confirmed. "They have gone so far as to pollute their [women's] persons in the presence of their aged fathers," an Alabama captain wrote from Middle Tennessee. Such reports, no matter how vague or unsubstantiated, incited fear and even panic. In early 1862, a Hoosier volunteer blamed Confederate leaders, especially General Sterling Price, for spreading rumors of pillage and rape that caused people in southern Missouri and northwestern Arkansas to flee their homes.[16]

How often sexual assaults did occur is impossible to say, and enslaved women and poor whites were frequently the victims. Although there is no evidence that Union troops viewed rape as a weapon of war, and the military justice system dealt with at least 450 cases, realities hardly mattered to Confederates eager to paint their enemies in the darkest possible hues.[17] Southern newspapers reported men being shot by northern soldiers while defending the honor of wives and daughters. In some cases, a civilian had managed to kill one or more of the ravishers before being killed himself. As for Yankees caught in the act and taken prisoner, they surely deserved summary execution.[18]

By the same token, those who would commit rape could just as easily commit murder. In Fredericksburg, Virginia, shortly before the battle,

General Thomas R. R. Cobb claimed that Federal batteries had fired at trains loaded with refugee women and children. Nor were families in private homes immune from Yankee artillery rounds. A South Carolina colonel speculated that the "Vandal hordes amuse themselves" lobbing shells into Atlanta "with the sole intension of injuring the town and frightening the poor defenseless women." The juxtaposition of "amuse" with "artillery" in this statement merely proved how truly barbaric the enemy had become. Near East Point, Georgia, during the Atlanta campaign, terrified women and children scurried from their homes, begging for mercy, screaming, praying—utterly convinced that the Federals intended to kill them all.[19]

Such attacks—whether real, exaggerated, or imagined—convinced some Confederates that cold-blooded murder had become part and parcel of Union war policy. Even as Lincoln was being inaugurated, South Carolina plantation mistress Keziah Brevard had claimed that his black Republican friends "must have dreadful hearts to wish to cut our throats because we are sinners." These were just the sort of men who had cheered on John Brown. Such a dire prospect, it was hoped, must arouse true southerners to defend their homes and convince even Unionists that the Yankees were no better than bloodthirsty marauders. Two years later a Richmond newspaper excitedly reported that the Pennsylvania state senate had debated "paying negroes premiums, for the murder of white families in the South."[20]

The invaders supposedly displayed an insatiable appetite for blood, whether soldier or civilian. Cavalry regiments and more irregular outfits developed fearsome reputations, with border areas such as Missouri, Kentucky, and Tennessee appearing especially vulnerable. According to their official statements, even northern Christians—a Virginia Baptist editor charged—took "delight in war." The combined effects of actual atrocities, official propaganda, and relentless rumors exacted a severe psychological toll. Even as the war was winding down, an Illinois sergeant wrote to his wife that the people in one south Alabama town seemed genuinely surprised that the Yankees did not eat them up, having heard so many tales of young women being ravished along with old men and children being murdered.[21]

Reports of brutal slayings regularly appeared in the newspapers. The common practice of reprinting articles meant that some stories—even the most implausible—quickly circulated across the Confederacy and then became topics of local gossip and dinner-table conversation. In early 1862, a poor shoemaker was burned to death in his own home near Centreville, Virginia. In an 1864 incident near Bermuda Hundred, Virginia, two men were captured, bayoneted to death, and their bodies nailed to a tree. Accounts of torture preceding death seemingly proved how the Yankees conducted warfare on the most uncivilized basis imaginable. And they naturally chose the most defenseless victims. Cowardly raiders would sneak about, avoid Confederate soldiers in the field, and then enter homes and towns to prey on unarmed civilians, sparing neither age nor gender.[22]

The case of a Natchez woman (known only as a "Mrs. Sanderson") well illustrates how tales of murderous Federals were told and retold. A Mississippi correspondent for an Atlanta newspaper reported that a Yankee lieutenant and two enlisted men had barged into this young woman's house. After she refused to tell where her husband was, the soldiers strung her up with the lieutenant's scarf and left the body hanging for the neighbors to find. An "old citizen of Natchez" visiting Atlanta was the supposed source of the story. Both Emma Holmes and Catherine Edmondston read about this along with an incident involving Federal troops searching the home of another Mississippi woman—an elderly widow. In this case, the soldiers had heard rumors (untrue as it turned out) about $40,000 hidden in the house, and her adamant denials availed nothing. The men whipped her bare back (Holmes claimed with five hundred lashes) and ended up killing the poor woman. Surely God would punish such wretches, Edmondston hoped, and both women poured out their shock and anger in diary entries. Here was one more reason for fighting to the death and never surrendering, Holmes decided.[23]

Killing women and children was just like the Yankees according to the standard Confederate narrative, and politicians played up the atrocity stories. Early in 1862 with Confederate fortunes lagging, Georgia governor Joe Brown knew how to reach the anxious, the fearful, and the angry by hitting on all the major themes of anti-Yankee polemics: "In their attempt to subjugate us, the Northern troops have been permitted to disregard all the established rules of warfare. They have not only stolen our property and laid waste the country behind them, where they have advanced within our territory, but with fiendish malignity, they have, on several occasions, in cold blood, shot down unarmed and unoffending women and children. Not only have they disregarded all the dictates of humanity, but, with sacrilegious infidelity, they have even desecrated the altars of God and have defiled and polluted our churches and places of public worship." That Yankee soldiers would not even respect southern white women—invariably described as "innocent," "helpless," or "unoffending"—revealed their true character and again showed why the war must continue until southern independence was won. To avenge these manifold crimes, Confederate soldiers must fight all the harder.[24]

No murderous ruse seemed too low or excuse too shopworn for the dastardly Yankees. According to an official Louisiana report on the conduct of Union troops in the western part of the state, army surgeons had created a vaccine designed to spread smallpox among the civilian population. On the pretense of hunting for Confederate guerrillas, soldiers had dragged men from their houses and summarily executed them. And by all accounts, southern Unionists (often dubbed "Lincolnites") were even more bloodthirsty.[25] Surely "it cannot be God's will to expose us to the treacherous and fiendish malice of a band of robbers & murderers," a young Baptist minister wrote plaintively. Even on supposed days of national thanksgiving, northerners entered churches with murder in their hearts. A Mississippi editor summed up their errant hypocrisy: "Brutality is the watchword with these people, they who, in times past, professed to teach the South, their superiors, Christianity and correct morals."[26]

Confederates repeatedly accused their enemies of ignoring the rules of "civilized warfare." Whether those two words actually belonged together or not, the Yankees' vicious proclivities received wide attention. As early as the summer of 1861, there were both official and unofficial complaints about Union soldiers summarily executing captured Confederates. Charges of prisoner abuse (all too real in many instances) became staples of propaganda on both sides throughout the war and long after, but Confederates fit them into a larger narrative of Yankee barbarism. In an early 1863 message to Congress, for example, Jefferson Davis singled out General John McNeil for killing seven prisoners "in cold blood" during a campaign against guerrillas in Missouri.[27] Leaving Fort Delaware aboard a steamer on a stifling August day and suffering for lack of air, space, and food, James McMichael made the expected comparison to the legendary "Black Hole of Calcutta." Returning prisoners graphically described conditions in northern prisons; civilians recounted and embroidered these stories. Accounts of starvation, heartless guards, and other examples of cruelty greatly angered Confederates, who saw their enemies descending ever lower on the ladder of civilization rung by rung. The comments of young South Carolinian Grace Brown Elmore spoke for many others: "The Yankees are a perfect outrage to everything noble in the nature of man, they are a blot upon the whole creation. Even the savage has a respect for a fallen foe, but the Yankee takes pleasure in petty insult, and the smallest spites against the man whose life is in his power."[28]

None of this mistreatment appeared isolated or unintentional. Smallpox-infected blankets, prisoners stripped to the waist in front of ladies, officers forced to clean privies, sparse meals with tainted meat, men covered with loathsome sores—it all added up to a policy of brutalizing human beings for sadistic amusement or out of simple meanness. The Confederate Treasury Department reportedly had compiled a list of "soldiers and citizens . . . murdered by cold, starvation, and most cruel intentional neglect" in northern prisons. Here were cases "numbering in the thousands" that presented the full range of Yankee villainy.[29]

Characterized by the abuse of prisoners, rape of women, and murder of soldiers and civilians, the war had degenerated into savagery, and Confederates readily talked of it in just such terms.[30] To ardent secessionists, all that had been apparent even before the first shots had been fired. The Yankees' goal was "extermination," South Carolinian Sue Sparks Keitt predicted. This logically meant that "submission" to such a people was both unthinkable and suicidal. What a Georgian termed the "vandal spirit" sought to annihilate southerners.[31] Such thinking might literally make the war a struggle to death: some Rebels defined the stakes as the very survival of the southern people.

Indeed, it did not take long for leading Confederates to describe the conflict as a literal "war of extermination," words that appeared repeatedly in private and public statements, including the appeals made by political candidates. This phrase carried multiple but uniformly frightening connotations. It would be a war with no quarter given. It would be a war in which the defeated southerners would retain neither rights nor property. It would be a war marking an apocalyptic clash between "barbarism" and "civilization." It would be a war of "numberless" atrocities.[32] In Confederate minds, a "war of extermination" meant most any series of terrors that one cared to imagine.

Only days after the firing on Fort Sumter, Joe Brown declared that the Yankees intended to subjugate or exterminate the southern people because "we are slave-holders." Indeed many white southerners literally (and ironically) feared their own enslavement at the hands of the enemy. The choices were grim, though variously defined: reunion, coercion, death by "fire and sword." Fears aroused by wartime propaganda persisted, but as the struggle became increasingly desperate and bloody, brave words often rang hollow. After the burning of Columbia, South Carolina, the *Edgefield Advertiser* hoped that the whole country would rise up to resist Sherman because the issue now boiled down to "extermination or slavery."[33]

Or perhaps even the enslavement of white southerners would no longer satisfy the rapacious enemy. The Yankees might rail against slavery, preach emancipation, and claim to be fighting for the glorious Union, the prominent Georgia Methodist James O. Andrew charged, but their real purpose was "the destruction of the white population of the South." Never one to avoid rhetorical excess, the editor of the *Charleston Mercury* declared that Confederates were fighting for the most basic right of self-preservation. The alternative was stark and horrifying: "We perish as a people the moment the struggle is abandoned for the deliberate, declared purpose of the enemy is to *exterminate* the pestilent race of rebels and to replace them with negroes first and Yankees afterwards." As the northern government moved toward a policy of general emancipation, a Georgian glimpsed a future filled with untold terrors. The North had failed to "subjugate" the South and so now sought to "inflame and direct the passions of a peaceful race against those whom they previously have obeyed and loved. They will exterminate the one race, in order that it may become, in the process of annihilation, the instrument of their revenge upon the other."[34]

However confusingly outlined, the true objective of the enemy had been unmasked. Abolition and extermination had become key parts of a single diabolical scheme, a policy conceived by northern fanatics and carried out by the despotic Lincoln and his minions. Catherine Edmondston even traced the problem back to old John Quincy Adams, whom she deemed the proverbial entering wedge of abolitionism. The defense of slavery had long rested on a deep fear of emancipation, a fear rooted in racial, economic, social, cultural, and political assumptions and ideology. The conflation of Republicans with abolitionists had helped fuel the secession movement along with alarms about anarchy and violence. In this view, every aspect of northern society from the churches, to literature, to the halls of Congress had become saturated and contaminated with antislavery zealotry.[35]

Yet a fundamental inconsistency was also at work here. Remarks both public and private spoke of Yankee abolitionism in the most frightening tones, while at the same time many Confederates could hardly imagine a world without slaves and ridiculed the very idea of emancipation. Slavery served as the rock solid foundation of southern society, and therefore abolition was simply inconceivable. As the prolific writer Frank Alfriend observed midway through the war, slavery and states' rights would protect the South against "leveling agrarianism" and an "abolition oligarchy." That statement alone sounded contradictory, but bold assertions about the perpetuity of slavery bespoke insecurity as much as confidence, despite assertions that the Yankees had only resorted to emancipation out of desperation. The long-held belief that the abolitionists would turn the South into another Saint-Domingue, and that white families would face impoverishment, extermination, or exile, appeared right alongside claims that the Yankees could never succeed in destroying slavery.[36]

Confederates hardly acknowledged such tensions and inconsistencies, instead claiming that their enemies manifested these same weaknesses. After all, abolitionists were the worst kind of hypocrites: the descendants of slave traders who dared cast moral judgment on southerners; religious fanatics who ignored the Bible; the ostensibly pious who pretended to worship God but in fact worshiped money. The present-day Yankees were the true heirs of the Puritans, a Mississippi editor asserted. "They hate slavery not because it gives pain to the slave, but because it gives pleasure and profit to the owner of the slave." That particular charge became a steady refrain for Confederates eager to link abolitionism with other northern character flaws. The cultural critique of New England's Puritan heritage gained intensity and saliency as the Federals embraced emancipation. But whether to take the Yankees at their word remained unclear. Writing a week after Lincoln issued the final Emancipation Proclamation, Virginian

Nancy Emerson dismissed the long agitation over slavery as nothing but a "monstrous humbug." All these varying assessments of northern policy went hand in hand with a defense of slavery that took on millennial and even apocalyptic overtones. Even before the war began, an Atlanta editor argued that the "grandeur of this system of African slavery" had incited the "lust of power, envy and hatred of the institution, by the Puritans of the North." Should they succeed in destroying slavery, the result would be "more distress in the civilized world than all the civil wars recorded in the book of Time." Abolition would "desolate the Eden of the earth, avert the progress of the arts and sciences, sow deep the seed of infidelity, efface the proud boon of Christianity, beggar the rich, starve the poor, and erect upon the ruins the altar of beastliness, shrouded in the mantle of the dark ages!"[37]

Tirades against northern abolitionism complemented a wide-ranging apologia for slave society that antedated but also reacted to decades of sectional conflict. Slavery remained the cornerstone of a harmonious social order, according to a popular line of argument that conveniently ignored how a system that treated human beings as both property and persons was inherently fraught with conflict. Ideologues such as George Fitzhugh had extolled a commonality of interest between capital and labor in the southern states—an abstraction that lacked many tangible examples but kept cropping up in wartime discussions of slavery. Everything from character to manners to white democracy depended on the existence of the peculiar institution, and though reformers might preach against abuses of the system, there was little political support for meaningful change. In sermons and various official statements on the master-slave relationship, paternalistic and familial themes still appeared, but such idealized portraits revealed much more about human rationalization than about the realities of bondage.[38]

Nevertheless, in theory at least, southern slaveholders remained quite literally the guardians of their African slaves. The prominent Episcopalian Stephen Elliott expressed the point succinctly: "We are fighting to protect and preserve a race who form part of our household, and stand with us next to our children." According to Jefferson Davis, Confederates were battling Lincoln and his abolitionist allies, who would ensure that "peaceful and contented laborers" were "doomed to extermination."[39] The slaveholders themselves worked hard to convince "their people" that the Yankees were a treacherous and dangerous lot. Masters and mistresses duly noted their slaves' apparent fright without considering that there might be a good deal of dissembling and manipulation at work. A regimental quartermaster stationed in Arkansas met many "negroes . . . endeavoring to make their own escape from the common enemy of them & mankind," but one wonders whether they were fleeing from or to the "enemy."[40]

Some slaves recalled being terribly scared and fleeing from Union troops, and well they might given the unpredictability of the situation along with all the wild rumors afloat. Masters, mistresses, and overseers (and sometimes older slaves) had described the Yankees as veritable monsters with horns sprouting on their heads. Having been told such tales by her "old Miss," Mittie Freeman was quite curious about such creatures and asked a soldier to take off his hat so she could see the horns.[41] Slaveholders warned their slaves that the Yankees would leave them to starve or worse. In North Carolina, Hannah Cresson's mistress told her that the Federal troops "were going to kill every nigger in the South."[42]

Equally far-fetched was the rumor of a Yankee plot to send all the slaves to Cuba, though a few slaveholders apparently believed it, and more tried to use such stories to keep their slaves from absconding into Union lines. Various northern colonization schemes lent a veneer of credibility to such tales, and they continued to circulate until the end of the war. Escaped slaves told Union officials how their masters had tried to deceive them by playing on old fears of separation and sale. One slaveholder had even warned his people that the Federals would cut off the slaves' ears before shipping them to Cuba.[43]

To portray the enemy as pitiless hypocrites carried certain practical advantages and perhaps reassured wavering Confederates of their own rectitude. Indeed, many slaveholders pointed to examples of Union soldiers stealing the property of poor slaves as prime evidence of their enemies' bad faith. In Phillips County, Arkansas, General Gideon J. Pillow claimed, Federal troops not only "rob and plunder the houses" but drive the slaves off the plantations, "shoot the negroes attempting to escape, and handcuff and chain those refusing to go." The blacks should therefore realize that they could place no reliance on the empty promises of smooth-tongued

FEMALE CONTRABAND, AS SEEN AMONG HER ABOLITION FRIENDS, SWEEPING THE STREETS OF NEW YORK FOR BREAD.

HAPPY MAID SERVANT AT HER COMFORTABLE HOME IN THE SOUTH, WHO DID NOT GO AMONG HER YANKEE "FRIENDS."

Top image: "Female contraband, as seen among her abolition friends, sweeping the streets of New York for bread." Bottom image: "Happy maid servant at her comfortable home in the South, who did not go among her Yankee 'friends.'" *Southern Punch*, August 29, 1863.

Yankees. On the eve of the Atlanta campaign, Joe Brown offered a touching appeal couched in the idiom of southern paternalism: "They [the Yankees] have robbed us of our negro women and children who were comfortable, contented and happy with their owners, and under pretext of extraordinary philanthropy, have in the name of liberty congregated thousands of them together in places where they could have neither the comforts nor the necessaries of life, there neglected and despised, to die of pestilence and hunger."[44] Black men forcibly taken from their families to become soldiers or to serve as laborers for the northern armies had shattered the supposedly affectionate and harmonious relations between master and slave. "These are their friends, the Abolitionists!" a woman living in Huntsville, Alabama, remarked sarcastically. Jefferson Davis sneered at "these pretended friends of human rights and liberties" who now preyed on the "unfortunate negroes."[45] Reports of families separated, with women and children left to perish or starve, showed how heartless the Yankees were and contrasted sharply with slaveholders' images of themselves as humane masters. Yet ironically some of these accounts also echoed stock descriptions found in abolitionist condemnations of slavery—though with the villains in the story obviously reversed.

Particular cruelties received much attention in the Confederate press and evoked no little private comment. Runaway slaves found to be infected with smallpox who had crossed several streams to reach Union camps were reportedly forced by northern soldiers to swim for their lives and drowned. One especially implausible tale claimed that a hospital in Georgetown, District of Columbia, "containing 500 negroes afflicted with small pox," had been burned down to "exterminate the negroes and the disease."[46] In Pickens County, Alabama, two young slaves whose ears had been cut off by the Yankees came running back to their masters. Stories of Union soldiers shooting and stabbing black laborers seemed to confirm the old axiom that Yankees turned out to be the most brutal of masters. In East Tennessee, Eliza Fain predicted that the Federals would "fasten upon them [the slaves] a bondage more cruel, more exacting than the Egyptian."[47]

When slaves ran off to the enemy and then returned after being mistreated, Confederates found their assumptions about both the Yankees and the blacks reaffirmed. In the trenches of Petersburg, a sergeant major in a Georgia regiment told of a "negroe boy" of "about 12 or 14 years" who had escaped from the Federals and entered the Confederate lines "anxious to get back to his old mistress and his Mammy." The word "deluded" frequently occurred in descriptions of slaves who absconded when Union armies appeared. A Virginia woman concluded that the "poor darkeys" seemed "deranged" and somehow thought that "this tremendous war is on their account." They could hardly understand that a "natural repugnance" between northerners and southerners made a separation inevitable. In Confederate accounts, the Yankees were always "enticing" ignorant and gullible slaves to act against their own best interests by promising some imaginary paradise of freedom. A newspaper correspondent described a group of blacks in Jacksonville, Florida, as the "poor victims of Puritan philanthropy."[48] Such stories reinforced slaveholders' sense of themselves as humane, enlightened, and Christian masters, later feeding into the lovingly told Lost Cause tales of faithful slaves who stood by their owners and shunned Yankee blandishments.

Dreams of emancipation spelled nothing but disaster for a people incapable of grasping notions of independence and responsibility. That assumption colored many Confederate accounts of slaves "deserting" to the Yankees. Georgian Susan Cornwall's views on the subject were typical: "Freedom which is to the white man the 'Open Sesame' to a career of honor and everything else desirable or conducive to happiness is with the African merely a synonym for idleness." In any area where the Federals had gained a foothold, Confederates estimated that the black population had declined by roughly one-half. Leading theologian James Henley Thornwell predicted that the black man "will slowly pass away, as the red man did before him, under the protection of Northern philanthropy."[49] Thus the dire warnings about future annihilation applied to southern blacks as well as to southern whites.

Confederates placed ultimate responsibility for these calamities on Abraham Lincoln, whose Emancipation Proclamation marked the culmination of a conspiracy to destroy southern civilization. The crude and uncultured Illinois rail-splitter would go down in history as a lying politician who had once promised to leave slavery alone but turned out to be in league with the wild-eyed abolitionists. Lincoln stood willing, a Mississippi editor asserted, to "destroy his own people, civil liberty, the negro, and every sentiment,

"Masks and Faces: King Abraham before and after Issuing the Emancipation Proclamation," *Southern Illustrated News*, November 8, 1862.

moral and political, which have made the Western Republic a beacon of light to the nations of the earth." To compound the crime, there was sheer hypocrisy because the infamous proclamation only applied to areas not controlled by Union forces.[50]

Lincoln and his allies were accused of unleashing a series of almost unimaginable horrors. A Texas cavalry officer charged northern politicians with pursuing a mad scheme to make the blacks free "even though it be over the corpses of their masters and the ashes of their ruined homesteads." The obvious historical analogy was the bloody Haitian revolution. For several decades slave rebel Toussaint L'Ouverture, along with the specter of Saint-Domingue, had come to symbolize the slaveholders' ultimate nightmare. Lincoln clearly intended to incite a slave rebellion, in the words of a Georgia editor, "drenching the whole South in blood." Florida governor John Milton explicitly linked the Emancipation Proclamation with Yankee efforts to "to drive off, rob or murder the citizens, and to colonize the State with negroes and foreigners."[51]

Bloodcurdling imagery had long been standard fare in southern anti-abolition rants, and it presumably would serve to rally soldiers and civilians against the northern invaders. Congress and the public made immediate calls for retaliatory measures against the Emancipation Proclamation, regardless of any practical difficulties involved. The reactions were unfocused if mostly predicable. Confederate senators introduced resolutions and blustered a great deal, with wild talk of raising the black flag and launching a war of extermination. In the absence of a larger and more definite response, however, an Alabama editor rejoiced over stories of "insubordination" among the Yankees' "own free negro population and the negroes they have stolen" because this marked a "just retribution" for "their criminal and cruel intentions." Some Confederates recommended trying captured Union officers for felonious slave tampering or simply hanging them. Others speculated on Lincoln's ultimate fate. "I think there is little chance of a happy hereafter for President Lincoln," Kate Stone wrote in her diary. "A thousand years of repentance would be but brief time to wipe out his sins against the South. How can he ever sleep with the shades of the thousands he has consigned to a bloody death darkening his soul?"[52]

Fantasies of revenge and retribution grew out of a sense that the world was simply out of joint; the Yankees had gone insane and now worshipped the African. Confederates seemed to think that a kind of madness had swept over their enemies. Northern soldiers even touched their hats when they met a black man on the street, an unimaginable courtesy in southern white society. The *Richmond Dispatch* reported a "negro mania . . . raging in Yankeedom," an obsession that almost but not quite defied description: "The negro is everything at the North. He is the grand centre of attraction, towards which the universal Yankee nation gravitates. Laws are made for nobody but him. This war is for nobody but him. All the blood that has been shed was shed for him. He has been not only placed on a level with the Yankee, but is made his superior. The white Yankee must succumb to him. If he wants anything, it must be given to him. If he owe anything, he must not be asked to pay. He lives at free quarters, eats of the best, dresses in the highest style, associates with the best of the codfish aristocracy, is haughty and overbearing in his manners. In a word, he is master of the situation, and he knows it. The stateliest houses are thrown open to him. He is the

"Rev. Africanus Ism: A Model Miscegenator of New England," *Southern Punch*, May 14, 1864.

welcome guest at the lordliest board, the favorite beau of the most splendid drawing-rooms, almost openly courted by the most lovely women, the favorite in the boudoir, the admired of all beholders in the salon.—The illusion is horrible, but it is complete. Under its effects the Yankee natives are urging on the most infamous war ever waged upon a free and noble people."[53]

Cultural boundaries mattered little to northern fanatics. Emancipation would mean black workers competing with white workers, and if one could imagine it, "social equality" between the races; this would all lead to a kind of Mexican "mongrelization," another fear that had long resonated in proslavery literature. As two Union soldiers strolled with two young black women in Winchester, Virginia, Kate Sperry could only shake her head: "To think that white men could place themselves upon equality with niggers! Bah, it makes me shiver all over." Accounts of once-enslaved women consorting with Yankees received considerable notice, and tongues wagged with shock and disgust over what were quickly termed "miscegenation balls."[54]

That word *miscegenation* first appeared in a pamphlet published in New York. Presumably written by an abolitionist at the end of 1863, *Miscegenation: The Theory of Race of Blending of the Races, Applied to the American White Man and Negro* was in fact the brainchild of two conservative Democrats who worked for the *New York World*. The authors purported to favor "the practical recognition of the brotherhood of all the children of the common father." No longer would Christians deny the "social equality of the colored man" because science had clearly "demonstrated that the intermarriage of diverse races is indispensable to a progressive humanity." Indeed "miscegenetic or mixed races" would be "superior, mentally, physically, and morally, to those pure or unmixed." Thus the war had become a contest not only "for the Negro" but for "amalgamation." Even Confederate military success to this point rested on a long association between blacks and whites in the South that had produced a superior governing class built on "illicit unions" going back several generations. And if this all were not enough, the pamphlet claimed that southern white women displayed a "strange infatuation" for black men and even dressed to attract their attention.[55]

How many people were fooled by this publication is impossible to say. Its purpose was to embarrass Republicans and abolitionists during the upcoming northern presidential campaign, but the author's wild and implausible statements likely made this a less then effective hoax. Yet *Miscegenation* played into the Confederate narrative of Yankee extremism, and word of the infamous document spread quickly. A Confederate prisoner on Johnson's Island read the pamphlet and found the whole thing "damnable" and "hellish." Expressions of disgust and revulsion hardly seemed an adequate response to such abominable notions. Not mincing any words, a South Carolina newspaper spelled out exactly what miscegenation—this term "of recent Yankee manufacture"—meant: "white people marrying niggers, and niggers marrying white people—while men, Yankee white men, taking odoriferous sable wenches to share their bed and board, and while women, Yankee white women, taking big, black, reeking Sambos and Pompeys and Bucks to become the fathers of their children." Expressing great shock—whether genuine or feigned—that this new-fangled doctrine was widely preached and practiced in the northern states, Confederates claimed it had been endorsed by such bête noires as Harriet Beecher Stowe, Theodore Tilton, Anna Dickinson, and Frederick Douglass.[56]

It seemed wonderfully ironic that these Yankees might fall victim to their own crack-brained race mixing—those who had threatened to exterminate white southerners could be sounding their own death knell. Thus the parade of horrors so common in Confederate propaganda could also be used to ridicule the Yankees. The Africanization of the southern states would drown the northern abolitionists in a great black sea, or so some Confederates predicted. However that might work out in the long run, in the short term the unsettling effects of an abolition war on the master class had become apparent. In early 1865, in the wake of Sherman's march, Georgian Mary Jones, who considered herself the most humane of mistresses, found her servants in a "perfect" state of "anarchy and rebellion." The anger and befuddlement expressed by many slaveholders over the mildest signs of slave independence lacked all sense of proportion, but then hyperbole had often been their stock in trade. Early in 1862, a racial revolution was reportedly sweeping through occupied Winchester, Virginia. Cornelia McDonald described the social upheaval: "Negroes can assemble in any numbers, and if they choose can jostle and crowd ladies off the pavement into the gutter as may suit their convenience. They are the only people who have any rights or liberty, and of the latter they have an undue share." It is worth noting that McDonald obviously did not believe that black women could possibly be "ladies." Each day seemed to bring some new outrage: a Yankee officer in Mississippi, looking on with approval as two slaves whipped their mistress.[57] The Emancipation Proclamation, Union armies of liberation, or any signs of assertiveness by black folks all produced dismay and fear accompanied by a redoubled defense of the southern economic, social, and racial order, along with intense speculation about a frightening future.

What would come next? A political revolution, perhaps, with black men wielding ballots rather than hoes. At the end of 1861, a Kentuckian serving on General Albert Sidney Johnston's staff warned Jefferson Davis that the radical Republicans in Congress sought to confiscate southern lands and enfranchise slaves. Even before the war had begun, a delegate to the Virginia secession convention sketched out what he saw as the inevitable consequences of abolition: "By the time the North shall have attained the power, the black race will be in a large majority, and then we will have black governors, black legislatures, black juries, black everything." Nor would the revolution stop there. Near the end of the war, one Georgia editor predicted that in another four years Frederick Douglass would be elected president of the United States.[58]

What made all this seem ever more likely was the appearance of African Americans in uniform. It made "my blood boil," a woman in New Orleans claimed, to see black soldiers parading on the streets. "Of course the white man had to step aside to their '*superiors*,'" she noted with disgust. "A great black negro called to the crowd of whites 'Now shout for Jeff Davis if you dare you d—— rebels.'" A world turned upside down if there ever was one. This mad attempt to arm slaves clearly grew out of the Yankees' unreasoning hatred for white southerners. Confederates could barely find the terms of opprobrium to express their fury over this turn of events, though several familiar themes reappeared. The cowardly Federals afraid to face the brave Confederates would now enlist the unwary black man, and as a Georgia volunteer put it, "send the poor nigger down south to get killed." Here were the logical fruits of fanaticism, of infidel Yankees moving at Satan's beck and nod. To complete the sacrilege, Union officers in Beaufort, North Carolina, gathered their hapless recruits in the old African Church.[59]

Always boastful, the enemy now appeared determined to rouse the vindictive passions of an inferior race, taking the war in an especially savage direction. Abolitionists had long been accused of attempting to incite slave insurrections, and the Emancipation Proclamation had intensified such fears, but the enrollment of black troops provoked even more fury and alarm. House burnings, murders, and a general slaughter of the white population must surely follow in the wake of these African American regiments. In arming the slaves, the Federals were clearly launching a "war of extermination," a phrase that had already cropped up in other contexts but one that seemed most apropos here.[60]

Some Confederates predicted that black troops would prove especially merciless, but more assumed that slaves would never make good soldiers. Such contradictory views, however, hardly seemed to matter because both outrage and argument combined to drive home the most important points, and in any case conveyed the warnings about an incipient social and political revolution. The Yankees were working to turn a simple and harmless people against their masters, attempting to transform contented bondsmen into veritable John Browns. According to a Virginia chaplain, Union officers must have used "force" to lead the "ignorant and timid negroes to help them," adding with some condescension that he felt far more sympathy for the blacks than for their new northern masters. Such statements sounded disingenuous, and in fact Confederates could not quite make up their mind about what this great northern experiment signified. Their alarm over impending insurrection hardly seemed convincing when in the same breath they declared their slaves natural cowards who would never stand up and fight white men. Even so, the Yankees reportedly placed their new black recruits in the front lines as cannon fodder, so whether colored troops were in fact more or less brave than the Yankees remained an open question for Confederates.[61]

One thing did appear certain: the supposed liberators would be the cruelest of taskmasters. Defenders of slavery had long adopted this line of reasoning against the abolitionists, and any evidence of black troops being mistreated by the bluecoats confirmed what many Confederates already believed or at least claimed to believe. Reports of black men confined in filthy quarters, kept in irons, or executed for minor offenses elicited expressions of paternalistic sympathy.[62] Even so, uncertainty and contradiction often characterized Confederate descriptions of black soldiers. Were they monstrous or merely ludicrous? A judicial officer in North Carolina noted how his neighbors variously described northern free blacks recruited into Union ranks: "a degraded looking set of wretches of various colors from the light mulatto to the sooty black, filthy as hogs in their persons, hideous in their forms and faces, cowardly looking in their general aspect, and with the look of demons in their eyes." One Virginia woman noticed a mulatto "boy" who had "fled from the best of masters. . . . there he rode at the head of the detachment as grandly as the first officer among them, and he looked as if he felt a savage satisfaction in thus coming back to his old home and lord where he had once served." In Winchester, Virginia, Laura Lee found the appearance of the much dreaded black troops to be a "revolting spectacle." But her outrage gave way to ridicule: "such rambling, shambling, tumbling for marching, such grinning and grimacing. There is nothing which so clearly exhibits, to me, the madness and folly of the Yankee Government, as the idea of expecting such creatures to fight. There were white officers riding down each side of the column, and they looked as if they were driving a flock of black sheep."[63]

Such sights struck observers as simply unbelievable. To imagine "such a thing in civilized warfare," a Tennessee private marveled as black troops guarded Confederate prisoners at Point Lookout. From the beginning of the war, the Yankees had snatched European immigrants right off the boats to fill their armies, but putting black men in uniform—especially former slaves—marked a new low. "Think of it, armed negroes!" Catherine Edmondston raged. "And this is the nineteenth century! and the proposers of this infernal act call themselves enlightened Christians."[64]

The simple presence of black soldiers enraged white southerners and posed a striking and unexpected challenge to a social order resting on chattel slavery and racial hierarchy. Little wonder that Confederates complained loudly and circulated wildly exaggerated stories of various enormities. Perhaps in one sense, the enlistment of black soldiers had been an almost immediate success—it had certainly captured the Rebels' attention. "The Yankees know they made it ten times worse for us by sending Negroes to commit these atrocities," Louisianan Kate Stone admitted. Pillaging by white soldiers was bad enough, but when white officers allowed their black troops a free hand in plundering farms and homes, that added worse insult to the original injury. Reports of sacking and burning again drew comparisons to the Sepoy rebellion in India. "The negroes were suffered to wander about from house to house without control, and wherever they went ladies were insulted, cursed, and reviled," some citizens in Virginia's Northern Neck advised Jefferson Davis. "The most disgusting proposals were made to some, others were subjected to indecent familiarities or rude and revolting embraces; twelve or fifteen escaped almost miraculously from successful violence, and four at least became unfortunate victims of brutal lust." After the burning of Columbia, South Carolina, and the garrisoning of that city by black troops, Emma LeConte claimed that even their white officers had grown disgusted and some thirty soldiers had been "shot for violating women."[65] She did not seem to think much about the improbability of that report, but the rage involved was largely blind to such considerations.

Given all the pent-up indignation over the mere idea of black men in uniform, such reports fueled demands for retaliation. "If these niggers are brought out into the state," a Florida enlisted man informed his brother, there will be the "damdest fights" and "every man of us is determined to do his best towards *wiping them out completely*." Now was not the time for what a Georgia editor termed "sickly sensibility." He considered the issue difficult but clear-cut: "It may be a terrible duty, and require vast strength of nerve to perform it, but true statesman [*sic*] will be equal to the task." It soon became clear that black troops could expect little mercy from Confederates who at times adopted a "take no prisoners" policy. Rebel officers hardly knew what to do with captured African Americans, though some were inclined to execute them on the spot. During fighting around Suffolk, Virginia, in early 1864, women waved handkerchiefs at passing Confederate troops, urging them to "kill the negroes." The refusal to treat these men as prisoners of war not only brought an end to prisoner exchanges but also led to calls for fighting under the "Black Flag."[66]

Wild talk was cheap, and bold promises of action often proved impractical, but the reality was gruesome enough. By the summer of 1864, Confederate ordnance chief Josiah Gorgas noted how the cavalry routinely killed black prisoners. For nearly two years, Confederate generals had tried to figure out what to do with such captives, and some officers sought to avoid a bloodbath, but others exerted little control over their men. With the suspension of prisoner exchanges as a convenient excuse, a Texan stationed in Mississippi simply recommended taking "every negro found in arms, and every man connected with them, into some thicket and swamp and hang them up as soon as captured."[67]

The war had unleashed such uncontrollable passions that no one should have been shocked or surprised at such a suggestion, but it also reflected the deep-seated values of slave society. An inhumane war had in large part grown out of an inhumane institution. And certainly many Confederates viewed black soldiers as less than human. Yet at the same time, in public statements, private reflections, and official propaganda, Confederates described themselves as the innocent victims of Yankee savagery. The invaders were attacking hearth and home; women and children had become the chief sufferers. Anyone reading the southern press could readily find accounts—many of them unreliable or overblown—of robberies, rapes, and murders committed by Union soldiers. A war of extermination became the logical outcome of Yankee fanaticism, and outcries about abolitionism and miscegenation completed this catalogue of unspeakable horrors. Of course the horrors were not exactly unspeakable because Confederates did speak about them, often at length in the most strident language. When Yankees began sending black soldiers into the field, that decision only gave rise to more fear and made the rhetoric all that more heated. Denunciations of "outrages," not to mention actual encounters with the enemy, generated an intense hatred and calls for retribution that would in turn lengthen the war and cast a long shadow on the defeated and subjugated South.

CHAPTER 5

Hatred and Vengeance

Eliza Frances Andrews was not yet twenty-five years old as the final year of the war began. The daughter of a superior court judge in Washington, Georgia, she had grown up in a genteel upper-crust family and had graduated from LaGrange Female College. But during the war, she sounded less and less like a refined young woman, especially when it came to the subject of Yankees, who "thwart all my plans, murder my friends, and make my life miserable." Wrath came pouring out in her diary: "Yankee, Yankee, is the one detestable word always ringing in Southern ears. If all the words of hatred in every language under heaven were lumped together into one huge epithet of detestation, they could not tell how I hate Yankees." She could loathe the invaders in part because she saw them as an undifferentiated mass, not real human beings but inhuman monsters.[1] This hardening of hearts went far beyond harsh words and angry outbursts, and calls for vengeance quickly followed, as did acts of vengeance.

The sectional conflict of the antebellum decades had heightened a sense of southern identity and intensified hostility to the "universal Yankee nation." It had fostered stereotypes of the grasping, bigoted, infidel, fanatical northerner, the abolitionist incendiary, the monstrous foe of the southern people. Here were mortal enemies of the Constitution who would repudiate the sacred heritage of the American founding fathers and ultimately destroy the republic. Thus early in the war, a Georgian living in Florida wrote back to his hometown newspaper pointing out how "our once sincere allegiance and devotion to the government of the United States as it existed in the days of our forefathers, has been changed by the corruptions and vandalism of a dominant Abolition party to a hatred as deep and implacable as the Poles have for Russia." Overstatement and hyperbole abounded in such comments, but the detestation for the enemy was real enough and throughout the war only intensified. When the notorious Ohio copperhead Clement L. Vallandigham was arrested by General Ambrose Burnside and banished to the Confederacy by Lincoln, an Atlanta editor feared that this supposed friend of the South had shown "too much love for the Union." As for receiving the exile: "Till he hates, loathes and abhors the Union, he cannot be a good Southern man, and we don't want him." The most ardent Confederates maintained there was no longer any sense of concord or brotherhood with the northern people. How could a true nation be held together solely by force? Just think about the American Revolution and how sturdy patriots had come to abhor their British oppressors. And the present war only magnified sectional divisions and further alienated two quite distinct peoples. As an Alabama officer held prisoner on Johnson's Island put it, "I live to hate the U.S. government & its agents."[2]

For many Confederates, the U.S. flag—what they once would have called "Old Glory"—had become a loathsome rag. They had truly loved that banner, and that made it all the harder when their enemies waved it in their faces; displaying Confederate flags in occupied territory in turn became an act of defiance, a weapon of the weak to be shaken impotently at the foe. The stars and stripes now conveyed only misery. When some women remarked that the old flag was still "sacred in their eyes," nurse Kate Cumming could hardly believe it. To her, it had become "the most hateful thing which I could look at; as every stripe in it recalled to my mind the gashes that I had witnessed upon our men." And when the infernal Yankees occupied a town and then raised their nasty colors, what a sense of degradation. Beset by a host of domestic troubles and frustrated over their inability to join their menfolk on the battlefield, women especially raged and fumed at such sights. The enemy somehow seemed to imagine that southerners still cherished the old flag and had some lingering affection for the old Union, but the most staunchly Confederate women quickly disabused them of that illusion. With some fanfare, they would walk out of their way and even through the mud to avoid the humiliation of passing under the hated banner. If that incensed the local Yankee garrison, so much the better. When Union troops came marching into Murfreesboro, Tennessee, young Alice Ready fantasized about stomping on their flag and shooting down the soldier who had dared raise it on the courthouse.[3]

Any signs of defiance no matter how pointless or ineffective became important in the legend of the "secesh female," a woman who at once repelled and attracted the Yankee occupiers. In expressing his own detestation for the stars and stripes, a Confederate soldier offered an indirect compliment to such patriotism: "I live to hate the U.S. Flag. I will marry no woman who has the least respect for it."[4]

It might seem odd to boast about hatred in oneself or others, but Confederates readily deflected any guilt onto their enemies. After all, the Yankees were the real haters, and Confederates could hold forth at some length and in some detail on northern hatred of southerners. The jealousy and enmity of the northern people was of long standing, the prominent divine Benjamin Morgan Palmer advised the South Carolina legislature at the end of 1863, and its intensity and ferocity had become all too apparent during the present war. That in turn made it easy to rationalize hating the Yankees. Indeed their crimes and atrocities reflected an unending and unlimited enmity for innocent southerners, an odium growing out of everything from Puritanical fanaticism to foreign-born infidelity. In an order to his troops, former Episcopal bishop turned Confederate general Leonidas Polk drove this point home: "The hate of these men has not been abated by the plunder and desolation and bloodshed upon which it has fed" but had instead "been deepened and intensified." Quotations from northern publications reinforced these views and proved effective propaganda tools in their own right. The effects could be Orwellian. On April 12, 1864, an Alabama soldier wrote in his diary: "3 years ago the Yankees fired on Ft. Sumter—the inauguration of the war of invasion of the South and its people."[5] Such historical revisionism reflected more than a simple obliviousness to fact; it revealed a powerful enmity untethered from self-examination, let alone self-criticism or indeed any real analysis of the Confederate cause itself and its prospects.

Religious faith occasionally softened such views and even led the especially upright to eschew hatred of the Yankees. Living in East Tennessee, Eliza Fain was a devoted Confederate but also a pious Christian. She took Christ's command to love your enemies seriously and wrestled with its implications along with her own darker impulses. Even Yankees had precious souls, but she deplored their self-righteousness and indeed saw them as enemies of the faith. Could she then still love them? Other Confederates struggled with such questions and could only pray that somehow northern hearts might be changed.[6] But suppressing a natural hatred for the foe was not any easier and indeed far more difficult than resisting other sins. "It takes very long for a proud heart to bend in submission to misfortune, and I fear I do not feel as a Christian should about our enemies," Virginian Mary Stribling confessed. "I cannot but think it right to pray that they may be driven back but still I feel far more angry and vindictive against them than a Christian should." Confederates might try to overcome their bitter feelings yet found it all but impossible. A quartermaster in Lee's army well captured this internal tug of war between piety and patriotism, between compassion and hardheartedness. "I sometimes think the avenging anger of a righteous and just God will ultimately blot them [the Yankees] out of existence or make them a prey to their own miserable and fiendish hearts," Robert Taylor Scott wrote to his wife. "My heart is bitter against them, yet dearest, I try, yes try hard to suppress its bitterness and soften my feelings. I cannot feel as if my feelings were sinful, yet Christ blessed those who cursed, reviled and heaped misery upon him."[7] However much such Confederates tried to manage these contradictory thoughts and impulses, the battle to control wartime hatred often proved to be a hopeless one even for the most devout.

Some simply admitted to losing any Christian feeling they had ever had toward their enemies. The war's enormous costs and sacrifices certainly tested religious faith and often left little room for Christian charity toward a despised and irredeemable foe. There had simply been too much destruction, too many deaths. Expressing a common enough sentiment, Eliza Andrews dealt with the matter head-on: "I can't believe that when Christ said 'love your enemies,' he meant Yankees."[8] Human beings have always been able to rationalize hatred for other human beings, and flimsy excuses are often presented as profound and even tragic dilemmas. Some Confederates drew a distinction between private and public enemies, with the latter deserving no forgiveness. A Baptist editor even maintained that southerners could still love their enemies even as they proceeded to slay them in a purely defensive war. For a time, praying for Yankee souls might reassure the pious that they truly followed the Lord's commandment about loving enemies, though that too wore thin. "Feeling as I do," Georgian William White admitted, "I cannot continue even that prayer. God forgive me if I sin in hating as I do." If it were indeed a sin to hate such fiends, another soldier figured he was "guilty of the unpardonable one."[9]

Of course hatred in some cases has a much greater effect on those doing the hating than on the object of their hatred, a psychological insight not lost on thoughtful Confederates. Bitter reflection and a desire for retribution could become all consuming. It might be hard if not impossible to love one's enemies, but self-examination could also be painful. Virginian Kate Sperry felt herself becoming "stonehearted and everything, hard and pitiless—never knew I was so revengeful." Members of divided families were especially sensitive to how blackguarding the Yankees could itself prove degrading—especially to women who had been taught to cultivate gentler virtues.[10]

Yet many a second thought about despising the foe gave way to hair-splitting rationalization and often unalloyed justification. After all, the vile Yankees clearly deserved to be hated.[11] "Robberers, murderers, and outlaws," a Mississippi editor asked, "how can we otherwise than detest them?" Confederate hospital steward John Samuel Apperson could simply not feel much compassion for wounded Federals. This might not be right, "But who can forbear to feel hatred towards such a race [?] It requires more than humanity to bear the sight of those who burn our homes [and] turn our mothers and sisters out in the woods. . . . Here now they share the attention of our surgeons and nurses while our own wounded suffer, the few medicines that we catch and grab at different points and now must be used for the purpose of saving the life of the very men who would starve us for the want of it." Perhaps such reasoning offered psychological release because the presence of Federal troops both infuriated and frustrated Confederates, especially civilians. A Union general solicitously offered a woman safe passage across the Rappahannock during the occupation of Fredericksburg, but she indignantly refused because she had "no more business beyond that river than a Yankee has in heaven." Stories of resistance and defiance served to promote political unity and social cohesion, or at least that was the hope. Such tales also helped cement Confederate identity and commitment by identifying and excoriating the common enemy. Thus the Yankees became the true authors of southern woes, and so carping against one's neighbors, Confederate generals, or political leaders was worse than useless if not treasonable. No one despised the abolitionists more than the South's non-slaveholding whites, the *Charleston Mercury* stoutly maintained. "With them, it is not only the patriotic *hatred* of a public foe who would involve the country in convulsion and ruin, but it is also the *hatred* of a social, personal enemy—the Black Republican—who would force upon them the alternative either of the most terrible degradation and barbarism, or of slaughtering the negro, or being slaughtered by him, in a war of extermination."[12] Here were the old themes of anti-Yankee polemics deployed to rally the white population in the great hour of danger.

The longer the war lasted, the more hatred intensified. It grew stronger each day, some Confederates claimed, though such statements were undoubtedly designed to hearten the wavering. A Mississippi volunteer simply informed his mother, "I am getting to hate the Yankees in earnest."[13] According to another soldier, the Yankee was "surely the most despicable being on earth." Aside from generalized hatred, Confederates readily pointed to specific Union policies and actions. Everything from the blockade, to the desolation of homes, to Sherman's campaigns through Georgia and the Carolinas only produced greater enmity and a desire for revenge.[14]

"I live to hate the Yankees," an embittered Confederate prisoner remarked. "I am willing to spend my days in killing Yankee vandals." From an early age, southerners must learn to loathe the northern people and everything they stood for. In a letter to his wife, a Confederate commissary officer left no doubt on that score: "Teach my children to hate them & despise them [the Yankees], as not only our worst & meanest enemies but as the enemies of God & mankind. I consider it a solemn duty that our children and all the rising generation should be brought up in this spirit, for peace will come, and after it this base hypocritical and detested race will endeavor to bring about the old state of things and our children should be taught to hate them to prevent their infernal designs." Anecdotes featuring little boys and girls saying ugly things about the Yankees proved amusing but carried a decided edge, because for their parents, this hostility was deadly serious. Passing these beliefs from generation to generation, southerners would presumably never get over their abhorrence of a merciless foe. They hardly paused during the war to explore the implications of such an attitude, but it required no great prescience to realize that such an unwavering enmity might well affect southern politics and society for decades to come. In the meantime, hatred might help unite an often factious people in a determination to resist the invaders at all costs.[15]

For some southerners it became a matter of great pride that not a drop of Yankee blood flowed in their veins. How one could be sure of such a thing raised some unanswerable but seemingly irrelevant questions. The larger point centered on unswerving Confederate identity and loyalty along with a deepening and widening hatred of the Yankees extending into the indefinite future. "Something more than just resentment and aggression inflames the soldiers of the South," William Naylor McDonald perceptively noted near the end of the war. "Ours is a hate in which contempt is the master feeling; an aversion unconquerable, a feeling of loathing like that which the human family feels for reptiles." The emotions were visceral and the reactions at times physical, especially for women unable to go into the field and face the enemy directly. "I feel as if I could fight myself," a young Tennessee woman wrote. "[I] never see a Yankee but what I roll my eyes, grit my teeth, and almost shake my fist at him, and then bite my lip involuntarily and turn away in disgust." The presence of Benjamin Butler's troops in New Orleans so enraged one "pretty Creole lady" that she wished to "trample on their dead bodies and spit on them."[16]

That was to be expected from those whom the infamous Butler had labeled "she-devils," but the problem ran much deeper. To many Confederates, one other word summed up their abhorrence of the Yankees: "inextinguishable." Hatred had become a fire inside that would not be tamped down any time soon. To shift the metaphor, mutual enmity had opened such a chasm between the North and South that reunion was not only impossible but unthinkable. Such sentiments ignored the internal divisions in both sections as the war continued, but even so the imagery grew ever more vivid. After so many horrendous battles, it seemed that a "river of blood" had formed what William Henry Trescott deemed a "fearful barrier between two hostile nations." It would therefore be easy enough (rhetorically at least) to consign the entire Yankee nation to hell, as some Confederates clearly wished, but for now, the point was to kill as many of the viperous brood as possible.[17]

Reading about the northern dead piled high on some great battlefield brought a perverse pleasure, especially for those who did not have to bloody their own hands and risk their own necks. Women admitted welcoming reports of Yankee casualties yet also wondered what had become of their gender's supposedly more merciful qualities. Hearts grew bitter, and perhaps such feelings were sinful, but it was easy enough to view them as unavoidable. "I rejoice when I hear of their slaughter by the thousands," Catherine Edmondston remarked as the Overland Campaign unfolded. Relieved that her young brother had come safely through a recent battle, Louise Wigfall still had to ask her mother, "Did he kill any Yankees? I hope so." The most coldhearted admitted to having no pity at all for the Federal sick and wounded.[18]

These words expressed a callousness carried to chilling lengths. "Their [the Yankees'] flesh will fatten the Buzzards of the South, and their bones will be left to bleach on Southern soils," a Georgia editor hoped. Or perhaps the bones would not be left lying about because body-strewn battlefields created opportunities for gathering macabre souvenirs. Some people reportedly fashioned jewelry from enemy bones or used skulls for drinking cups; according to Confederate nurse Phoebe Pember, one woman took comfort in waking each morning to the sight of a "pile of Yankee bones lying around her pump." These tales—many no doubt apocryphal or embroidered—often appeared in northern newspapers and soldier letters. Historically, there is nothing all that extraordinary in such stories. War hardens soldiers and civilians alike, leading to the treatment of human enemies as little more than animals whose remains deserve no respect.[19] Obviously, such callousness is far from universal, but during the Civil War, many participants on both sides observed the phenomenon in themselves and others.

The display of grisly mementoes received occasional criticism in Confederate circles, though many people simply dismissed the more lurid accounts as enemy propaganda.[20] Surely good southerners would not behave in such a way, but even "a Yankee skull drinking cup," one South Carolina woman maintained, hardly compared "with any one of the million atrocities daily committed by *them*." No fear of overstatement there, and it proved an easy step from discounting such practices to defending them. "I tried to cut a ring off a dead Yankee's finger, but my knife was too dull," a Virginia private wrote to his young fiancée. "This may appear revolting to you but if you had seen as much of the scoundrels as I have you would think otherwise."[21]

According to the Bible, vengeance belongs to the Lord, and it became an article of faith among Confederates that their enemies would ultimately face divine punishment. "The North need not expect to escape the universal law of retribution," the *Richmond Dispatch* intoned. "It will one day have to drink the same bitter cup which is now pressed upon the lips of the South, aggravated by the punishment of its crimes in the present war. It is inconceivable that the Almighty should fail to visit such gigantic wickedness as the present invasion, and the inhuman and atrocious manner in which it is carried on, with His most signal displeasure." Surely the Yankees would be rewarded according to their deeds. Their moral arrogance boggled the mind, leading southern divine Benjamin Morgan Palmer declared. "The North has, for more than a generation, challenged the most High God. Claiming for themselves a purity superior to his own, they have presumptuously pronounced against the Divine administration from the beginning of time." The fanatical abolitionists had sought to "make the world more perfect than God would have it to be." All Confederates need do was wait, "trusting in that Almighty arm which is pledged to strike down the haughty and the proud." An ever-lengthening list of northern transgressions was all the more reason to believe that God's wrath would not be stayed forever. Individual sinners might face everlasting torment in hell, but sinful nations must receive condign punishment in the here and now. Yet the question then became how long would the Almighty allow the Federals free rein for persecution, plunder, and destruction, how long would the day of judgment be delayed. The Yankees' crimes would become notorious, as one Virginia minister put it, "until the North is scourged and scarred so as to retain the marks for generations."[22]

But human beings have seldom waited for God to avenge their wrongs, and Confederates obviously believed that the Lord needed assistance in rebalancing the scales of justice. Calls for retaliation against northern barbarians had appeared in the press before the war was well underway or many outrages of any kind had even been committed. Should the Yankees appear in Greenville, Mississippi, one Confederate volunteer advised the home folks to "take double barrell shotguns & pepper them like smoke.

Kill, slay & murder them. Give them no peace; for unless we do, we do not deserve God's mercy." Whether it be a particular injury or a whole series that called forth cries for retaliation, all the responsibility lay with the Yankees. "By their own infamous conduct," a Tennessee editor sharply noted, "they have placed themselves beyond the pale of civilization, and should be treated as barbarians who are incapable of generous or humane emotions." In the latter stages of the war as even diehard Confederates weighed the possibility of defeat, there was talk of painful memories, of avenging spirits, and of future retribution.[23]

Enraged Confederate soldiers longed to meet the Federals in battle so enemy blood could atone for unspeakable crimes against innocent southerners. The loathing poured forth in letters home, in pledges to redress the wrongs suffered by defenseless civilians; calls for divine chastisement were accompanied by promises of all too human vengeance. After Union forces began bombarding Charleston in August 1863, a South Carolina lieutenant vowed that if the opportunity offered, "I shall neither give nor ask quarter, but slaughter every wretch that comes within my power." A good deal of dramatic posturing and simple venting appeared in such statements, and promises to avenge the enemy's many crimes naturally poured out as the military situation deteriorated. In the bloody summer of 1864, a Georgia soldier recaptured the raw emotions involved. "When I come in sight of their blue yankee uniforms a feeling more like that of a fiend than human takes possession of me," Barrington King informed his mother. "I only feel an intense desire to kill, to strike to the earth all that comes in my reach." Like many other Confederates he spoke of the Yankees desolating homes and polluting southern soil. After the battle of Fredericksburg, one of General James Longstreet's staff officers noted how it was "doing my soul good" to see the enemy's "severed limbs, decapitated bodies, and mutilated remains." Increasingly, however, such statements sounded ever more desperate. In a speech to Confederate troops in late October 1864, General Patrick Cleburne did not mince words: "Hereafter I intend to fight, not for rights, but for revenge. You had as well talk religion to a heathen as right—Southern Rights—to a Yankee. Revenge, Revenge! for ruined homes, violated wives and daughters, desecrated graves and altars, land laid waste and our fair cities burned and sacked and ruined. Can we ever be remunerated? Never!

But vengeance upon them henceforth, until not a Yankee live[s] on Southern soil."[24]

Some Confederates recoiled from such harsh words and from their own vengeful thoughts. Gentler souls among the civilian population wondered what would become of compassion and mercy should blood lust rule the day. Lee's notably pious staff officer Walter Taylor observed the stark contrast between a natural desire for revenge and scriptural admonitions about forgiving enemies. Succumbing to baser impulses meant in effect questioning God's sovereignty by substituting human for divine judgment. In more sensitive hearts, wartime passions prompted self-reflection. Hatred for the enemy and calls for retribution could become all consuming, produce a dangerous lethargy, or worse yet devolve into savagery. How could southerners then stake out the moral high ground against their enemies? In the end, many loyal Confederates put aside such worries and simply rationalized the adoption of more draconian measures against a relentless foe. One could readily justify resentment and retaliation, one Baptist writer suggested, by simply reflecting on the "putrid qualities of the Northern heart."[25]

And nowhere were those qualities more evident than in the most notorious and despised Yankee generals. In the summer of 1862, both Charleston newspapers warned that the conflict was degenerating into a "war of extermination" carried out by Benjamin Butler, David Hunter, John Pope, and others of their ilk. Dramatic accounts of plundering, arrests, and various outrages increasingly led to calls for retaliation, for punishing enemy generals according to their deeds. "Is there no Brutus in New Orleans?" a Georgia headline screamed; a young Tennessee woman would have rejoiced to hear that Butler "was dead and buried so deep that the Lord could not find him at the resurrection day." Confederates often disagreed about which Yankee general deserved the greatest punishment and also differed on an appropriate penalty, some preferring that Union commanders be executed, others that they rot in prison while being forced to meditate on their evil deeds.[26]

Confederates talked of patience being exhausted, the time for temporizing at an end. And of course it was easy to cite Edmund Burke's famous remark about forbearance ceasing to be a virtue. In any case, the Yankees no longer deserved mercy, and any leniency by Confederates would only encourage their worst tendencies. "Fear is the only motive by which they can be restrained," a Richmond editor maintained. "What consideration, what common courtesy even; do we owe to such savages? If we had carried on the war from the beginning upon the most rigid principle of retaliation, the Yankee barbarians would long since have slunk back to their dens and caves. It is not too late now to learn a lesson from history, and from our own experience."[27]

Calls for retaliation, however, faced a formidable obstacle in the Confederate administration. Jefferson Davis's most vociferous critics regularly condemned the government for its halfhearted response to the enemy's darkest deeds. Edward Pollard wrote of a "feeble sentimentalism" that greatly contrasted with the "stern spirit of a people fighting for their liberties." Apoplectic editorials in the always acerbic *Charleston Mercury* and even in the usually friendlier *Richmond Dispatch* railed against the kid glove treatment of a brutal foe. When Confederates actually declared the Yankees "enemies of all mankind," it seemed high time to align deeds with words. Yet even high-ranking southern generals had taken no effective countermeasures against the ruthless invaders, claiming that local commanders were in the best position to deal with specific incidents and determine appropriate responses. In reality, lethargy and hesitation reigned, and Congress proved no more willing to tackle the issue than the president or his generals. The politicians talked incessantly about Yankee barbarities, an Alabamian fumed, but did nothing. "Mercy shown to our enemies is cruelty, bitter cruelty to our mothers, wives, sisters and people of all classes in these Confederate states, whether white or black." What the Confederate government truly demonstrated was weakness in the face of a pitiless adversary. Jefferson Davis threatened retaliation but then failed to follow through, further encouraging the Yankees to proceed with impunity.[28]

From the beginning, some Confederates had concluded that only retaliation and punishment could stay the enemy in his course, and as the fighting continued that conviction only grew stronger. The war brought forth calls for Old Testament justice. Impatient Confederates appealed to the ancient standard of "an eye for an eye." After Benjamin Butler ordered the hanging of the professional gambler William Mumford, who had torn down an American flag in New Orleans, Catherine Edmondston recommended similar treatment for a captured Union general. At the same time, a War Department official raised those stakes by proposing the execution of two Federals for every Confederate put to death. To a Savannah editor, the justification appeared obvious: ""The law of retaliation is a fearful one, but in a war like the present, against a barbarous and unscrupulous foe, its enforcement is necessary." If Yankees sought a contest of annihilation so be it; the guilt would fall on their heads.[29] Once again Confederates could portray themselves as wounded innocents. If the war continued with ever greater bloodshed, responsibility lay with the enemy.

As early as the summer of 1862, some Confederates proposed executing any white man found in the company of armed blacks. Turncoats under Union protection attempting to exercise civil authority in a seceded state (one might easily point to military governor Andrew Johnson in Tennessee) merited similar treatment. Rather than showing mercy to a band of robbers and murderers, Confederate leaders should show mercy to their own people by retaliating against such fiendish outlaws. "War to the knife, and to the last," wrote one aspiring poet. Even as hope for southern independence rapidly faded during the spring of 1865, an up-country South Carolina editor—striking a note of pathetic desperation—recommended a war without mercy against Sherman's men: "hang them if caught, and . . . give them no quarter on the field of battle. If we are to be exterminated, let our extermination cost the enemy as much as possible. Do not let them slay us and not slay them in return."[30]

In late 1861, a newly organized infantry company in New Orleans carried a black flag inscribed, "We gave no quarters [*sic*] and we ask none." Besides its association with pirates, the "black flag" traditionally signified no mercy shown and no prisoners taken; for some Confederates, early reports of Yankee atrocities raised that ominous specter. Barbaric behavior on one side seemingly necessitated an equally harsh response. During the summer of 1862 with the northern Congress's passage of the Second Confiscation Act along with calls for emancipating slaves and enrolling black troops, the discussion grew more serious. "Now it only remains for the Yankees to cease their outrages or enter into a war of no quarter, of a war to the knife," a young Mississippi volunteer informed his mother. "It is awful to contemplate such a state of things. Still, we are ready for the alternative." By fall, senators were publicly discussing the possibility of raising the black flag.[31]

Though fiery Confederates called for iron-fisted measures without worrying too much about the consequences, this all worked better in theory than it ever did in practice. From the beginning, more thoughtful voices asked if the Confederacy really wanted to adopt a "no prisoner" policy and get caught up in a cycle of endless retaliation. The raising of the black flag would mark an abandonment of civilized values and would hardly win over the western world to the southern cause. The natural tendency to seek vengeance against a bloodthirsty enemy should not override moral and practical objections. By the summer of 1863, Union armies had penetrated deeply into many parts of the Confederacy. How would southern civilians in occupied territory fare if their own government suddenly began executing prisoners or worse? Would not suffering women and children face new and deadlier dangers?[32]

A Georgia private stationed in Virginia who had heard a great deal about Yankee abuse of Rebel prisoners nevertheless shared these reservations. He fought to defend "our rights under a Civilized Banner" and was "very much opposed to the Black Flag." Yet he added an important caveat: if the enemy "raises it first," he would "fight [under] it." Confederates recalled the example of the late lamented Stonewall Jackson, a fearsome warrior whose bloodcurdling comments had become widely known and admired. In a long conversation shortly after John Pope had arrived in Virginia and issued his notorious orders, Jackson had discussed changing the nature of the war and what he considered the excessively mild policies favored by General Lee and the Confederate administration. From the beginning of the war, he confessed to having favored a "black flag" approach to the Yankee invaders, and this was no isolated sentiment. Cries for vengeance echoed from the press and the camps, fueled by each fresh and often unreliable report of Yankee outrages. Jefferson Davis would never embrace the need for retaliation, one Alabamian feared, but it had become absolutely necessary to "hoist the black flag."[33]

The easiest and most practical form of revenge would be against Union prisoners. Early in the war each side charged the other with mistreating captives, and therefore debates about appropriate retaliation began almost immediately. In a broader sense, Yankee outrages seemed to justify a much tougher policy on prisoners. In response to John Pope's orders, Jefferson Davis himself had suggested that if captured, Pope and his officers should not

“Contrast: Confederate Prisoner, Ohio Penitentiary; Federal Prisoners, Belle Isle,” *Southern Illustrated News*, October 10, 1863.

be considered prisoners of war and therefore not subject to exchange. The invasion of southern territory and the accompanying depredations formed the backdrop for any discussions about the treatment of prisoners. In the fall of 1861 Edmund Ruffin went off on a tirade against “an army of robbers, house-burners, . . . slave-stealers & inciters of negro insurrection, ravishers & murderers.” Such crimes would justify “refusing to make many prisoners, & putting to death, as felons, robbers & murderers, all who may be in our power in battle.” Once Lincoln had issued the Emancipation Proclamation, even that pious slaveholding paternalist Reverend Charles Colcock Jones, favored “putting every prisoner taken to instantaneous death, unless the war be wholly altered in its character and the proclamation be withdrawn.” During the war’s final year, young Eliza Andrews met a Confederate who “with a wink” explained how his men took Yankee stragglers into the woods and “lost ’em” or sometimes “the guns *would* go off an’ shoot ’em in spite of all our folks could do.” Pleas of necessity appeared in editorial calls for summary justice.[34]

"Personification of the Yankee Proposition for the New Cartel of Exchange," *Southern Punch*, October 3, 1863.

Perhaps even the early establishment of an exchange cartel with the enemy had been a mistake, and criticism of Davis for being too tender-hearted persisted throughout the war. Indeed the very reluctance of the government to retaliate before the Federals had gained a preponderance of prisoners after the fall of Vicksburg had proven to be a costly blunder. Retaliation might have become the last resort but also the best recourse. To give the Yankees a bitter taste of their own medicine would surely make them sue for peace and presumably bring the fighting to an abrupt end. The collapse of the exchange cartel brought about worsening conditions in both northern and southern prisons, and that in turn led to more cynical if not deliberately cruel treatment. There was public pressure to remove Federal prisoners from various places—especially Richmond—and even calls to reduce rations. Both sides believed that the mistreatment of prisoners had become intentional, and so justifications and rationalizations multiplied. Limited resources compounded by incompetence and neglect caused places like Andersonville to deteriorate rapidly.[35] Whether the official indifference to prison conditions reflected a policy of retaliation or not, the results were horrific.

Then too more pragmatic considerations cut both ways, and a desire for vengeance at times meant ignoring not only moral but practical consequences. The Union enrollment of black troops offered a case in point. This challenge to the southern racial, political, and social order aroused furious passions but also became part of the larger debate over retaliation. No quarter should be given a Yankee "fighting by the side of armed negroes," a North Carolina editor advised. Whether the enemy would actually send black troops into combat remained an open question for skeptical Confederates, but should they do so, the *Richmond Enquirer* warned, "none will be taken prisoners." That view received official sanction in late November 1862 from Secretary of War James A. Seddon, who, after consulting the president, declared that commanders had discretion to order the "summary execution" of armed slaves in Federal uniforms. Davis later softened this policy by ordering that black prisoners (along with their white officers) be handed over to state authorities. Members of Congress heatedly called for stronger measures and eventually adopted a resolution declaring white officers commanding black troops to be guilty of "inciting servile insurrection." If captured, these men could be executed. As for the African American troops themselves, "all negroes and mulattoes . . . taken in arms against the Confederate States" would be dealt with by the states.[36]

In truth, practice could be harsher than these official statements suggested. Much depended on commanders and their troops, and reports of atrocities appeared almost immediately. On the Olustee battlefield in Florida, Confederates stripped the dead and bayoneted wounded blacks; a Confederate memoirist candidly admitted to "fighting under the black flag" against African American troops near Yazoo City, Mississippi; after a skirmish in Jackson, Louisiana, young Celine Frémaux heard that some captured blacks had been executed, and on her way to fetch a doctor for a sick child stumbled into a thicket where "two niggers were hung to a tree limb."[37]

By no means the bloodiest but certainly the most politically charged affair occurred at Fort Pillow along the Mississippi River north of Memphis. Surrounded by Nathan Bedford Forrest's cavalry on April 12, 1864, a greatly outnumbered Union garrison was in desperate straits when surrender negotiations broke down, and Confederate cavalry swarmed into the fort. What followed amounted to wholesale butchery of black troops and their white officers. "The poor deluded negroes would run up to our men fall upon their knees and with uplifted hands scream for mercy but they were ordered to their feet and then shot down," Achilles V. Clark of the 20th Tennessee Cavalry informed his sisters. "The white men fared but little better. Their fort turned out to be a great slaughter pen. Blood, human blood stood about in pools and brains could have been gathered up in any quantity." A regimental surgeon added that "it was decidedly the most horrible sight I have ever witnessed." Another of Forrest's men admitted that "the negroes were shown no mercy."[38]

Eyewitnesses left little doubt about the fury that consumed some of the Confederates, a rage that had been building up ever since they had learned that Federal armies were enlisting black men. According to the testimony of a lieutenant from a Tennessee Union regiment, "several black soldiers [were] shot after they were wounded; as they were crawling around, the secesh would step out and blow their brains out." A white Union private attempted to surrender, but one Rebel shouted, "God damn you, you fight with the niggers and we will kill the last one of you." Some Confederate officers apparently yelled at their men to "give no quarter."[39]

However shocking the "Fort Pillow Massacre" (as it soon became known) might appear to northerners, Confederates claimed that it paled beside the outrages routinely perpetrated by Yankee generals and their minions. The debate over what actually happened and who was to blame began immediately and has never entirely died down, but in the meantime the carnage continued. A little over a week after Fort Pillow, Confederates overran Federal forces along the North Carolina coast at Plymouth; Rebel troops hunted down native whites who had joined the bluecoats along with many black soldiers, killing an unknown number. Interestingly enough, the *Charleston Mercury* justified the slaughter while laying some of the blame on the Davis administration. "At Fort Pillow, our soldiers killed all the white officers commanding negro troops, and at Plymouth, all the negro officers captured prisoners, are taken out and shot," the editor noted with apparent pride and approval. "Our soldiery, thus, have taken into their own hands, despite the weak complicity of the Confederate Government with our foes, the vindication of our rights." An equally fiery editorial in another South Carolina newspaper agreed that "the Federals themselves are responsible for all the retribution visited upon their heads." It all came back to the character of the enemy: "We are fighting highwaymen, burglars, criminals, who, having broken into our fair homes, would brain every man, woman and child to accomplish what remains of their desperate task. In other words, they have invaded our land, blockaded our ports, starved our people, occupied our cities, in loathsome dungeons imprisoned our sons and daughters, pillaged, burnt and ravished, violated every rule of legitimate warfare, and carried their deviltries as far as devils dare." The victims of Fort Pillow had received their just deserts, some soldiers and civilians concluded. Mounting hatred of the enemy had brought on calls for retribution, and finally retribution itself. Reading about how the retreating enemy had "been bayoneted, shot, sabred," Catherine Edmondston could only hope that "it is all true."[40]

That last statement reflected a key dilemma in a war of revenge: stirring up an insatiable bloodlust meant the atrocities would continue along with the war itself. "Repeat Fort Pillow," the *Richmond Examiner* cried. "Repeat Plymouth a few times and we shall bring the Yankees to their senses." The killing of black prisoners occurred elsewhere, and in some cases African American troops exacted their own payback. Near Charleston in early July 1864, Union and Confederate forces, whites and blacks alike, bayoneted prisoners.[41]

The reprisals continued on July 30, 1864, when the detonation of the famous Petersburg mine created enough death, destruction, and confusion that the resulting fury and carnage seemed all but inevitable. Going down into the crater created by the explosion, some black troops bayoneted and shot Confederate prisoners. Sent to plug the gap in the Rebel line, General William H. Mahone's men heard that black soldiers had shouted "Fort Pillow" and "No Quarter." Confederates quickly turned the tables, smashing skulls and wielding the bayonet with abandon. One Confederate officer recalled how his men were "utterly frenzied with rage" and that "nothing in the war could have exceeded the horrors that followed." A Georgian admitted that "butchery" had taken place but concluded it was "perfectly right." For many Rebels, it was their first contact with black troops; given memories of John Brown and fears of servile insurrection, the reaction was ferocious. Even black men allowed to surrender might be shot later. Mahone may have tried to halt the slaughter, but soldiers kept thrusting bayonets and swinging rifle butts. Several hundred black troops were likely killed after they had thrown down their arms.[42]

Abusing or killing black prisoners continued for the rest of the war, though Confederate practice was never consistent. Some Rebel outfits dealt mercifully with black captives while others adopted a "no quarter" policy, at least unofficially. At Saltville, Virginia, after being routed by Confederates on October 2, 1864, the Federals left behind a large number of wounded. The following morning in the midst of a dense fog, some Confederates went onto the field and began shooting black soldiers. Orders from no less a figure than General John C. Breckinridge were ignored, and a staff officer laconically wrote in his diary: "Our men took no negro prisoners." To make matters worse, the notorious guerrilla Champ Ferguson reportedly roamed about firing at white and black Federals alike.[43]

Ferguson's presence was hardly surprising because almost from the beginning, guerrilla raids and reprisals had become a larger part of the war than either side publicly acknowledged. In early 1862, Virginia governor John Letcher summoned the "loyal citizens" in the western part of his state to exact "vengeance upon the foe." Forbearance would never work against the Confederacy's ruthless enemies, so most any retaliatory measures became legitimate. The historically knowledgeable pointed to the successful guerrilla war against Napoleon in Spain (including night attacks) as an object lesson for the southern people. That the Yankees loudly complained about guerrillas and bushwhackers only strengthened the case for irregular warfare. With Jefferson Davis always hesitant to retaliate, the guerrillas took matters into their own hands. Even Edmund Ruffin admitted how painful it was to read about the exploits of William Clarke Quantrill and other bloodthirsty fighters, but Confederate civilians increasingly concluded that the southern people had no choice in the matter. "Horrible yet necessary" became their watchwords.[44]

Hunt down the Yankees like wild beasts, and other bloodcurdling suggestions, flowed from southern pens and out of southern mouths. As Confederate soldiers marched along, women exhorted them to kill *all* the Yankees. Elevating such an admonition to a higher moral plane, a Virginian urged her husband to shoot the "devil furies" whenever he got the chance: "It is God's will and wish for you to destroy them. You are his instrument and it is your Christian duty." Some men responded by urging folks at home to take up arms against any Federals who appeared in their neighborhood. Young women learned to shoot and dreamed of fighting off the northern demons with a pistol or even a carving knife. "Every man, woman and child in the Confederacy, is bound by every consideration of religion and patriotism to slay every Yankee he sees," an Alabama editor advised his readers. Even prayers called down pestilence and various calamities on the northern people. The famous Confederate mapmaker Jedediah Hotchkiss heard one poor woman with tears rolling down her cheeks imprecating the Lord that by June 1, 1863, "not one of the [Yankee] race might be left on the face of the earth."[45]

Confederates had often accused northern troops of waging a war of "extermination," but some thought that had now become a legitimate goal for Rebel armies. In response to a question about disinterring the bodies of Union soldiers, Robert E. Lee remarked that he "did not want a single Yankee on our soil *dead or alive*." As the Army of Northern Virginia prepared to enter Maryland and Pennsylvania at the beginning of the Gettysburg campaign, a terrible retribution was eagerly anticipated. Here was the chance to seize livestock, to destroy mills, to burn barns, and to cut a path of destruction through enemy territory. Retaliation and vengeance, an invasion that would lay waste to Yankeeland, such a vision fired the southern imagination. To see the Pennsylvania capital of Harrisburg in flames, that would truly be glorious. At the same time, less sanguinary Confederates might take pride in Lee's strict orders against pillaging (however much they might be violated), and worries about a war without mercy lingered; but such old-fashioned ideals were all too often honored in the breach.[46]

Reservations and second thoughts were rapidly dissipating even among Lee's worshipful admirers. Perhaps a few salutatory hangings of Yankee raiders might be in order, and by early 1864, soldiers in the Army of Northern Virginia, who despite the defeat at Gettysburg still anticipated a future offensive into Pennsylvania, declared that no longer would enemy property be protected.[47] Such sentiments were by no means new. Even before the Confederacy had been formed, Jefferson Davis had warned his Senate colleagues that the densely populated, industrialized cites of the North would be especially vulnerable to "torch and sword." Hotspurs had longed for Confederate armies to move on Washington after the first great victory at Manassas, but more was at work here than a preference for the offensive. Even during the first year of the conflict, some Confederates pressed their leaders to carry destruction and terror northward. A Texas cavalryman dreamed of hoisting the "black flag" and advancing on Washington, Philadelphia, New York, and Boston. Aside from simple vengeance and bloodlust, such a policy would surely strengthen the peace faction of the Democratic Party and convince the enemy that his cause was truly hopeless.[48]

In July 1864, a final raid into Pennsylvania by cavalry in General Jubal Early's command resulted in the burning of Chambersburg. That news heartened soldiers in the Petersburg trenches who thought it was about time, at last an act of well-deserved retribution. Cries of anguish from the North greatly pleased impatient Confederates who relished the thought of Yankees receiving their just deserts. Though she found this news frightening, Eliza Fain speculated that the conflagration might be part of God's plan to bring the enemy to their senses. Other Confederates hoped the fires of Chambersburg would mark the start of a more general policy of carrying the war to northern doorsteps and beyond.[49]

Clearly Confederate imaginations raced far beyond their fledgling nation's military capabilities. A Tennessee editor hoped to see "our cavalry trooping through every city, village and hamlet of the Yankees to see their women begging protection" or to witness "the plows torn from the hands of their farmers and broken to pieces—their fences laid waste and homes in flames," to watch as "their wives and children [are] driven into exile and hooted from their own territory by an invading enemy." Such dreams of vengeance turned ever more fanciful. Weeping throughout New England—there was a scene for beleaguered Confederates to conjure. Those who had endured so many destructive raids found psychological release if not momentary comfort in the thought of northern families suffering similar indignities. "When our Armies invade the North I want them to carry the torch in one hand & the sword in the other," a North Carolina woman wrote shortly after the Army of Northern Virginia had surrendered. "I want desolation carried to the hearts of their country. The widows and orphans left naked and starving just as ours were left."[50]

Long before war's end, however, beleaguered Confederates had dreamed of their troops sweeping through northern towns and cities, perhaps even to the Canadian border. Surely the artillery bombardment of northern cities would force the Yankees to make peace. It seemed only fair that Philadelphia or New York or Boston receive the same treatment that had been meted out to Fredericksburg or Charleston or Atlanta. But for Confederates who imagined how their enemies might be suitably punished, fire became the preferred method. Burning the great cites of the North, to see them reduced to ashes and turned into a vast wasteland—that became an all too common fantasy. Send a few veterans north to do the work, and soon the flames would be licking at the very foundations of the haughty and arrogant Yankees' supposedly superior civilization. Or perhaps to envision fires raging through lush valleys destroying crops, just as Union armies had devastated the southern countryside. Such images especially appealed to newspaper readers and disheartened civilians.[51]

They also revealed the depth of hatred—the inevitable consequence of persistent demonizing of the enemy compounded by the all too real ravages wrought by Union armies. Words had from the start become weapons against the enemy, and in turn words had led to the use of deadly weapons; hatred and avenging anger had inspired acts of retribution. Such strong emotions could not dissipate quickly, and one could readily imagine that loathing of the Yankees and a settling of scores would continue after the war. People had grown used to violence, and violence might well remain a political instrument.

As it was, to revile the northern people and to witness the war's destructiveness elicited cries for vengeance, but calls for retaliation just like the fanatical diatribes against the Yankees came with a cost. They solved nothing, yet in fundamental ways distorted Confederate thinking. To imagine that the dastardly enemy might ultimately triumph just did not fit in with pervasive ideas about virtuous Confederates who would eventually prevail over evil Yankees. Clear-eyed assessments of the Confederate military and political situation became difficult if not impossible when looking through the clouded lenses of sectional chauvinism and righteous anger.

CHAPTER 6

Subjugation

Fantasizing about acts of retaliation helped keep the emphasis on enemy misdeeds rather than Confederate weaknesses. No need to acknowledge the possibility of defeat, so long as one could dwell on the northern government's evil intentions and how to avenge them. From the beginning of the war, editors, politicians, soldiers, and civilians had all asserted that the Yankees were really aiming at the "subjugation" of the South.[1] That ominous word resonated from the late antebellum period, throughout the war, and well beyond. In many ways, it encapsulated the enemy's true character and intentions.[2] "The bare idea of subjugation by Yankees is enough to freeze the hottest blood that ever bounded through Southern veins," a Virginia plantation mistress wrote in early 1862 as she tried to absorb reports of losses in the western theater. Warnings about the dangers of subjugation had been a staple of secessionist rhetoric, but the war gave the term much more tangible meanings. Confiscation, emancipation, murder, and rape would surely follow; so would the obliteration of state boundaries and the establishment of a military despotism. In the midst of gloomy news about the fall of Fort Donelson and the surrender of Nashville, young Sarah Wadley, living near Monroe, Louisiana, envisioned a stark choice: "Victory, or death is our only alternative, worse than death would be our conquest by the Yankees, that is now the most hateful word in our language."[3] Wadley described but two choices at this early stage of the war, and it is remarkable how easily she (and many other Confederates) failed to envision any other possibilities. Given southern views of the Yankee enemy, it logically followed that defeat at the hands of such a foe could not fail to yield the most nightmarish results.

Initially at least, subjugation seemed inconceivable and Confederate resolve unshakeable. "The forces of the World in arms can never conquer our people," declared the *Atlanta Southern Confederacy* before a shot had been fired. "If we could be conquered, we would all die in the last ditch before we would yield one inch to the dictation of the Nigger-Republican-Lincoln Government." Like the French Jacobins, the *Southern Illustrated News* predicted, the great northern despotism would be swept away, and there was even speculation that it might be the Confederates who would end up subjugating the Yankees. Such brave avowals thundered from courthouse steps and pulpits and porches as troops were being sent into the field, but Confederates also developed what they considered a universal axiom of political science. "A free people thoroughly united, who are true to themselves, can never be subjugated," a Georgia editor asserted with disarming simplicity. One volunteer serving near Yorktown, Virginia, in early January 1862 restated the principle more colorfully: "I have no more idea that the Yankees will whip us than that a chicken can teach Latin." The noble character of the southern people made such an eventuality all but impossible, though it is certainly notable how such statements simply assumed there would be social and political unity in southern ranks. Even after defeats, passionate Confederates declared that the idea of subjugation or reconstruction was simply not part of the southern vocabulary. And in any case, Almighty God would hardly allow his chosen people to be vanquished by the diabolical Yankees.[4]

The course of the war, the loss of territory, and bloodshed on an unprecedented scale undermined such assertions or at least made them more conditional. "Never, no never will the South yield to Northern rule while there are *strong* men to fight her battles," Virginian Susan Caldwell declared in the spring of 1862 as the Confederacy moved toward conscription. Other Confederates cited early setbacks and the evacuation of cities during the American Revolution to show how it was quite premature to speak of final defeat. Some thought that women's patriotism alone would prevent such a result or pointed to the revolt in the Netherlands against Spain's Phillip II as an inspiring historical example. A faith in the ability and willingness of soldiers and civilians to keep making sacrifices for the cause of southern independence showed remarkable persistence. Although some Confederates expressed their confidence in a more qualified way, others doubled down.

The whole world had come to realize that what many termed the "Abolition Government" could never conquer the South, and now the fanatics of the North just had to acknowledge that reality. The purblind Yankees placed great faith in their physical prowess while ignoring the moral strength of the southern people. Even into 1864 and 1865 a few diehard Confederates clung to the "impossibility" of the South's subjugation.[5]

As much as Yankee actions, Yankee intentions remained a potent rallying cry. "They had gradually unfolded their final purpose," a South Carolina minister informed his grandson stationed at Corinth, Mississippi. "We must either make up our minds to disappoint and defeat them, or to die." The course of the war revealed Federal plans in a clearer and clearer light, as southerners pointed out repeatedly in speeches, editorials, orders, diaries, and correspondence. Each description of northern objectives would, it was hoped, foster a renewed fighting spirit. Early in the war, General Leonidas Polk boldly asserted that "all ages and conditions are united in one grand and holy purpose of rolling back the desolating tide of invasion." With the enemy unmasked, Jefferson Davis called for a show of popular support for the government, and public meetings adopted resolutions detailing the price of subjugation. Throughout the war, officers sought to inspire their troops with vivid descriptions of how defeat would bring about seemingly unimaginable but somehow readily described consequences.[6]

For shame, if people understood how the Yankees intended to impose a heavy yoke on once free men yet still hesitated to enlist or evaded service with some devious stratagem. An Alabamian in a camp near Tupelo, Mississippi, could only shake his head over such a prospect and conclude that any cowards would "deserve all that Lincoln's fanatical rule could bring upon them." Confederate propagandists reminded southerners of their moral and racial superiority in a war against a degenerate enemy bent on conquest and plunder. Surely, weak-kneed patriots should remember that the Yankees had left southerners no choice but to secede and now sought their utter destruction.[7]

How then to explain the indecision and weakness of so many southerners? How could there be any reluctance to retaliate in kind when the character of the foe was so abundantly clear? On one level, the explanation seemed obvious. A war that brought great economic hardships, infringement on civil liberties, and horrendous bloodshed had naturally produced weariness and despair, if not disaffection. Yet ending the fighting and submitting to the yoke of Yankee rule (including emancipation) still seemed unacceptable—at least until very late in the war—to many Confederates. Loyalty to the nascent southern nation had come at tremendous cost, but whether that price was unacceptable when compared to the alternative of submission to the enemy remained the most difficult question that had to be faced. A hard choice for sure, but for many Confederates, horrific sacrifices seemed preferable to surrender and reconstruction.

To unyielding Confederate patriots, an appeal to history was obviously in order. The glorious memories of the American Revolution, and the noble role played by southerners lovingly recounted by William Gilmore Simms and others, must mean something to the present generation. Surely they would not become the degenerate heirs of their noble sires—or at least that became a common rallying cry. Newspapers printed letters from women seeking to shame men into reenlisting. A congressional candidate in 1863 adopted an equally emotional appeal: "Are there Georgians ready to crawl to his [Lincoln's] feet and with less than the spirit of whipped hounds, to pray for such mercy to their vile bodies, as he may see fit to grant?"[8]

The answer to that question might in fact be "yes." A literary-minded North Carolinian who served to the bitter end remarked that "if the South is ever subjugated it is purely and simply the fault of the people." Slightly paraphrasing Shakespeare, he added, "It is in ourselves and not in our stars, dear Brutus, that we are underlings." Perhaps the Yankees assumed they could wear down southerners to the point of submission, though that idea sparked strong demurrers. "The character of our people forbids this conclusion," a Virginia editor maintained in the aftermath of Gettysburg and Vicksburg, but such a blanket denial could be interpreted either as wishful thinking or dogged persistence. It ran up against substantial evidence of internal divisions, steady murmuring, and growing disaffection, but public statements at least (and many private ones for that matter) failed to acknowledge such realities. What now kept Confederates going, the hopeful editor added, was "the deep and growing and incurable hated of our people to the dominion of the Yankees." Various historical parallels came to mind: Spanish hatred for the Moors; Dutch hatred for the Duke of Alva.[9]

European examples proved a useful guide as Confederates paused to consider what would surely follow their subjugation. "Our history will be worse than that of Poland and Hungary," James Henley Thornwell warned. "It is a night of thick darkness that will settle upon us." Yankee oppressors would easily rival the Russians in cruelty or even shame the Vandal hordes who had rampaged across the continent and sacked Rome. But none of these comparisons seemed adequate to a Virginia minister who on an early Confederate fast day observed that if the northern enemy somehow succeeded, "history furnishes no page so dark and bloody as that which would record the result." For want of any more pertinent historical precedent, some Confederates simply predicted that the Yankees would turn the South into a vast, howling wilderness.[10]

Radical Republicans had talked of reducing the southern states to territories, and some Confederates maintained that was exactly what would happen. "We should have no political rights, except such as our masters chose to permit us to exercise," Georgia governor Joe Brown predicted. Such alarms became standard political fare, and dire prophecies echoed from speeches and editorials. Northern leaders would turn the southern states into colonies governed by bayonets, and with a military dictatorship in place, a long train of abuses would follow. Not surprisingly fire-eater William Lowndes Yancey could foresee everything from disfranchisement, to confiscation, to mass rape. Some observers expected powerful Yankee generals to be ensconced in each state while others simply anticipated mob rule. In a long and widely reprinted editorial on what subjugation would mean for the southern people, the *Richmond Examiner* predicted a Federal garrison in every town, with martial law in place and Yankee judges in the courtrooms. Confederates would lose all their rights and become little more than serfs under the thumb of northern masters.[11]

As the war ground into its final year, prophecies grew ever grimmer. Official statements and political speeches alike painted a more and more frightening picture. "Subjugation involves everything that the torturing malice and devilish ingenuity of our foes can suggest," a widely circulated address by Congress advised the southern people. "The destruction of our nationality, the equalization of whites and blacks, the obliteration of State lines, degradation to colonial vassalage, and the reduction of many of our citizens to dreary, hopeless, remediless bondage. A hostile police would keep 'order' in every town and city. Judges . . . would hold our courts, protected by Yankee soldiers. Churches would be filled by Yankee or tory preachers. Every office would be bestowed on aliens. Absolutism would curse us with all its vices. Super-added to these, sinking us into a lower abyss of degradation, we would be made the slaves of our slaves, hewers of wood and drawers of water for those upon whom God has stamped indelibly the marks of physical and intellectual inferiority." Texas senator Williamson S. Oldham cast the future in even darker hues: "It [subjugation] means the erasing of our name and country from the map of the world; the conclusion of our history, with no future; the destruction of our governments both State and Confederate, and the provincializing of our States, to be governed by a triumvirate, consisting of the whining, canting, hypocritical Yankee, the red republican, infidel German, and the superior of the trio, the African negro."[12]

Speculation about Yankee political intentions seemed scattershot compared to what Confederates concluded about their enemies' economic objectives. In fact one word, "confiscation," pretty well summed up the great fear on that score. Northerners were plotting to seize southern lands and all others forms of property—a point that seemed obvious to many from the beginning and even more so during the course of the war. Farms and plantations would be handed over to Union soldiers, white and black alike. How else could the Emancipation Proclamation be interpreted? Yet a few Confederates predicted that government-seized lands would be worked by slaves and so pointed to what they considered the utter hypocrisy of northern "freedom shriekers."[13]

The Yankees would need all this wealth to help pay the staggering costs of their war against the southern people. Everyone from Joe Brown to the *Charleston Mercury* warned of onerous taxes that would be imposed to finance the northern war debt. "But as long as they declare that our property shall pay the expenses of this war I will fight them as long as I can crawl," a North Carolina lieutenant promised. The prospect of being ground into the dust by a combination of confiscation and taxation became a call to patriotic sacrifice. The ruination that would follow a Yankee triumph should presumably convince those with a significant economic stake to remain steadfast.[14]

Confiscation, moreover, carried broader connotations: loss of property equaled loss of freedom. When asked what the Federals would do once they had conquered the southern people, a New York colonel told a Virginia woman, "Make serfs of you." That might well be, yet the more pervasive and deeper worry was "enslavement," a word that resonated deeply with virtually all white southerners. It was one thing to talk about the end of liberty in a general sense, but soldiers remarked how they were literally fighting to prevent their families from being enslaved. In late 1864, a Florida Unionist observed how Confederates played on just such a fear in a vain attempt to stem the tide of desertion. From private correspondence to poetry to editorials, images of chains being prepared for the vanquished made the threat appear quite real. With several choice and familiar epithets to hurl against the enemy, a Mobile editor summed up the danger: "Egyptian bondage would be sweet [compared] to the cruel subjection of this proud race to the psalm singing, puritanical devils, who with God and liberty on their lips come to us with lust, cupidity and hatred in their hearts."[15]

The enslavement of white people would inevitably follow the emancipation of black people. That proposition had always been part of the proslavery gospel, and even if the Yankees were phony liberators, the principle still applied. Southerners had long conflated Republicans with abolitionists, and even before Lincoln had cited military necessity to move against slavery, Confederates had accused their enemies of waging an abolition war.[16] Indeed emancipation and confiscation would go hand in hand. Not only would several million slaves be ostensibly freed, North Carolina governor Zebulon Vance warned, but some 200,000 black men who had taken up arms against their masters and against the Confederacy would "be turned loose at once in our midst." Early in the war, a Louisiana editor had pithily summed up the consequences: "freedom to slaves and slavery to freemen."[17]

A world turned upside down—or "bottom rail on top" as the saying went—that prospect thoroughly frightened Confederates even as it baffled them. Near the conclusion of an argumentative correspondence with General William T. Sherman about the evacuation of Atlanta, General John B. Hood let loose a final blast against northern war policy: "You came into our country with your army avowedly for the purpose of subjugating free white men, women, and children, and not only intend to rule over them, but you make negroes your allies and desire to place over us an inferior race." To imagine southern white men laboring in the cotton fields or even worse women and children toiling under the supervision of Yankee overseers boggled the Confederate mind. Northerners would in essence elevate former slaves to mastery and then dictate the future of southern race relations.[18]

With Confederate prospects sinking in August 1863, Jefferson Davis spread the alarm by pointing to the horrific consequences of defeat and adding a distinct element of racial fear. He latched onto staples of proslavery ideology and applied them in most desperate circumstances: "They [the Federals] design to incite servile insurrection and light the fires of incendiarism wherever they can reach your homes, and they debauch the inferior race, hitherto docile and contented, by promising indulgence of the vilest passions as the price of treachery." More than a year earlier with worries about lagging reenlistments and increasing desertions, the *Charleston Mercury* in an equally predictable way had played on the anxieties of non-slaveholders. Should the Yankees succeed in subjugating the Confederacy, the "poor white people" would face a terrible choice between "amalgamation with the negro, or a strife of extermination." Once the theme of racial menace was well established, fertile imaginations went to work. Not only would the slaves be emancipated, they would sit on juries, testify against whites, and help enforce Yankee rule. Any racial clash would be adjudicated on the basis of what a Mobile editor dubbed the new "claims of negro superiority." Congress would soon force social equality everywhere from streetcars to churches with worse still to come. Sexual anxieties bubbled near the surface, and a Texas soldier, after making the usual reference to the tyrants' clanking chains, warned that Confederate laggards dare not "wait till we are all bound hand and foot and the fair daughters of the south reduced to a level with the flat footed thick-liped negro." Southerners would then have to live, a Mississippi volunteer predicted, "in a land where the inter-mixture of races will breed a long train of evils which were fairly illustrated in the history of Jamaica."[19]

A South Carolinian recoiled at the "emancipation horrors" that would follow any Yankee triumph but was equally worried about the fate of southern "religious privileges." This was no afterthought. The sectional division of the churches before the war, and continuing appeals by both sides to divine favor, naturally led to speculation about the religious consequences of subjugation. Given the southern belief that heresy and infidelity had long infected the northern states, the thought of Yankee missionaries colonizing the South struck a sensitive nerve. The northern crusade against the Bible and true faith could only assume more ominous forms with religious freedom in the southern states quickly snuffed out. Wartime orders by Secretary of War Edwin Stanton and the aggressive efforts of several northern denominations were but preludes to a general takeover of southern churches and the forcible removal of southern ministers. In the fall of 1864 a children's magazine even warned that Yankees might confiscate Bibles and interfere with family prayers.[20]

Such alarms added an important religious element to a discussion of subjugation that remained wide-ranging and anxiety-ridden. Military despotism, confiscation, emancipation, and miscegenation—all received attention in Confederate propaganda, and all became sources of public and private lamentation. There was little detailed attention paid to any particular danger. Instead, speeches, newspaper editorials, and even private correspondence rattled off a litany of dreadful consequences that must surely come in the wake of northern victory. A language of warning and dread along with calls for renewed commitment reinforced well-established notions about the enemy while making any hint at surrender or even negotiation unacceptable.[21]

At first glance, the idea of "reconstruction" might appear less frightening than subjugation, but zealous Confederates spurned semantic distinctions. Early in the war, a Savannah newspaper haughtily observed that Confederates could hardly conceive of even "the slightest political connections with the puritanical fanatics and blackguards whose wrongs have forced us to a separation." The gulf between the northern and southern peoples had simply grown too wide for papering over by any attempt at reconstructing the old Union. After all, in the Confederate mind the enemy warred against civilization itself. "These imps of Satan," a Mississippi soldier wrote early in 1865, made reunion inconceivable. "The vilest savage, the basest negro, the greatest infidel and diabolical robber of virtue, is a fitter companion for Southern men than a 'Reconstructionist' on any terms." Cowardly submissionists deserved hanging, a Georgia volunteer declared. The whole idea of reconstruction appeared absurd, and in any event would simply become slavery by another name.[22]

Dreams of reunion were no more than a wicked delusion. Only those fools willing to suffer the deepest degradation would consider swearing the Yankee oath of allegiance in a futile effort to save their property. Reconstruction would ultimately amount to nothing less than surrendering all rights to the South's most bitter enemies. As an Englishman serving as a Confederate staff officer in Charleston pithily expressed it, "Reconstruction means subjugation." Who could imagine that the Yankees' malignant hatred would suddenly give way to magnanimity once the bullets stopped flying? "We will have no fellowship, we will pledge no faith, with the plunderers of our property—the murderers of our sons, and the despoilers of our wives and daughters," a Georgia politician avowed during an 1863 election campaign. Anyone who sought to restore relations with such a people was an enemy of the South. These fervent sentiments reflected a mounting desperation stemming from worries about disaffection and desertions. By the summer of 1863 there were growing signs that some Confederates might be willing to parley with the enemy, and so leading politicians scrambled to shore up public morale. Even later, with the southern nation tottering toward destruction, the language of hatred and resistance remained powerful. In February 1865, Louisiana governor Henry Watkins Allen sounded the expected note of defiance: "Can I trust men who have committed every crime in the Decalogue? Can I shake hands with murderers and robbers? Can I sit down with thieves, and house burners, and assassins, and break bread with those who have insulted my wife, my mother, my sister? No, never! never!! never!!!" And once the war was over, matters would only grow worse. Who then could expect the northern barbarians to show any restraint at all?[23]

That left the southern people with clear choices: despotism or freedom, extermination or independence. The war against the Yankees and all they stood for naturally fed into this Manichean rhetoric, both lengthening the war and poisoning an eventual peace. Lincoln had left Confederates no alternative but to keep up the struggle because there was really no basis for negotiations, much less reasonable compromise. In the summer of 1864, an Ohio soldier perceptively concluded that desertion had drained many of the weak-kneed and disloyal from the Rebel armies and that the remaining troops would keep up the fight because they viewed their options in just such stark terms. To a resolute Texas cavalryman, complete destruction seemed preferable to submission.[24] If all these brave words cannot be taken literally, and the exaggeration and overkill are obvious, even stripped of excess, they present a picture of grim determination to keep up armed resistance as Confederate fortunes sagged.

Declining prospects, however, only intensified fears of subjugation and hatred of the enemy. The Yankees' barbarous character—so long detailed and denounced by Confederates in almost every imaginable way—made the possibility (and increasing likelihood) of defeat more humiliating than words could describe. But tongue and pen did try to describe what many Confederates considered to be the ultimate loss of "honor," a word that did not skip lightly over southern tongues. In February 1865, Governor Zebulon Vance of North Carolina spoke of the "dishonor" that would surely accompany the "degradation" and "ruin" of defeat. Even some three years earlier a South Carolina planter who had eagerly enlisted in the army had similarly sketched out the consequences of a Yankee triumph: "we would be an humbled, down trodden and disgraced people. Not entitled to the respect of any body, and have no respect for ourselves. In fact we would be the most wretched and abject people on the face of the Earth." Everyone—men, women, and children—would face an almost unimaginable humiliation, forced to don what a prominent minister termed "the badge of a conquered race." The word *race* of course resonated deeply, but generals such as Earl Van Dorn and Patrick Cleburne also warned their troops that failure to repulse the invaders would mean a loss of manhood, a loss that carried its own particular disgrace. Resolutions adopted by Confederate soldiers near the end of the war declared that submission would create an everlasting mark of shame on the southern character.[25]

Here were raw emotions and words of utter desperation. To the very end, some Confederates bravely maintained that they could not be conquered by such a foe because for one thing, the Lord would not allow it. "We need have no fears of being enslaved by so brutal and cruel enemies as those against whom we are fighting," Louisiana volunteer Reuben Pierson assured his father. "God who rules the destiny of all things and is a God of wisdom and of justice will never suffer a determined and Christian people to be overcome by a cruel Tyrant but be their deliver[er] as in the days of old. He led the children of Israel dry-shod through the Red Sea." But there was also a gnawing fatalism because whatever the outcome, the Almighty's plans would be fulfilled. By March 1865, a public meeting in Augusta County, Virginia, had reduced patriotism and perseverance to a familiar and not exactly reassuring litany: "Placing our trust in the Lord of Hosts; relying upon the justice of our cause; preferring death to dishonor—determined to bequeath the precious boon of Independence which we inherited from our Fathers, to our children, or die in the effort; willing to lay our all if need be upon the altar of our country, resolved never to submit to the yoke of such a people as those with whom our brothers and sons have been engaged in deadly struggle for four years, and who have delighted in sacking and destroying our houses, devastating our lands, insulting our women and murdering our citizens." Proposals to enlist black soldiers reflected a frightening desperation even in the minds of the most loyal Confederates. Soldiers willing to admit that many of their comrades had lost hope or even deserted still claimed that there were enough stalwart fellows left to keep the armies in the field. In April 1865, a letter published in a Louisiana newspaper could only offer a less than inspiring cliché: "To will is to accomplish."[26]

Confederates simply had trouble acknowledging the facts on the ground. Official and semiofficial statements presented a far too rosy picture of the military situation or explained away defeats and casualties with breathtaking sophistry. From the war's earliest days, editors, politicians, and military leaders had told the southern people that any fate would be preferable to Yankee rule, and yet with whatever logic or illogic was at hand, continued to deny that such an eventuality was likely or even possible. When Confederate prospects appeared bright, such bold assertions along with the usual blackguarding of the enemy showed an apparent confidence. "There is no people on God's green earth we would not call brother," a Georgia editor crowed, "before we would the God-forsaken, lying, thieving, butchering dogs of the nigger-stealing North." As the war entered its third year, the Confederate Congress declared that far better for the southern people to be "conquered by any other nation than by the United States." Anything to avoid Yankee domination became last-ditch cries, and some firebrands even vowed (whether truthfully or not) to die before facing such a catastrophe.[27]

Would armies then fight to the death? Better death than subjugation was easy enough to say, especially for politicians and civilians far from battlefields, and especially for newspaper editors who had uttered that plea long before the military situation had become so perilous. How seriously to take such calls presents any number of interpretative problems. Were they simply the empty braggadocio of people who had not thought very seriously about what they were saying? Were these only words carelessly spoken? Did such statements merely express the standard themes of wartime propaganda? Perhaps so, but when some soldiers swore to fight to the last man, their sentiments carried a little more weight. Even North Carolina governor Zebulon Vance, who steered a careful course between the Confederate administration and the peace faction in his own state, spoke of fighting to the "last extremity."[28]

What that meant exactly, no one explained, but an expressed determination to fight to the bitter end had appeared early in the war and never died out. After the defeats at Fort Henry and Fort Donelson, a North Carolina editor had set the tone: "Better that the last Southern man be buried beneath the soil in whose defence he died, than become the slave of Yankee tyrants." Mississippian Amanda Worthington went one step further, preferring to "have every man, woman and child in the Confederacy killed" rather than returning to the despised Union. Governor Charles Clark of Mississippi wildly imagined a mass suicide after the last soldier had died with old men, women, and children "join[ing] hands together, marching into the sea, and perish[ing] beneath its waters."[29] Such flights of fancy offered little psychological comfort. Advice from home to kill the blue devils or South Carolina governor Andrew Magrath's summons to slaughter the Yankees as Sherman's army was about to enter the state were predictable but also pathetic.[30] By the same token, they indicated a deep, relentless hatred, and such calls for vengeance often took on a life of their own.

A South Carolina editor had even suggested the Palmetto State "should make the freest offering of blood and treasure." As the cradle of secession, and not coincidentally the southern state most despised by the enemy, South Carolina would pay a fearful price. Not only would Columbia, the capital, be burned, but Sherman's troops would show little restraint in rampaging through the state. The very destructiveness of the war along with all the demonization and hatred of the enemy, as historian Jason Phillips has perceptively argued, made surrender all that more difficult.[31]

Defeat would mean losing everything, the most stalwart Confederates feared. "Reconstruction," according to an April 1865 statement attributed to General Nathan Bedford Forrest, "would require the soldier to destroy the proud ensigns of his glory, to stack his arms, lower his head in dishonor and pass under the yoke of abolition tyranny. It would require confiscation, imprisonment and death! It would turn into our families bands of detectives to ferret out the household secrets! It would suppress the freedom of speech—deprive us of arms and the elective franchise. Every office would be filled by Yankees, the churches by Yankee, tory (or negro) preachers and we would be made the slaves of our slaves, who would be lurking spies over all our conduct! Our homes, land, property, all taken from us! I cannot see how continued resistance will bring upon us greater 'destruction' than that which would follow 'reconstruction.'" Such obliviousness to practical considerations, the political future, or to the all too real price of continued resistance mattered a great deal as the war finally ended. This made adjustment to the new order especially painful and difficult, and for some impossible. Word of Lee's surrender seemed beyond belief, especially to the thousands of civilians who considered Marse Robert's army to be invincible. Now indeed, "subjugation" had come and that dread word continued to evoke horrors that haunted the dreams and waking hours of Confederates who still could not imagine that the day of doom had arrived.[32]

To acknowledge that the insufferable Yankees had won the war was hard even for soldiers who had been present at Appomattox. North Carolina captain Henry Chambers wrote of hopes "blasted" and "bitter humiliation." But that was not the half of it. "Worse than all . . . these worthless fellows whom we have so often whipped, whose cowardly backs we have so often seen, have at last by sheer force of numbers, numbers swelled by contributions from almost every race and color on the face of the globe, have compelled us to come to this, can now lord it over us and ours, can pass, with the airs of conquerors, through our camps and here throughout our whole country." Aside from elements of what would soon become the Lost Cause, Chambers's diary entry revealed how some Confederates refused to accord the long-despised enemy any respect. Surely some terrible retribution awaited this "motley crew who have waged upon us so unjust, so barbarous a warfare! upon this soldiery who have burned our houses, desecrated our altars, plundered our wealth, waged unrelenting warfare upon the aged, the weak and the helpless, insulted and dishonored our lovely women! upon that heartless and fanatical people who have by every means in their power, by money, by chicanery, by fraud, by passion, by superstition, by a fanatical religion, by the hope of immense rewards, and by the blandishments of beauty urged on those hell-hounds in their fiendish work!" Cries for vengeance persisted, especially among distraught women. As early as 1863, a Georgia editor had speculated that, in the unlikely event of northern forces prevailing, "it will be our chief happiness to render their supremacy a curse, by devoting our whole time to the work of revenge."[33]

After all, it would simply be impossible to live under Yankee domination. More than a month after Lee's surrender, a Georgia woman claimed to be a "hotter rebel than ever" and could not resign herself to going "back into the Union with such a corrupt people." Others feared seeing the South thoroughly Yankeeized and dominated by what a North Carolinian dismissively termed a "shoddy aristocracy." This of course carried echoes of the corrupt contractors who had cheated the U.S. government and been lampooned in the northern press, and in fact had been responsible for bringing the word "shoddy" into the American lexicon. What would it be like for supposedly pure and innocent southern children to grow up in such a degraded society? That question had disturbed thoughtful Confederates even before Appomattox.[34]

In the meantime the postwar world appeared shrouded in darkness. For many Confederates, Abraham Lincoln had come to symbolize the Yankee character at its worst, but now he was dead, struck down by an assassin's bullet. Perhaps this marked the righteous retribution for which so many Confederates had been praying. In March 1862, a North Carolina woman had told some Union officers that she would happily "blow Abe Linkon's brains out with a pistol." Throughout the war there had been much speculation about the northern president's eventual day of reckoning. Surely he would face eternal damnation, and the thought of Lincoln cast into the lake of fire seemed heartening enough, though even the flames of hell could hardly pay for his sins. Yet there was little open rejoicing over his death—in part from fear of Federal authorities but also out of real doubt and apprehension about what the assassination portended. A goodly number of southerners foresaw nothing but disaster, and the elevation of the equally despised Andrew Johnson to the presidency hardly boded well.[35]

Defeat and military occupation meant the Confederacy had at last been subjugated. Lincoln's assassination made easing tensions between the two sides more difficult, of course, but sectional animosity and wartime hostility would have persisted regardless. Demonization of an enemy often has lasting effects. Even during the surrender ceremony at Appomattox that has long been celebrated as the first grand act of reconciliation, one Confederate officer candidly remarked to Joshua Lawrence Chamberlain, "There is rancor in our hearts . . . which you little dream of. We hate you, sir." And indeed that emotion would linger for years and even decades. In speaking to a northern writer on a tour of the former Confederate states in late 1865, a South Carolinian was equally blunt: "They [the Yankees] left me one inestimable privilege—to hate 'em. I git up at half-past four in the morning, and sit up till twelve at night, to hate 'em." Dramatic and no doubt overblown, such statements nevertheless revealed an important but often ignored legacy of the war. For years historians and teachers have recounted the story of fire-eater Edmund Ruffin's suicide as a kind of last shot of the American Civil War, but equally worthy of attention are the sentiments Ruffin scribbled in his diary before taking his life, sentiments expressed in the most extreme language but that were not all that uncommon. "I here declare my unmitigated hatred to Yankee rule—all political, social & business connection with Yankees—& to the Yankee race," he wrote. "Would that I could impress these sentiments, in their full force, on every living southerner, & bequeath them to every one yet to be born!" Here were familiar themes dating back to the antebellum period that had only intensified during the war: the emphasis on hatred, the Yankees as a separate race, and the importance of implanting in future generations all the classic elements of anti-northern invective. Indeed, Ruffin hoped that this worldview would survive the Confederacy's demise and his own. "May such sentiments be held universally in the outraged & down-trodden South, though in silence & stillness, until the now far-distant day shall arrive for just retribution for Yankee usurpation, oppression, & atrocious outrages—& for deliverance & vengeance for the now ruined, subjugated, & enslaved Southern States!"[36]

And on more than one occasion, deeds followed words. A Virginian assembled a scrapbook of newspaper clippings with sections on Yankee "vandalism" and "atrocities" as a historical record of enemy barbarism. There were reports that the northern soldiers' graves had been desecrated, headboards removed, or bodies stolen for anatomical study. In some places, corpses had simply been left unburied. Even worship services became venues for venting sectional hatred and expressing Confederate loyalty. At Washington, Georgia, in June 1865, tongues wagged when a Yankee marched up to the altar to pray with an ex-Confederate soldier who had experienced the call of salvation. On hearing about the incident, Eliza Frances Andrews reflected on her own still smoldering emotions: "It is dreadful to hate anybody so, and I do try sometimes to get these wicked feelings out of my heart, but as soon as I begin to feel a little like a Christian, I hear of some new piece of rascality the Yankees have done that rouses me up to white heat again."[37]

It has become a historical commonplace to observe that Confederate nationalism at times seemed stronger after the war was over, but however that might be, the attitudes expressed by Eliza Andrews and countless others would shape the tortured history of the Reconstruction period and leave an even longer lasting legacy. More than half a century ago, Robert Penn Warren wrote brilliantly about what he termed the "Treasury of Virtue," the North's "psychological heritage" from the Civil War.[38] Yet it seems obvious that the South was also left with its own treasury of virtue in the conflict's aftermath. The sense of the Confederacy as a righteous, indeed holy, cause long survived the war, as did the rhetoric that had fired southern hearts and sent young men off to fight and die.

In the postwar world, stories of Yankee barbarism and atrocities only grew in the telling. The critique, or perhaps more accurately, the assault on the character of the northern people remained intense, and the language did not change much. The central refrains of anti-Yankee invective not only survived but flourished and indeed shaped both the rhetoric and the political strategies of the Reconstruction era.[39] At the end of 1865 an anonymous woman poet offered a preface to a familiar theme:[40]

It is the soul that sorrows o'er
A sad heart-broken nation,

> It is the genius that portrays
> The woes of subjugation

That final word still carried so many potent, frightening, inflammatory connotations. Subjugation was still the North's primary goal—as it had been all along—and this remained an article of faith for many white southerners. The conflict between Andrew Johnson and the Republican majority in Congress simply marked the latest round in the continuing battle against despotic power. *DeBow's Review* pointed to the great "apprehension of the reign of the 'universal Yankee nation.'" Whatever doubts they harbored about the Democratic Party (especially after its abandonment of brave Confederates in the midst of secession and war), southern politicians would yet rally to the party of Jackson as a hoped-for bulwark against the tyrannical tendencies of the age.[41]

Just as had been prophesied during the war, the enslavement of southern white people would proceed apace. In the war's aftermath, this bedrock assumption undergirded the thoughts (and emotions) of many white southerners. Each new step toward "reconstruction"—however small—would serve to slowly but surely accustom southerners to life as a subjugated people. Such acquiescence signified the ultimate degradation, and each concession would only encourage broader assertions of absolute power over a conquered land.[42] Acts of Congress and constitutional amendments all pointed toward a "centralized despotism," another ominous phrase that reverberated from the antebellum period and war years. Everything from congressional committee investigations to the Freedmen's Bureau revealed an unremitting hatred for the South and the Yankees' grim determination to subdue and oppress a long-suffering people. That was the true platform of the supposedly "radical" congressional majority.[43]

To carry out this program, Republican politicians would have to rely on a large military force, or so some outraged southerners maintained. Ironically, even as the number of the troops stationed in the southern states steadily declined, this hardly slowed the editorial blasts against Yankee officers as Persian satraps or Turkish janissaries. "Blue coated dogs of despotism," sneered one woman. By its very nature "military Reconstruction" required a "standing army"—a phrase that echoed from the history of colonial resistance to British tyranny. In an odd twist on this argument, a New Orleans editor even ridiculed the Federal government for sending troops into areas rife with yellow fever, risking "useless death" to show that "negro rights [are] so much more important than white men's lives."[44] Yet ex-Confederate cabinet officer and former senator Robert M. T. Hunter readily conceded that he preferred "military government" to the "control of the colored race." At least soldiers commanded by Grant and Sherman had won the grudging respect of their erstwhile foes on the battlefield. Better to be ruled by such men at least in the short term than by an unholy alliance of blacks, carpetbaggers, and scalawags.[45]

An increasingly violent resistance to reconstruction gathered strength from long-held assumptions about the northern people and their government. That the Yankees hated southerners and were determined to deprive them of all political rights remained axiomatic—regardless of the fact that the very incompleteness and in some cases moderation of congressional measures gave the southern states considerable leeway in mapping out their political future. Did Congress intend to make citizens of the most ignorant blacks and disfranchise the most intelligent whites? Such claims appeared regularly and further inflamed the raw emotions that so easily welled to the surface as the political battles of the Reconstruction period raged. First the denial and then the delay in the restoration of the southern states to representation in Congress presumably proved that the Republicans primarily sought political advantage, a monopoly of offices, and indeed despotic power.[46]

During the war, Confederate propagandists had warned of "Negro rule" in the wake of a Union victory, and that dire prophecy appeared to be reaching a frightening fulfillment. Some newspapers spoke ominously of "Negro supremacy." This war upon the white race—at least according to many politicians and editors—was proceeding from implementation of the Reconstruction Acts and would turn the southern states into "subjugated provinces." According to the *Memphis Ledger*, "the negro is now uppermost in the mind of Congress. Shining through the Ethiopian skin, the Radicals behold the glimmerings of superior intelligence, and the glow of virtues most sublime." Republicans would humiliate southern whites and indeed make them pay taxes to support illegitimate governments filled with worthless scamps holding positions of public trust. This all marked, in the words of the always fiery Robert Toombs, "the subjugation of the Caucasian to the African and the Scalawag."[47]

And former slaves would now have to be recognized as not only political but social equals—just as supposedly farseeing secessionists and Confederates had long predicted. Bad enough to have black voters, legislators, and judges, one Georgia editor remarked in the midst of the congressional efforts to counter President Johnson's conservative restoration measures. He vividly imagined how the "descendants of Ham" now envisioned their future: "Mine is the right to sit by your fastidious daughter in church. I may eat at your tables, visit your parlors, ride in your carriages and marry your lovely damsels!" Restaurants, theaters, ands schools would suddenly be thrown open to both races. By the same token, the political proscription of white people must inexorably lead to what to a Louisianian termed "social degradation."[48]

The northern triumph was seemingly complete, but this in turn might entice a vast horde of Yankees to descend on the southern States. "They want to dissolve and reconstruct our whole social system," a Richmond editor noted with alarm. They would then make southerners "conform" to the "Puritianical, Pharisaical system of Praise-God Barebones New England."[49] More broadly speaking, the comparisons to various foreign tyrannies remained as common, creative, and implausible as they had during the height of the war. Was the condition of the South more comparable to that of Ireland, Hungary, or Poland? Some still preferred analogies to the barbarians' sack of Rome or the Norman conquest of Saxon England. Whatever the reference point, a Mobile editor predicted that the result would be a "bitter and undying hate."[50]

The United States should simply be renamed "Yankeeland," one angry Confederate suggested. After all, the Radicals were treating the southern states as nothing more than occupied territory. And the more unreconstructed could foresee the obliteration of the southern states themselves if not the obliteration of the southern people. Wild talk about a "war of extermination" hardly ended at Appomattox. Early in 1866 a Memphis editor wrote of Republican plans to "emasculate, to eviscerate; nay, more—to wipe out the South." With some relish, southern newspapers quoted the most extreme statements by their political enemies to drive this point home.

Seldom was there any hesitation in making the most hyperbolic responses. Indeed newspaper readers would often learn that congressional attacks on Andrew Johnson grew out of a Republican drive toward both "confiscation" and "extermination."[51]

This might all produce a "war of the races," another dreadful prophesy that editorial writers and politicians regularly bandied about. References to Saint-Domingue fed traditional fears of black insurrections but also led to contradictory claims that in any racial clashes, the poor deluded blacks would be the principal victims. In this case, it would be the former slaves, not their masters, who would face extermination.[52]

Not surprisingly, southern politicians and editors repeatedly referred to the Republicans (and not just the Radical faction) as Jacobins. They might cast Thaddeus Stevens or Charles Sumner in the role of Robespierre and throw in references to guillotines for good measure. In 1869 an Alabama editor claimed that a nascent economic recovery proved southerners' "pluck and courage over which the gates of a Jacobin hell have not been able to prevail." And indeed this use of the term "Jacobin" remained alive and well in the historical literature on Reconstruction into the 1940s.[53] Perhaps a more apt analogy might have compared the unreconstructed (and unreconstructable) to the famous House of Bourbon who, according to a pithy saying usually attributed to Talleyrand, "had learned nothing and forgotten nothing." Obviously the recent past weighed heavily on many ex-Confederates, but their memory was decidedly selective and subject to some jarring historical revision. "Do not let us forget," declared "General" W. K. Easley (who had never risen above the rank of lieutenant colonel), "that our cause was a good and noble cause; that it was for the right of self-government we struggled." And as always, the noble Confederates stood in sharp contrast to their ignoble enemies. A poem written shortly after the war in the midst of a controversy in North Carolina over wearing Confederate uniforms neatly summed it all up:

> Their hireling troops let others boast,
> Who fought for spoil and prey,
> Our southern lads we love the most,
> In a private's suit of grey.

Such memories were powerful and politically potent, and became the foundations for the Lost Cause. Of more immediate concern, those who summoned forth colorful descriptions of venerated Rebels and despised Yankees urged southerners to bravely face the future, to watch and wait for liberation and vindication.[54]

Familiar stories about a sacred past became potent arguments for making no concessions or compromises in the present. In fact they served to justify resistance. Attempting to explain (and in part justify) the rise of the Ku Klux Klan, the editor of the *New Orleans Picayune* offered what he considered to be an irrefutable lesson from history: "Oppressed races have never voluntarily submitted to become the serfs of the conqueror." Defiance of the northern "tyrants" became inevitable, though such statements ignored the considerable divisions in the southern states over political strategy in the wake of the Reconstruction Acts. Indeed, warnings about the consequences of any compromise over "rights" or "honor" kept pouring forth. Should southerners suddenly kowtow to their oppressors, their subjugation would be complete and permanent. Those who could somehow acquiesce in the latest congressional outrage were not men at all, but rather pusillanimous puppies eager to make concession after concession even to the point of paying for the pensions of those hireling soldiers who had invaded their homes. By refusing consent to their own degradation, ex-Confederates could at least retain their honor.[55]

Spurning submission, calling for resistance, and using violence to achieve political ends reinforced the claims of many northern politicians that the southern states remained hotbeds of disloyalty. But that hardly mattered to the most defiant. Despotic rule, the *Memphis Appeal* declared, "had released" southerners "from all obligations and duties of loyalty and allegiance." More ominously, a Petersburg editor warned: "Let our fetters be riveted, for treated as felons and slaves, we will be dangerous."[56] Such statements obviously more than hinted at serious and perhaps extralegal resistance. These threats would be carried out not only by the Ku Klux Klan but by the White League in Louisiana, the White Line in Mississippi, and the rifle clubs in South Carolina among other paramilitary groups.

Campaigns to drive the Republicans from power in the southern state and local governments through intimidation and terror rested on familiar images of the "enemy." And despite war's end, those images remained vibrant. Denunciations of the Yankees showed remarkable staying power in postwar politics and served to rally opposition against the reconstruction experiment. "The man who believes that a people will long submit to such a tyranny and to rulers so execrably low and base, is a fool," a Tennessee editor raged. "Even the Tartar hordes that subjugated the millions of China, had some virtues and much manhood. The creatures who domineer over the white men of the South have none. They are the very excrements of humanity, the lees and dregs of the race." Such barely coherent rants were all too common and reflected deeper problems that posed often insuperable obstacles to transforming the South, reforming governments, and molding biracial political coalitions that could effectively wield and maintain power. Proving that though there may not be poetry in hatred, there can be hatred in poetry, a Mississippian recalled earlier attacks on New England civilization when in a bit of doggerel, he described the attitudes of his fellow southerners: "What hates the Cotton Mather and the Roger Williams stock, / That dirty pile of hell's manure first dumped on Plymouth Rock."[57] It is worth noting how little the language and themes had changed despite Confederate defeat. Thus the legacy of anti-Yankee tirades remained remarkably consistent and persistent, casting a long shadow over southern history.

Not long ago at the University of Alabama where I teach, an old time capsule was opened and inside was a clipping from an early twentieth-century newspaper that referred to the burning of the campus by General John T. Croxton's Union cavalry. The article termed these men a "vandal soldiery."[58] Additional examples are disparate but revealing. A recent book written by an author who channeled the Confederate rhetoric of the 1860s claimed that "warring against noncombatants" was the "stated policy and deliberate practice of the United States in its subjugation of the Confederacy." In the process, the "shelling and burning of cities, systematic destruction of entire districts, mass arrests, forced expulsions, wholesale plundering of personal property, even murder all became routine." The author approvingly quoted another writer who saw a direct link between northern crimes and Nazi atrocities.[59] Only a couple years ago, a Confederate reenactor in Birmingham, Alabama, observed to this writer that the Yankees had really been Puritan agnostics and infidels, echoing a contradictory description that had circulated during the antebellum years and Civil War. In his mind as in the minds of his Civil War–era ancestors, such folk remained "damn Yankees." For sure, the harsher opinions have over the years become rarer and marginalized, sometimes more bizarre and amusing than threatening, but they keep cropping up and serve to confirm William Faulkner's famous line, "The past is never dead. It's not even past."[60]

Acknowledgments

An invitation to deliver the Walter Lynwood Fleming lectures at Louisiana State University was a singular honor, and doubly so for an LSU graduate. When the History Department extended the invitation, I had little time to celebrate before the sobering realization set in that I had to come up with a subject. My deep affection for LSU and especially for the History Department made the task especially daunting.

For some years, I had noted with passing interest how Confederates commented regularly and vividly on their northern enemies. After mulling this over, considering some other possible topics, and consulting friends and colleagues, I finally decided that I would focus the lectures and book on *Damn Yankees!* Indeed the title came first. Over the years, the Fleming lecturers have produced both longer and shorter works, and it seemed that the best strategy here was to write the book and then boil it down for the lectures. When the manuscript grew in both length and complexity, that seemed even more necessary. As I proceeded with the project, Michael Bernath, Glenn Brasher, Gary Gallagher, John Hall, Guy Hubbs, Larry Kohl, Chris McIlwain, and Christian McWhirter shared sound advice, helpful suggestions, and invaluable sources. John Coski from the Museum of the Confederacy kindly helped out with illustrations.

At LSU Press, Executive Editor Rand Dotson showed great interest in this project and moved it through the editorial process with remarkable efficiency. Gary Gallagher generously took time out of his hectic schedule to serve as an outside reader, and as is his wont offered both needed encouragement and excellent recommendations for revisions. Gary Von Euer copyedited the manuscript with great care and attention to detail.

My wife Kay and I had a wonderful time in Baton Rouge, where we once lived for nearly seven years. During our time in graduate school we made friendships that have endured more than forty years. Three charter members of this group—Chip Dawson, Will Greene, and Frank Wetta—took time out of their busy lives to attend the lectures and even behaved reasonably well. I was deeply touched by their presence, but value their friendship along with that of the rest of the LSU gang even more. Geaux Tigers!

I much appreciated having such a receptive audience for the lectures, and several excellent questions forced me to rethink aspects of the project both large and small. The chair of the History Department Victor Stater and his assistant Darlene Albritton kindly handled the logistical details. William J. Cooper Jr., Paul Paskoff, and Aaron Sheehan-Dean made generous introductions. Bill and Patricia Cooper graciously hosted a reception at their home, complete with excellent food, good drink, and fine conversation. Kay and I greatly appreciated and will long remember their warm hospitality. I first met Bill Cooper when I was a scared and naïve first-semester graduate student in the fall of 1972. I was immediately impressed by his fine qualities as a teacher and his high academic expectations. Satisfying Bill's exacting standards for scholarship has always proved challenging, but his prodding, encouragement, and assistance over many years meant that I simply had to dedicate the lectures and this book to him.

Only a few days after our marriage in Greenwich, Ohio, Kay and I drove a U-Haul trailer to Baton Rouge to begin our new life together. Since then we have become parents and most recently grandparents. Our daughters Anne and Katie, and son-in-law Dave, at least read the acknowledgments to my books, so I make sure that I mention them. But of course they along with Kay deserve much more than a mere mention. All have proven to be the choicest of God's blessings in ways both imaginable and unimaginable. As I was putting the final touches on the lectures, our grandson Lincoln Rable Bernath was born. He is a fine young fellow in every way, and for many more details (including pictures and video) you can just ask me.

Notes

INTRODUCTION

1. *Congressional Globe*, 36th Congress, 2nd Session, 12.

2. Abraham Lincoln, *The Collected Works of Abraham Lincoln*, ed. Roy P. Basler, 9 vols. (New Brunswick, N.J.: Rutgers University Press, 1954), 4:271.

3. Robert J. Sternberg and Karin Sternberg, *The Nature of Hate* (Cambridge: Cambridge University Press, 2008), 34, 137–40; William Gaylin, *Hatred: The Psychological Descent into Violence* (New York: Public Affairs, 2003), 21, 33–36, 173–87. For still helpful accounts of efforts to define the enemy during the American Civil War, see James W. Silver, *Confederate Morale and Church Propaganda* (Tuscaloosa, Ala.: Confederate Publishing, 1957), 82–92; Randall C. Jimerson, *The Private Civil War: Popular Thought during the Sectional Conflict* (Baton Rouge: Louisiana State University Press, 1988), 124–79. On this subject, I have found the excellent work of Jason Phillips to be especially valuable and insightful. *Diehard Rebels: The Confederate Culture of Invincibility* (Athens: University of Georgia Press, 2007), 147–77; "A Brothers' War? Exploring Confederate Perceptions of the Enemy," in Aaron Sheehan-Dean, ed., *The View from the Ground: Experiences of Civil War Soldiers* (Lexington: University Press of Kentucky, 2007), 67–90.

4. For a useful discussion of emotion and reason with particular application to the French Revolution, see William M. Reddy, *The Navigation of Feeling: A Framework for the History of Emotions* (Cambridge: Cambridge University Press, 2001), 142–43.

5. David Hume, *A Treatise of Human Nature*, 1739–40, http://www.gutenberg.org/files/4705/4705-h/4705-h.htm.

6. Joshua Searle-White, *Psychology of Nationalism* (New York: Palgrave, 2001), 91; Sternberg and Sternberg, *Nature of Hate*, 18, 43, 58ff.

7. *New York Times*, February 14, 1862. These comments were reprinted in the *Richmond Daily Dispatch*, February 19, 1862.

8. Jill Lepore has written that "war is a contest of words as much as it is a contest of wounds." Jill Lepore, *The Name of War: King Phillip's War and the Origins of American Identity* (New York: Alfred A. Knopf, 1998), 47. For the use of language—including a rhetoric of conspiracy—in the French Revolution, see Lynn Hunt, *Politics, Culture and Class in the French Revolution* (Berkeley: University of California Press, 1984), 19–51.

9. George Orwell, *Homage to Catalonia* (New York: Harcourt, Brace, 1952), 65.

10. Sternberg and Sternberg, *Nature of Hate*, 3, 63–65, 131–33. On the role of journalism in dehumanizing the enemy, see David Livingstone Smith, *Less than Human: Why We Demean, Enslave, and Exterminate Others* (New York: St. Martin's Press, 2011), 20–25.

11. *Raleigh (N.C.) Daily Register*, August 10, 1861; *Little Rock (Ark.) Journal*, n.d., in *Milledgeville (Ga.) Southern Recorder*, January 14, 1862; *Richmond Daily Dispatch*, June 8, 1864; *Raleigh (N.C.) Weekly Register*, December 11, 1861. For a poem that touched on a goodly number of themes commonly found in anti-Yankee invective, see *Southern Illustrated News*, September 19, 1863.

12. William R. Taylor, *Cavalier and Yankee: The Old South and American National Character* (New York: George Braziller, 1961), 329; Jimerson, *Private Civil War*, 126; John W. Dower, *War without Mercy: Race and Power in the Pacific War* (New York: Pantheon Books, 1986), 16–32; Sternberg and Sternberg, *Nature of Hate*, 65–70.

13. Russell Jacoby, *Bloodlust: On the Roots of Violence from Cain and Abel to the Present* (New York: Free Press, 2011), ix, 7–9, 39–74, 128; Mary Chesnut, *Mary Chesnut's Civil War*, ed. C. Vann Woodward (New Haven: Yale University Press, 1981), 25.

14. Ernest Renan, http://en.wikipedia.org/wiki/Ernest_Renan.

15. For widely differing approaches to these questions, see Emory M. Thomas, *The Confederacy as a Revolutionary Experience* (Englewood Cliffs, N.J.: Prentice-Hall, 1971); Richard E. Beringer et al., *Why the South Lost the Civil War* (Athens: University of Georgia Press, 1986); Drew Gilpin Faust, *The Creation of Confederate Nationalism: Ideology and Identity in the Civil War South* (Baton Rouge: Louisiana State University Press, 1988); Gary W. Gallagher, *The Confederate War* (Cambridge, Mass.: Harvard University Press, 1997); Stephanie McCurry, *Confederate Reckoning: Power and Politics in the Civil War South* (Cambridge, Mass.: Harvard University Press, 2010).

16. Edward Everett Dale and Gaston Litton, eds., *Cherokee Cavaliers: Forty Years of Cherokee History As Told in the Correspondence of the Ridge-Watie-Boudinot Family* (Norman: University of Oklahoma Press, 1939), 134.

17. See the various discussions of sources, samples, and representative evidence in James M. McPherson, *What They Fought For, 1861–1865* (Baton Rouge: Louisiana State University Press, 1994), 13–18; Gallagher, *Confederate War*, 72; James M. McPherson, *For Cause and Comrades: Why Men Fought in the Civil War* (New York: Oxford University Press, 1997), vii–x; Phillips, *Diehard Rebels*, 4–6; Chandra Manning, *What This Cruel War Was Over: Soldiers, Slavery, and the Civil War* (New York: Alfred A. Knopf, 2007), 8–11; Gary W. Gallagher, *The Union War* (Cambridge, Mass.: Harvard University Press, 2011), 5–6, 62, 80–81.

18. On the importance of junior officers for the Confederate project, see Peter S. Carmichael, *The Last Generation: Young Virginians in Peace, War, and Reunion* (Chapel Hill: University of North Carolina Press, 2005).

19. Joseph T. Glatthaar, *General Lee's Army: From Victory to Collapse* (New York: Free Press, 2008), 19–21, 30–31, 203–4, 316, 359. See also the invaluable statistics and discussion in Joseph T. Glatthaar, *Soldiering in the Army of Northern Virginia: A Statistical Portrait of the Troops Who Served under Robert E. Lee* (Chapel Hill: University of North Carolina Press, 2011), 154–65.

20. Smith, *Less than Human*, 13.

1. THE UNIVERSAL YANKEE NATION

1. "Atlantic Steam Navigation," *Quarterly Review* (London) 52 (June and October 1838): 194.

2. *Milledgeville (Ga.) Southern Recorder*, May 14, 1861; *Milledgeville (Ga.) Southern Federal Union*, May 14, September 3, 1861; Daniel R. Hundley, *Prison Echoes of the Great Rebellion* (New York: S. W. Green, 1874), 186–87. To cite but one of many publications, the *Richmond Dispatch* repeatedly used the phrase "universal Yankee nation" to signify northern vices. *Richmond Daily Dispatch*, November 4, 13, 1861, January 23, October 2, 1862, August 2, 1864.

3. William R. Taylor, *Cavalier and Yankee: The Old South and American National Character* (New York: George Braziller, 1961), 47–48; March 6, 1863, Nancy Emerson Diary, Albert and Shirley Small Special Collections Library, University of Virginia; A South Carolinian [pseud.], *The Confederate* (Mobile, Ala.: S. h. Goetzel, 1863), 37–44.

4. Susan-Mary Grant, *North Over South: Northern Nationalism and American Identity in the Antebellum Era* (Lawrence: University Press of Kansas, 2000), 53–54.

5. In some ways, this discussion makes the long debate on the reality of sectional differences and southern distinctiveness beside the point. Likewise the endless arguments over the nature and strength of southern, or more properly Confederate, nationalism hardly matter here. The key point is perception. Whatever the shared history, cultural ties, common characteristics, or even complementary elements, the *perceived* gap between northern and southern civilization had widened. Even dealing with this question carries its own problems because people not only demonize those most unlike themselves, but in the case of civil wars demonize those remarkably similar to themselves by emphasizing and exaggerating real and imagined differences. See the classic discussions by some of our finest historians: Edward Pessen, "How Different from Each Other Were the Antebellum North and South?" *American Historical Review* 85 (December 1980): 1119–49; Forrest McDonald and Grady McWhiney, "The South from Self-Sufficiency to Peonage: An Interpretation," *American Historical Review* 85 (December 1980): 1095–1118; Thomas B. Alexander, Stanley L. Engerman, Forrest McDonald, Grady McWhiney, and Edward Pessen, "Antebellum North and South in Comparative Perspective: A Discussion," *American Historical Review* 85 (December 1980): 1150–66; James M. McPherson, "Antebellum Southern Exceptionalism: A New Look at an Old Question," *Civil War History* 29 (September 1983): 230–44; David M. Potter, "The Historian's Use of Nationalism and Vice Versa" in Potter, *The South and the Sectional Conflict* (Baton Rouge: Louisiana State University Press, 1968), 34–83.

6. John McCardell, *The Idea of a Southern Nation: Southern Nationalists and Southern Nationalism, 1830–1860* (New York: W. W. Norton, 1979), 141–76; Michael T. Bernath, *Confederate Minds: The Struggle for Intellectual Independence in the Civil War South* (Chapel Hill: University of North Carolina Press, 2010), 36–37. Bernath perceptively observes how the war increased the "urgency and scope" of attacks on northern civilization. Confederate propagandists presented "a wide-ranging cultural justification for separate southern nationality."

7. Drew Gilpin Faust, *A Sacred Circle: The Dilemma of the Intellectual in the Old South, 1840–1860* (Baltimore: Johns Hopkins University Press, 1977), 7–14, 45–60, 132–48; Paul Quigley, *Shifting Grounds: Nationalism and the American South, 1848–1865* (New York: Oxford University Press,

2012), 9–10; Jesse T. Carpenter, *The South as a Conscious Minority, 1789–1861: A Study in Political Thought* (New York: New York University Press, 1930), 7–33.

8. Nicholas A. Davis, *Chaplain Davis and Hood's Texas Brigade*, ed. Donald E. Everett (Baton Rouge: Louisiana State University Press, 1999), 147–48. Davis's account was originally published in 1863 in Richmond, and the anti-Yankee invective was quoted in Confederate newspapers. *Richmond Whig*, February 17, 1863; *Fayetteville (N.C.) Observer*, February 19, 1863. For other examples from early war soldier comments, see McPherson, *What They Fought For*, 19.

9. E. Merton Coulter, *The Confederate States of America, 1861–1865* (Baton Rouge: Louisiana State University Press, 1950), 81–82.

10. See the still useful discussion of literary sources in Taylor, *Cavalier and Yankee*, 15–22. An Alabama editor adopted an even more sweeping generalization, claiming that people from northern climes often launched wars of conquest against their southern neighbors. This geographical determinism apparently gained few adherents. *Mobile (Ala.) Register*, February 1, 1862.

11. Thomas W. MacMahon, *Cause and Contrast: An Essay on the American Crisis* (Richmond: West and Johnson, 1862), 65–66; Jefferson Davis, *The Papers of Jefferson Davis*, ed. Lynda Lasswell Crist, Mary Seaton Dix, and Kenneth H. Williams, 14 vols. (Baton Rouge: Louisiana State University Press, 1971–2015), 8:567; *Richmond Daily Dispatch*, September 11, 1861, September 18, December 12, 1862; Elizabeth Scott Neblett, *A Rebel Wife in Texas: The Diary and Letters of Elizabeth Scott Neblett*, ed. Erika L. Murr (Baton Rouge: Louisiana State University Press, 2001), 195–96.

12. L. Luckett to Alexander H. H. Stuart, September 2, 1861, Stuart Papers, Albert and Shirley Small Special Collections Library, University of Virginia; *Richmond Daily Dispatch*, February 6, 1861; George Fitzhugh, "The Message, the Constitution, and the Times," *DeBow's Review* 30 (February 1861): 162; *Atlanta Southern Confederacy*, May 24, 1861. On the racial element, see Ritchie Devon Watson Jr., *Normans and Saxons: Southern Racial Mythology and the Intellectual History of the Civil War* (Baton Rouge: Louisiana State University Press, 2008), 19–46, 72–92, 135–68.

13. *Athens (Ga.) Southern Watchman*, April 24, 1861; *Richmond Daily Dispatch*, March 23, 1862; *Petersburg (Va.) Express*, September 17, 1861; An Alabamian, "The One Great Cause of the Failure of the Federal Government," *Southern Literary Messenger* 32 (May 1861): 334. Such a contrast had been a central motif of antebellum fiction. Taylor, *Cavalier and Yankee*, 95–115. For problems and contradictions in this Confederate critique of northern character, see Bernath, *Confederate Minds*, 55–60.

14. *Richmond Daily Whig*, December 2, 1862; Mary Greenhow Lee, *The Civil War Journal of Mary Greenhow Lee of Winchester, Virginia*, ed. Eloise C. Strader (Winchester, Va.: Winchester-Frederick County Historical Society, 2011), 39; George Fitzhugh, "The Pioneers, Preachers, and People of the Mississippi Valley," *DeBow's Review* 30 (March 1861): 260.

15. For similar reasoning in a much different war, see Haruko Taya Cook and Theodore F. Cook, *Japan at War: An Oral History* (New York: New Press, 1992), 175.

16. Marion Hill Fitzpatrick, *Letters to Amanda: The Civil War Letters of Marion Hill Fitzpatrick, Army of Northern Virginia*, ed. Jeffrey C. Lowe and Sam Hodges (Macon, Ga.: Mercer University Press, 1998), 175; *Richmond Daily Dispatch*, March 28, 1862; Stephen Elliott, *New Wine Not to be Put into Old Bottles: A Sermon Preached in Christ Church, Savannah, on Friday, February 28th, 1862* (Savannah, Ga.: John M. Cooper, 1862), 8–9; Margaret Ann Vogtsberger, ed., *The Dulanys of Welbourne: A Family in Mosby's Confederacy* (Berryville, Va.: Rockbridge Publishing, 1995), 152.

17. Randall C. Jimerson, *The Private Civil War: Popular Thought during the Sectional Conflict* (Baton Rouge: Louisiana State University Press, 1988), 142. Another soldier promised to bring the ardently Confederate Lizzie Hardin a "pet Yankee." Elizabeth Pendleton Hardin, *The Private War of Lizzie Hardin: A Kentucky Confederate Girl's Diary of the Civil War in Kentucky, Virginia, Tennessee, Alabama, and Georgia*, ed. G. Glenn Clift (Frankfort: Kentucky Historical Society, 1963), 19.

18. *Richmond Daily Dispatch*, April 29, 1861, September 1, 1863. One wag suggested that West Point should establish a "Chair of Casuistry," and students could then work toward "the degree of L.D.D., or Learned Doctor of Lies." *Southern Illustrated News*, March 14, 1863.

19. South Carolinian [pseud.], *The Confederate*, 6–7; *Richmond Daily Dispatch*, September 11, 1861; "The True Question: A Contest for the Supremacy of the Race, As Between the Saxon Puritan of the North and the Norman of the South," *Southern Literary Messenger* 33 (July 1861): 19–27; Lafayette McLaws, *A Soldier's General: The Civil War Letters of Major General Lafayette McLaws*, ed. John C. Oeffinger (Chapel Hill: University of North Carolina Press, 2002), 159–60.

20. Ida Powell Dulany, *In the Shadow of the Enemy: The Civil War Journal of Ida Powell Dulany*, ed. Mary L. Mackall, Stevan F. Meserve, and Anne Mackall Sasscer (Knoxville: University of Tennessee Press, 2009), 14; James B. Griffin, *A Gentleman and Officer: A Military and Social History of James B. Griffin's Civil War*, ed. Judith N. McArthur and Orville Vernon Burton (New York: Oxford University Press, 1996), 105; April 15, 1862, Alice Ready Diary, Southern Historical Collection, University of North Carolina, Chapel Hill; July 25, 1863, Kate D. Foster Diary, Rubenstein Rare Book and Manuscript Library, Duke University.

21. L. Luckett to Alexander H. H. Stuart, September 2, 1861, Stuart Papers; William Henry Holcombe, "The Alternative: A Separate Destiny, or the Africanization of the South," *Southern Literary Messenger* 32 (February 1861): 86.

22. William A. Hall, *The Historic Significance of the Southern Revolution. A Lecture . . . in Petersburg, Va., March 14th and April 29th, 1864* (Petersburg, Va.: A. F. Crutchfield, 1864), 22, 25. For a superb analysis of the problems with these arguments, see Robert E. Bonner, "Roundheaded Cavaliers? The Context and Limits of a Confederate Racial Project," *Civil War History* 48 (March 2002): 34–59.

23. *Richmond Daily Dispatch*, January 7, 1861; A South Carolinian [pseud.], *The Confederate*, 22–29; Frank Moore, ed., *Songs and Ballads of the Southern People* (New York: Appleton, 1886), 15; Dr. Stuart, "Anglo-Saxon Mania," *Southern Literary Messenger* 37 (November–December 1863): 673–74, 687; Arthur James Lyon Fremantle, *Three Months in the Southern States: April–June 1863* (Edinburgh, Scotland: William Blackwood and Son, 1863), 320. For an account that emphasizes the popularity and influence of the Cavalier legend, see Jason Phillips, *Diehard Rebels: The Confederate Culture of Invincibility* (Athens: University of Georgia Press, 2007), 43–46.

24. *New Orleans Daily Picayune*, April 24, 1861; [William Naylor McDonald], *The Two Rebellions; or, Treason Unmasked. By a Virginian* (Richmond: Smith, Bayley, 1865), 9; *Weekly Raleigh (N.C.) Register*, January 22, 1862; *Milledgeville (Ga.) Southern Recorder*, March 26, 1861; Catherine Ann Devereux Edmondston, *"Journal of a Secesh Lady": The Diary of Catherine Ann Devereux Edmondston, 1860–1866*, ed. Beth G. Crabtree and James W. Patton (Raleigh, N.C.: Division of Archives and History, 1979), 181–82; A South Carolinian [pseud.], *The Confederate*, 3. For a long diatribe against Yankee Puritanism that connected it to every variety of disorder and fanaticism, see *Richmond Whig*, May 22, 1863.

25. Gamble McCorkle to his mother, July 7, 1862, Bumgardner Family Papers, Albert and Shirley Small Special Collections Library, University of Virginia; Emma Holmes, *Diary of Miss Emma Holmes, 1861–1866*, ed. John F. Marszalek (Baton Rouge: Louisiana State University Press, 1979), 231–32; *Augusta (Ga.) Daily Chronicle and Sentinel*, August 16, 1861; *Mobile Register*, n.d., in *Fayetteville (N.C.) Observer*, January 22, 1863; D. H. Hill, *Elements of Algebra* (Philadelphia: J. B. Lippincott, 1857), 151.

26. MacMahon, *Cause and Contrast*, 65–66; William Archer Cocke, "The Puritan and the Cavalier; or, The Elements of American Colonial Society," *DeBow's Review* 31 (September 1861): 211–12; *Savannah (Ga.) Daily Morning News*, August 29, 1863; *Weekly Raleigh (N.C.) Register*, September 2, 1863; A South Carolinian [pseud.], *The Confederate*, 3, 30–36, 47; Samuel S. Cox, *Puritanism in Politics. Speech of Hon. S. S. Cox, of Ohio before the Democratic Union Association, January 13, 1863* (New York: Van Evrie, Horton, 1863).

27. Augusta Jane Evans Wilson, *A Southern Woman of Letters: The Correspondence of Augusta Jane Evans Wilson*, ed. Rebecca Grant Sexton (Columbia: University of South Carolina Press, 2002), 37; [McDonald], *Two Rebellions*, 14; August 11, 1861, George Anderson Mercer Diary, Southern Historical Collection, University of North Carolina; *Richmond Examiner*, n.d., in *Salisbury (N.C.) Carolina Watchman*, May 5, 1862; Peter Wellington Alexander, *Writing and Fighting the Confederate War: The Letters of Peter Wellington Alexander, Confederate War Correspondent*, ed. William B. Styple (Kearny, N.J.: Belle Grove Publishing, 2002), 181. Once freed of Yankee influence, Confederates could celebrate holidays such as Christmas without facing the censure of Puritan killjoys. *Charleston Mercury*, December 25, 1861.

28. *Richmond Daily Dispatch*, September 11, 1861; *Atlanta Southern Confederacy*, May 28, 1863; George Fitzhugh, "The Huguenots of the South of the South," *DeBow's Review* 30 (May and June 1861): 513–20; Quigley, *Shifting Grounds*, 140–41; *Christian Index* (Macon, Ga.), August 14, 1861; *Jackson (Miss.) Daily Southern Crisis*, February 21, 1863.

29. Sam Keen, *Faces of the Enemy: Reflections of the Hostile Imagination* (San Francisco: Harper and Row, 1986), 27–42; Quigley, *Shifting Grounds*, 141–42; *Atlanta Southern Confederacy*, May 16, 1861; *Charleston Mercury*, July 31, 1862; "The Future of Our Confederation," *DeBow's Review* 31 (July 1861): 37.

30. Eliza Rhea Anderson Fain, *Sanctified Trial: The Diary of Eliza Rhea Anderson Fain, a Confederate Woman in East Tennessee*, ed. John N. Fain (Knoxville: University of Tennessee Press, 2004), 11–12, 161–62; *Savannah (Ga.) Daily Morning News*, December 23, 1862; *Richmond Daily Dispatch*, April 20, 1862; H. M. Wharton, *War Songs and Poems of the Southern Confederacy* (Philadelphia: American Book and Bible House, 1904), 102; November 25, 1864, Nancy Emerson Diary, Special Collections Library, University of Virginia. The Yankees had become "infidels" to both the Bible and the Constitution. *Savannah (Ga.) Republican*, January 9, 1861.

31. *Augusta (Ga.) Daily Chronicle and Sentinel*, August 11, 1861; *Charleston Mercury*, December 19, 1862; *Christian Observer* (Richmond), February 4, 1864; "The Rev. Dr. Thornwell's Memorial on the Recognition of Christianity in the Constitution," *Southern Presbyterian Review* 16 (July 1863): 77–87; *Christian Index* (Macon, Ga.), August 7, 1861.

32. *Richmond Daily Dispatch*, July 6, 1861, July 3, 1862; Hundley, *Prison Echoes*, 167–68; William Howard Russell, *My Diary North and South* (Boston: T. O. H. P. Burham, 1863), 147–48.

Occasionally Confederates conceded that self-righteousness might also be a problem on their side. (Macon) *Georgia Weekly Telegraph*, May 9, 1862.

33. *Confederate Baptist* (Columbia, S.C.), October 29, 1862; Robert Manson Myers, ed., *The Children of Pride: A True Story of Georgia and the Civil War* (New Haven: Yale University Press, 1972), 689; Edward Mayes, *Lucius Q. C. Lamar: His Life, Times and Speeches, 1825–1893* (Nashville: Publishing House of the Methodist Episcopal Church, South, 1896), 637.

34. *Athens (Ga.) Southern Watchman*, July 8, 1863; Kate Cumming, *Kate: The Journal of a Confederate Nurse*, ed. Richard Barksdale Harwell (Baton Rouge: Louisiana State University Press, 1959), 168; A South Carolinian [pseud.], *The Confederate*, 45–52; *Richmond Daily Dispatch*, February 29, 1864; D. S. Doggett, *The War and Its Close: A Discourse, Delivered in Centenary Church, Richmond, Va., Friday, April 8th, 1864 . . . on the Occasion of the National Fast* (Richmond: Macfarlane and Fergusson, 1864), 11–15. Early in the war, a Louisiana captain maintained that the Confederates were waging a battle against the various "isms" that had so plagued the country. Colin Edward Woodward, *Marching Masters: Slavery, Race, and the Confederate Army during the Civil War* (Charlottesville: University of Virginia Press, 2014), 25. For a helpful discussion of how fear of various "isms" influenced conservative thought in both sections, see Michael F. Conlin, "The Dangerous *Isms* and the Fanatical *Ists*: Antebellum Conservatives in the South and the North Confront the Modernist Conspiracy," *Journal of the Civil War Era* 4 (June 2014): 205–33.

35. Hall, *Historic Significance of the Southern Revolution*, 14, 19, 44–45; *Richmond Daily Dispatch*, May 22, August 1, 1861; May 5, 1861, George Anderson Mercer Diary; *Milledgeville (Ga.) Confederate Union*, June 23, 1862; A. W. Miller, "Report on the State of the Church," *Southern Presbyterian Review* 15 (January 1863): 405–47.

36. Robert Newton Sledd, *Sermon Delivered in the Market Street M.E. Church, Petersburg, Va. Before the Confederate Cadets on the Occasion of Their Departure for the Seat of War* (Petersburg, Va.: A. F. Crutchfield, 1861), 21; *Savannah (Ga.) Republican*, May 8, 1861; Presbyterian Church, Synod of North Carolina, *Minutes of the Forty Eighth Sessions of the Synod of North Carolina, Held in the Church of Raleigh, October, 1861* (Fayetteville, N.C.: Presbyterian Office, 1862), 20–23; [William Falconer], "The True Question: A Contest for the Supremacy of Race, as between the Saxon Puritan of the North, and the Norman of the South," *Southern Literary Messenger* 33 (July 1861): 27; Fain, *Sanctified Trial*, 48; *Richmond Daily Dispatch*, April 5, July 25, 1864. For a first-rate analysis of how central the idea of "fanaticism" was to the Confederate critique of northern society, see Bernath, *Confederate Minds*, 37–40. During the war, some form of the word "fanatic" appeared 835 times in the *Richmond Daily Dispatch*.

37. *Richmond Daily Dispatch*, May 2, September 2, December 6, 1861, October 27, 1862; "The New Republic," *Southern Literary Messenger* 32 (May 1861): 397–98; *Charleston Mercury*, November 3, 1863. On the theme of northern fanaticism (including Puritanism) in wartime poetry, see Watson, *Normans and Saxons*, 213–15.

38. *Richmond Daily Dispatch*, March 4, 1861; Sue Sparks Keitt, "Sue Sparks Keitt to a Northern Friend, March 4, 1861," ed. Elmer Don Herd Jr., *South Carolina Historical Magazine* 62 (April 1961), 84; April 14, 1861, Meta Morris Grimball Diary, Southern Historical Collection, University of North Carolina; *Salisbury (N.C.) Carolina Watchman*, March 18, 1864; *Montgomery Mail*, n.d., in *Augusta (Ga.) Daily Chronicle and Sentinel*, November 5, 1864.

39. *Richmond Daily Dispatch*, February 13, 1865; *Charleston Mercury*, January 18, 1861; *Atlanta Southern Confederacy*, February 18, 1863.

40. *Raleigh (N.C.) Standard*, April 24, 1861 in *Salisbury (N.C.) Carolina Watchman*, September 28, 1863; James B. Sheeran, *Confederate Chaplain: A War Journal of Rev. James B. Sheeran, c.ss.r., 14th Louisiana, C.S.A.*, ed. Joseph T. Durkin (Milwaukee: Bruce Publishing, 1960), 4; Griffin Frost, *Camp and Prison Journal* (Iowa City, Iowa: Camp Pope Book Shop, 1994), 46; *Richmond Daily Dispatch*, May 28, 1862.

41. (Macon) *Georgia Weekly Telegraph*, May 24, 1861; *Mobile (Ala.) Register*, February 2, 1862; *New Orleans Daily Picayune*, June 25, 1861.

42. *Charleston Mercury*, January 12, 1861; *Richmond Daily Dispatch*, October 2, 1862; Holmes, *Diary of Emma Holmes*, 40; February 28, 1862, Fast Day sermon, Henry Champlin Lay Sermons, Southern Historical Collection, University of North Carolina.

43. Taylor, *Cavalier and Yankee*, 55–65; J. Quitman Moore, "National Characteristics—The Issues of the Day," *DeBow's Review* 30 (January 1861): 49–50; Fitzhugh, "Message, Constitution, and Times," 164; J. H. Easterby, ed., *The South Carolina Rice Plantation as Revealed in the Papers of Robert F. W. Allston* (Chicago: University of Chicago Press, 1945), 175–76; Laurence Keitt to William Porcher Miles, October 3, 1860, Miles Papers, Southern Historical Collection, University of North Carolina; *Journal of the Senate of South Carolina: Being the Sessions of 1861* (Columbia, S.C.: Charles P. Pelham, 1861), 23–25; *Southern Illustrated News*, September 19, 1863; *Richmond Daily Dispatch*, October 27, 1862.

44. Frank H. Alfriend, "A Southern Republic and a Northern Democracy," *Southern Literary Messenger* 37 (May 1863): 283–90; "Past and Present," *DeBow's Review* 30 (February 1861): 187–98; Atlanta Register, *Address of the Atlanta Register to the People of the Confederate States* (Atlanta: J. A. Sperry, [1864]), 2; "National Characteristics: The Issues of the Day," *DeBow's Review* 30 (January 1861): 42–53.

45. "The Union, Its Benefits and Dangers," *Southern Literary Messenger* 32 (January 1861): 3–4. See the fine analysis of southern intellectuals and the idea of agrarianism in Bernath, *Confederate Minds*, 42–44.

46. [Falconer], "The True Question," 19; *Atlanta Southern Confederacy*, June 12, 1861. Even the famous New England common schools had become nurseries of fanaticism "populating the mind with all sorts of crudities." Edward Alfred Pollard, "Hints on Southern Civilization," *Southern Literary Messenger* 32 (April 1861): 309–10.

47. George Fitzhugh, "Thoughts Suggested by the War—the Past and the Future," *DeBow's Review* 31 (September 1861): 302; Stephen D. Elliott, *Ezra's Dilemma. A Sermon Preached in Christ Church, Savannah, On Friday, August 21st, 1863, Being the Day of Humiliation, Fasting and Prayer* (Savannah, Ga.: Power Press of George N. Nichols, 1863), 14–15; Benjamin Morgan Palmer and W. T. Leacock, *The Rights of the South Defended in the Pulpits* (Mobile, Ala.: J. Y. Thompson, 1860), 7; *New Orleans Daily Picayune*, June 4, 1861; (Macon) *Georgia Weekly Telegraph*, October 24, 1862; *Richmond Daily Dispatch*, August 20, 1861; *Staunton (Va.) Spectator*, September 10, 1861.

48. *Savannah (Ga.) Republican*, August 7, 1862, June 13, 1863; September 29, 1862, Ann Wilkinson Penrose Diary, Louisiana and Lower Mississippi Valley Collection, Louisiana State Univer-

sity, Baton Rouge; *Milledgeville (Ga.) Southern Federal Union*, May 21, September 3, 1861; *Savannah (Ga.) Daily Morning News*, December 27, 1861; *Charleston Mercury*, June 5, 1861.

49. March 12, 1861, Susan Cornwall Book, Southern Historical Collection, University of North Carolina; Holmes, *Diary of Emma Holmes*, 10; *Richmond Daily Dispatch*, April 16, 1861; *Alexandria (La.) Constitutional*, May 4, 1861.

50. *Atlanta Southern Confederacy*, May 11, 1861; *Warrenton (Va.) Flag of '98*, May 21, 1861; Easterby, ed., *South Carolina Rice Plantation*, 175–76; Daniel I. Dreher, *A Sermon Delivered by Rev. Daniel I. Dreher, Pastor of St. James Church, Concord, N.C., June 13, 1861* (Salisbury, N.C.: Printed at the Watchman Office, 1861), 13; *War of the Rebellion: A Compilation of the Official Records of the Union and Confederate Armies* [OR], 128 vols. (Washington: Government Printing Office, 1880–1901), ser. 1, vol. 2:907. Confederate soldiers also were of two minds about Lincoln. Reid Mitchell, *Civil War Soldiers* (New York: Viking, 1988), 35.

51. *Athens (Ga.) Southern Banner*, June 5, 1861; Alexander, *Writing and Fighting the Confederate War*, 15; Lucy Rebecca Buck, *Shadows on My Heart: The Civil War Diary of Lucy Rebecca Buck of Virginia*, ed. Elizabeth R. Baer (Athens: University of Georgia Press, 1997), 31. "The despot's heel is on thy shore," began one of the war's most popular songs and one that expressed the long-held hope that the people of Maryland would rise up to support the Confederacy and throw off the Yankee yoke. James Ryder Randall, *Maryland! My Maryland! A Patriotic Song* (New Orleans: A. E. Blackmar, 1862?). This is one of at least eleven Confederate editions of what quickly became a southern standard. T. Michael Parrish and Robert M. Willingham Jr., *Confederate Imprints: A Bibliography of Southern Publications from Secession to Surrender* (Austin, Tex.: Jenkins Publishing, 1984), 603.

52. *Richmond Enquirer*, April 25, May 28, 1861; Robert H. White, ed. *Messages of the Governors of Tennessee*, 8 vols. (Nashville: Tennessee Historical Commission, 1952–1990), 5:282.

53. *Charleston Mercury*, April 19, June 5, 1861; *Augusta (Ga.) Daily Chronicle and Sentinel*, June 18, 1861; *Athens (Ga.) Southern Watchman*, June 19, 1861. Such descriptions found an echo in a border-state ditty, complete with sneering references to a tobacco-chewing, whiskey-guzzling president whose mouth spewed out endless lies as he plotted new schemes of oppression. Francis Orray Ticknor, *The Despot's Song!* [Baltimore, 1862].

54. *Savannah (Ga.) Republican*, October 19, 1861; *New Orleans Daily Picayune*, June 22, 1861; Jefferson Davis, *Jefferson Davis: The Essential Writings*, ed. William J. Cooper Jr. (New York: Modern Library, 2003), 219; Edmund Ruffin, *The Diary of Edmund Ruffin*, ed. William K. Scarborough, 3 vols. (Baton Rouge: Louisiana State University Press, 1972–1989), 2:110; Guy R. Everson and Edward W. Simpson Jr., *Far, Far from Home: The Wartime Letters of Dick and Tally Simpson, 3rd South Carolina Volunteers* (New York: Oxford University Press, 1994), 72; Susan Leigh Blackford, compiler, *Memoirs of Life In and Out of the Army in Virginia during the War Between the States*, 2 vols. (Lynchburg, Va.: J. P. Bell, 1894), 1:108. Logically the Confederacy stood as a bulwark against such onrushing centralization, but critics of the Davis administration soon turned these same rhetorical guns against their own government. "Proceedings of First Confederate Congress," *Southern Historical Society Papers* 46 (1928): 89–92; Wilson, *Southern Woman of Letters*, 91–92.

55. Allen D. Candler, ed., *The Confederate Records of the State of Georgia*, 5 vols. (Atlanta: C. P. Byrd, 1909–11), 2:188; MacMahon, *Cause and Contrast*, 156–57; *Staunton (Va.) Spectator*, Septem-

ber 3, 1861; Holmes, *Diary of Emma Holmes*, 84–85; *New Orleans Daily Picayune*, August 23, 1861; *Southern Illustrated News*, May 23, 1863; Davis, *Jefferson Davis: Essential Writings*, 225; *Athens (Ga.) Southern Banner*, September 4, 1861; *Daily Raleigh (N.C.) Register*, October 5, 1861; *Daily Richmond Examiner*, October 24, 1863.

56. *New Orleans Daily Picayune*, May 13, 1861; *Savannah (Ga.) Republican*, October 14, 1862; *Salisbury (N.C.) Carolina Watchman*, August 15, 1861, November 17, 1862; Blackford, *Memoirs of Life In and Out of the Army*, 1:68; *Milledgeville (Ga.) Southern Federal Union*, September 10, 1861.

57. *Staunton (Va.) Spectator*, September 10, 1861; Rosa Deloney to William G. Deloney, January 7, 1862, Deloney Papers, Hargrett Rare Book and Manuscript Library, University of Georgia; *Richmond Daily Whig*, December 9, 1862; *Augusta (Ga.) Daily Chronicle and Sentinel*, April 20, 1861; Joshua K. Callaway, *The Civil War Letters of Joshua K. Callaway*, ed. Judith Lee Hallock (Athens: University of Georgia Press, 1997), 79; *Chattanooga Daily Rebel*, February 18, 1863; Holmes, *Diary of Emma Holmes*, 56; Robert J. Trout, ed., *With Pen and Saber: The Letters and Diaries of J.E.B. Stuart's Staff Officers* (Mechanicsburg, Pa.: Stackpole Books, 1995), 35; *Richmond Daily Dispatch*, May 24, 1862.

58. *Charleston Mercury*, February 24, 1862; *Augusta (Ga.) Daily Chronicle and Sentinel*, September 15, 1863; Mills Lane, ed., *"Dear Mother: Don't grieve about me. If I get killed, I'll only be dead." Letters from Georgia Soldiers in the Civil War* (Savannah, Ga.: Beehive Press, 1990), 89; Ruffin, *Diary of Edmund Ruffin*, 2:291; *Camden (S.C.) Confederate*, September 18, 1863; Robert Watson, *Southern Service on Land and Sea: The Wartime Journal of Robert Watson*, ed. R. Thomas Campbell (Knoxville: University of Tennessee Press, 2002), 92. Jonathan Worth, a strong Unionist and most reluctant Confederate, concluded by 1864 that southerners would end up living under a military despotism no matter which side won. Jonathan Worth, *The Correspondence of Jonathan Worth*, ed. J. G. de Roulhac Hamilton, 2 vols. (Raleigh: Edwards and Broughton, 1909), 1:300.

59. *Atlanta Daily Intelligencer*, November 19, 1863; Edmondston, "*Journal of a Secesh Lady*," 236; *Richmond Enquirer*, n.d., in *Savannah (Ga.) Daily Morning News*, June 25, 1862; *Richmond Daily Dispatch*, December 27, 1862.

60. *Milledgeville (Ga.) Federal Union*, January 22, 1861; *Charleston Mercury*, January 24, June 5, 1861; *Milledgeville (Ga.) Southern Recorder*, July 2, 1861; Judith W. McGuire, *Diary of a Southern Refugee during the War by a Lady of Virginia* (New York: E. J. Hale, 1867), 35; Trout, ed., *With Pen and Saber*, 2; *Southern Illustrated News*, November 8, 1862; *Athens (Ga.) Southern Banner*, January 30, 1861; *Richmond Daily Dispatch*, April 16, July 11, 1861. There was even talk of changing the name of Scott County, Virginia to Davis County. *Richmond Daily Dispatch*, May 27, 1861.

61. *Daily Richmond Examiner*, July 16, 1861; Holmes, *Diary of Emma Holmes*, 6–7; *Albany (Ga.) Patriot*, July 11, 1861; *Montgomery (Ala.) Daily Mail*, February 12, 1861; June 17, 1861, Mary Ezell Diary, Edward Conigland Papers, Southern Historical Collection, University of North Carolina; *Richmond Daily Dispatch*, September 6, 1861.

62. *New Orleans Daily Picayune*, May 28, 1861; *Richmond Daily Dispatch*, July 6, August 8, 1861, February 26, 1862; *Staunton (Va.) Vindicator*, February 8, 1861; *Daily Raleigh (N.C.) Register*, September 4, 1861

63. Mary Chesnut, *Mary Chesnut's Civil War*, ed. C. Vann Woodward (New Haven: Yale University Press, 1981), 118; *Daily Raleigh (N.C.) Register*, August 3, 1861.

2. DEFINING AND DEFAMING THE ENEMY

1. Walter Herron Taylor, *Lee's Adjutant: The Wartime Letters of Colonel Walter Herron Taylor, 1862–1865*, ed. R. Lockwood Tower (Columbia: University of South Carolina Press, 1995), 68; *Columbia Daily South Carolinian*, August 7, 1864.

2. *Richmond Daily Dispatch*, January 7, 1861; *New Orleans Daily Picayune*, May 7, 1861; *Petersburg Express*, n.d., in *Raleigh (N.C.) Register*, June 15, 1861; *Fayetteville (N.C.) Observer*, July 1, 1861.

3. *Salisbury (N.C.) Watchman*, June 27, 1861; August 18, 1861, George Anderson Mercer Diary, Southern Historical Collection, University of North Carolina; *Charleston Mercury*, August 1, 1861; Jefferson Davis, *The Papers of Jefferson Davis*, ed. Lynda Lasswell Crist, Mary Seaton Dix, and Kenneth H. Williams, 14 vols. (Baton Rouge: Louisiana State University Press, 1971–2015), 7:262; *Richmond Examiner*, n.d., in *Fayetteville (N.C.) Observer*, September 5, 1861; S. H. Pressley to Robert Briggs Watson, August 1, 1861, Watson Family Papers, South Caroliniana Library, University of South Carolina; *Augusta (Ga.) Daily Chronicle and Sentinel*, September 21, 1861. A Unionist woman was shocked to hear "intelligent men" declare the war was virtually over with the Confederate victory at Manassas. Mrs. Eugene McLean, "A Northern Woman in the Confederacy," *Harper's Monthly Magazine* 128, February 1914, 445–46. See numerous short pieces alluding to northern cowardice at Manassas in the *Savannah (Ga.) Republican*, August 1861, passim.

4. *Official Records of the Union and Confederate Navies in the War of the Rebellion* [OR] (31 vols.; Washington: Government Printing Office, 1894–1922), ser. 1, vol. 15:502; John M. Daniel, *The Richmond Examiner during the War* (New York: printed for the author, 1868), 17; Robert J. Trout, ed., *With Pen and Saber: The Letters and Diaries of J.E.B. Stuart's Staff Officers* (Mechanicsburg, Pa.: Stackpole Books, 1995), 31–32; *Athens (Ga.) Southern Banner*, July 9, 1862; Anna Harden to Mary Ann Harden, October 19, 1861, Edward Harden Papers, Rubenstein Rare Book and Manuscript Library, Duke University; Robert Manson Myers, ed., *The Children of Pride: A True Story of Georgia and the Civil War* (New Haven: Yale University Press, 1972), 788; William Cowan McClellan, *Welcome the Hour of Conflict: William Cowan McClellan and the 9th Alabama*, ed. John C. Carter (Tuscaloosa: University of Alabama Press, 2007), 100; *Jackson Weekly Mississippian*, November 6, 1861. Early in the war, both sides sometimes assumed their enemies were cowards. Reid Mitchell, *Civil War Soldiers* (New York: Viking, 1988), 30.

5. *Milledgeville (Ga.) Southern Federal Union*, December 31, 1861; *Albany (Ga.) Patriot*, January 2, 1862; *Athens (Ga.) Southern Banner*, January 8, 1862; Samuel A. Burney, *A Southern Soldier's Letters Home: The Civil War Letters of Samuel A. Burney, Cobb's Georgia Legion, Army of Northern Virginia*, ed. Nat S. Turner III (Macon, Ga.: Mercer University Press, 2002), 98.

6. Robert Franklin Bunting, *Our Trust is in the God of Battles: The Civil War Letters of Robert Franklin Bunting, Chaplain, Terry's Texas Rangers, C.S.A.*, ed. Thomas W. Cutrer (Knoxville: University of Tennessee Press, 2006), 12; *Richmond Daily Dispatch*, February 14, 1862; McClellan, *Welcome the Hour of Conflict*, 235; Charles W. Turner, ed., *Civil War Letters of Arabella Speairs and William Beverley Pettit of Fluvanna County, Virginia, March 1862–March 1865*, 2 vols. (Roanoke, Va.: Virginia Lithography and Graphics, 1988), 1:22; Bryan Grimes, *Extracts of Letters of Major-General Bryan Grimes, to His Wife*, ed. Gary W. Gallagher (Wilmington, N.C.: Broadfoot Publishing, 1986), 43; *Mobile Register*, January 11, 1862, in *Savannah (Ga.) Daily Morning News*, January 31, 1862.

7. *Milledgeville (Ga.) Southern Recorder*, February 18, March 25, 1862; Myers, ed., *Children of Pride*, 850–51; *Richmond Daily Dispatch*, April 24, 1862, September 14, 1863; *Savannah (Ga.) Republican*, July 3, 1862; Davis, *Papers of Jefferson Davis*, 7:138.

8. *Richmond Daily Dispatch*, September 14, 1863; *Athens (Ga.) Southern Watchman*, March 2, 1864; Kate Cumming, *Kate: The Journal of a Confederate Nurse*, ed. Richard Barksdale Harwell (Baton Rouge: Louisiana State University Press, 1959), 142; William Dorsey Pender, *The General to His Lady: The Civil War Letters of William Dorsey Pender to Fanny Pender*, ed. William W. Hassler (Chapel Hill: University of North Carolina Press, 1988), 16.

9. *Milledgeville (Ga.) Confederate Union*, December 23, 1862; *Milledgeville (Ga.) Southern Federal Union*, August 19, 1862; *OR*, ser. 1, vol. 11, pt. 1:602, vol. 18:894, vol. 53:371; *Milledgeville (Ga.) Southern Recorder*, May 12, 1863, January 5, 1864; *Salisbury (N.C.) Carolina Watchman*, September 19, 1861; Stephen Dodson Ramseur, *The Bravest of the Brave: The Correspondence of Stephen Dodson Ramseur*, ed. George C. Kundahl (Chapel Hill: University of North Carolina Press, 2010), 121. In contrast, Jason Phillips sees more continuity in these notions of weak and cowardly Yankees than I have found. At the same time, he has perceptively noted how images of "inept enemies" and "barbaric foes" coexisted throughout the war. Although the idea of the "cowardly Yankee" declined, the notion of barbarism often encompassed moral cowardice. *Diehard Rebels: The Confederate Culture of Invincibility* (Athens: University of Georgia Press, 2007), 42, 46–52. For an argument that assessments of northern cowardice held steady during the war, see Bell Irvin Wiley, *The Life of Johnny Reb: The Common Soldiers of the Confederacy* (Indianapolis: Bobbs-Merrill, 1943), 313–15.

10. "Diary of Robert E. Park, Macon, Georgia, late Captain Twelfth Alabama Regiment, Confederate States Army," *Southern Historical Society Papers* 1 (May 1876): 374, 381; Grace Brown Elmore, *A Heritage of Woe: The Civil War Diary of Grace Brown Elmore, 1861–1868*, ed. Marli F. Weiner (Athens: University of Georgia Press, 1997), 102–3.

11. William R. Taylor, *Cavalier and Yankee: The Old South and American National Character* (New York: George Braziller, 1961), 133–37; Thomas W. Cutrer and T. Michael Parrish, eds., *Brothers in Gray: The Civil War Letters of the Pierson Family* (Baton Rouge: Louisiana State University Press, 1997), 190–91; John Hampden Chamberlayne, *Ham Chamberlayne—Virginian: Letters and Papers of an Artillery Officer for Southern Independence, 1861–1865*, ed. C. G. Chamberlayne (Richmond: Dietz Printing, 1932), 105; E. Merton Coulter, *The Confederate States of America, 1861–1865* (Baton Rouge: Louisiana State University Press, 1950), 12, 15; *Savannah (Ga.) Daily Morning News*, March 12, 1862.

12. Coulter, *Confederate States*, 12; Peter Wellington Alexander, *Writing and Fighting the Confederate War: The Letters of Peter Wellington Alexander, Confederate War Correspondent*, ed. William B. Styple (Kearny, N.J. Belle Grove Publishing, 2002), 32; A South Carolinian [pseud.], *The Confederate* (Mobile: S. H. Goetzel, 1863), 53–59.

13. Emma Holmes, *Diary of Miss Emma Holmes, 1861–1866*, ed. John F. Marszalek (Baton Rouge: Louisiana State University Press, 1979), 56; Edmund Ruffin, *The Diary of Edmund Ruffin*, ed. William K. Scarborough, 3 vols. (Baton Rouge: Louisiana State University Press, 1972–1989), 2:212–13; *Charleston Mercury*, November 3, 1863; *Richmond Daily Dispatch*, January 23, 1862.

14. Ruffin, *Diary of Edmund Ruffin*, 2:200; Burney, *A Southern Soldier's Letters Home*, 74; Jefferson Davis, *Jefferson Davis: The Essential Writings*, ed. William J. Cooper Jr. (New York: Modern Library, 2003), 227; *Charleston Courier, Tri-Weekly*, July 26, 1862; *Athens (Ga.) Southern Watchman*, August 13, 1862; Sarah Morgan, *The Civil War Diary of Sarah Morgan*, ed. Charles East (Athens: University of Georgia Press, 1991), 74–75.

15. *Richmond Whig*, n.d., in *Athens (Ga.) Southern Banner*, January 8, 1862; Burney, *Southern Soldier's Letters Home*, 102; *Athens (Ga.) Southern Banner*, July 3, 1861; *Columbia (S.C.) Guardian*, n.d., in *Augusta (Ga.) Daily Chronicle and Sentinel*, May 10, 1862. Jason Phillips has carefully pointed out how stereotypes about Yankee character and the supposed economic weaknesses and political divisions in the North led Confederates to underestimate their opponents. Phillips, *Diehard Rebels*, 73–75.

16. Mitchell, *Civil War Soldiers*, 30; *OR*, ser. 1, vol. 9:94; Henry Hotze, *Henry Hotze, Confederate Propagandist: Selected Writings on Revolution, Recognition, and Race*, ed. Lonnie A. Burnett (Tuscaloosa: University of Alabama Press, 2008), 139–40. During the war, the word *mercenary* appeared in one form or another at least 292 times in the *Richmond Daily Dispatch*. Southern newspapers happily reprinted numerous articles from the foreign press that parroted their own attacks on the Yankees and northern society.

17. *Atlanta Southern Confederacy*, May 2, 1861; *Charleston Mercury*, May 1, 1861. In a rather oddly crafted appeal to his troops, General Albert Sidney Johnston described the northern invaders as "agrarian mercenaries." *OR*, ser. 1, vol. 10, pt. 1:396.

18. A modern reflection of this viewpoint appears in the movie *Gods and Generals*, where it never becomes clear why the Union soldiers are fighting at all.

19. For an explicit use of this comparison, see *Savannah (Ga.) Daily Morning News*, October 30, 1861.

20. Benjamin Franklin Batchelor and George Q. Turner, *Batchelor-Turner Letters, 1861–1864. Written by Two of Terry's Texas Rangers* (Austin, Tex.: Steck Company, 1961), 29.

21. William F. Fox, *Regimental Losses in the American Civil War, 1861–1865* (Albany, N.Y.: Brandow Printing, 1898), 62; Benjamin Arthorp Gould, *Investigations in the Military and Anthropological Statistics of American Soldiers* (New York: Hurd and Houghton, 1869), 26–30.

22. [George Fitzhugh], "The Great Day of Manassas," *DeBow's Review* 6 (September 1861): 283; Augustus Pitt Adamson, *Sojourns of a Patriot: The Field and Prison Papers of an Unreconstructed Confederate*, ed. Richard Bender Abel and Fay Adamson Gecik (Murfreesboro, Tenn.: Southern Heritage Press, 1998), 42; Ruffin, *Diary of Edmund Ruffin*, 2:198; *Richmond Daily Dispatch*, October 26, 1861.

23. *Athens (Ga.) Southern Banner*, January 9, 1861; *Fayetteville (N.C.) Observer*, June 13, 1861; *Richmond Daily Dispatch*, March 19, July 31, 1861; Batchelor and Turner, *Batchelor-Turner Letters*, 11; James J. White, "Liberty Hall Volunteers, Co. I, 4th Reg. Va. Vols." A. S. Williams Collection, University of Alabama; *OR*, ser. 4, vol. 3:130–31; *New Orleans Daily Picayune*, April 24, 1861.

24. *Edgefield (S.C.) Advertiser*, June 3, 1863; George W. Davis to Rebecca Pitchford Davis, July 7, 1863, Rebecca Pitchford Davis Papers, Southern Historical Collection, University of North Carolina; Clement Anselm Evans, *Intrepid Warrior: Clement Anselm Evans, Confederate General*

from Georgia, Life, Letters, and Diaries of the War Years, ed. Robert Grier Stephens Jr. (Dayton, Ohio: Morningside, 1992), 380.

25. *Petersburg (Va.) Daily Express*, November 24, 1863; *Richmond Daily Dispatch*, July 27, 1861; May 7, 1861, George Anderson Mercer Diary; Catherine Ann Devereux Edmondston, *"Journal of a Secesh Lady": The Diary of Catherine Ann Devereux Edmondston, 1860–1866*, ed. Beth G. Crabtree and James W. Patton (Raleigh, N.C.: Division of Archives and History, 1979), 178; *Charleston Mercury*, July 28, 1863; Allen D. Candler, ed., *The Confederate Records of the State of Georgia*, 5 vols. (Atlanta: C. P. Byrd, 1909–11), 2:283–84; *Resolutions of the State of Texas, concerning peace, reconstruction, and independence* [Richmond, 1865], 2. Confederate leaders and editors bragged that their armies were not made up of "foreign scum." Southern solders were men of sterling character whose natural superiority seemed obvious. Indeed, assertions of these striking contrasts between soldiers on the two sides began before there had even been a major battle. *Athens (Ga.) Southern Watchman*, February 8, 1865; Randall C. Jimerson, *The Private Civil War: Popular Thought during the Sectional Conflict* (Baton Rouge: Louisiana State University Press, 1988), 127–28; *OR*, ser. 4, vol. 3:129; *Savannah (Ga.) Republican*, August 16, 1861; *Richmond Daily Dispatch*, May 3, 1861, January 18, 1864.

26. *Shreveport (La.) Semi-Weekly News*, October 28, 1862; Frank Moore, ed., *Songs and Ballads of the Southern People* (New York: Appleton, 1886), 32; *OR*, ser. 1, vol. 10, pt. 2:484; Jedediah Hotchkiss to Sara A. Hotchkiss, April 24, July 15, 1862, Hotchkiss Papers, Library of Congress; *Richmond Daily Dispatch*, July 23, 1861.

27. *New Orleans Daily Picayune*, October 8, 1861; *Richmond Daily Dispatch*, May 3, August 7, 1861; *Savannah (Ga.) Republican*, June 2, 1863; Myers, ed., *Children of Pride*, 916; Edmondston, *"Journal of a Secesh Lady,"* 413; W. R. M. Slaughter to his sister, January 4, 1863, Slaughter Papers, Virginia Historical Society. By the same token, these "real" Yankees bore more responsibility for all the destruction and bloodshed than their foreign-born dupes. This "Puritan breed" served an evil cause, "prompted by the basest passions in seeking the blood of the Southern people." *Richmond Daily Dispatch*, June 10, 1863.

28. April 30, 1862, Mary G. A. Stribling Diary, Library of Virginia, Richmond; "Diary of Robert E. Park," 372; *Richmond Daily Dispatch*, March 13, 1862, July 17, 1863, May 7, 1864.

29. *Richmond Enquirer*, May 29, 1863; *Atlanta Southern Confederacy*, May 31, 1861; *Athens (Ga.) Southern Banner*, March 27, 1861; *Staunton (Va.) Spectator*, March 18, 1864; *Richmond Daily Dispatch*, May 10, 15, September 5, 1861. Despite evidence of anti-Semitism that would soon appear in the Confederacy, the *Charleston Mercury* maintained that South Carolina had been especially hospitable to Jews. *Charleston Mercury*, February 1, 1861.

30. *Charleston Mercury*, February 26, 1863; George Fitzhugh, "Cuba: The March of Empire and the Course of Trade," *DeBow's Review* 30 (January 1861): 34; Cornelia Lockett to Samuel Henry Lockett, February 20, 1864, Samuel Henry Lockett Papers, Southern Historical Collection, University of North Carolina; *Journal of the Senate of South Carolina: Being the Session of 1862* (Columbia, S.C.: Charles P. Pelham, 1862), 22; *Journal of the Proceedings of the House of Representatives . . . of Florida . . . 1861* (Tallahassee: Office of the Floridian and Journal, 1861), 182–83.

31. *Richmond Daily Dispatch*, December 4, 1861, May 23, 1862; *Atlanta Southern Confederacy*, June 29, 1861; William R. Smith, *The History and Debates of the Convention of the People of Alabama*,

Begun and Held in the City of Montgomery, on the seventh Day of January 1861 (Montgomery: White, Pfiester, 1861), 225.

32. Frank H. Alfriend, "A Southern Republic and a Northern Democracy," *Southern Literary Messenger* 37 (May 1863): 289–90; *Milledgeville (Ga.) Southern Recorder*, February 25, 1862; *Savannah (Ga.) Daily Morning News*, March 12, 1863; *Mobile (Ala.) Register*, July 20, August 27, 1862; *Raleigh (N.C.) Daily Register*, August 17, 1861; *Weekly Raleigh (N.C.) Register*, May 6, 1863; *Atlanta Southern Confederacy*, June 29, 1861.

33. Edmondston, "*Journal of a Secesh Lady*," 72; Elizabeth Preston Allan, *The Life and Letters of Margaret Junkin Preston* (Boston: Houghton, Mifflin, 1903), 163; *Athens (Ga.) Southern Banner*, May 8, 1861; *Richmond Whig*, December 17, 1861.

34. Andy Brice, South Carolina, *Slave Narratives* CD-ROM (Orem, Utah: MyFamily.com, 2000); April 3, 1862, Kate S. Sperry Diary, Library of Virginia, Richmond; Chamberlayne, *Ham Chamberlayne*, 186; Sarah Jane Sams to Robert R. Sams, February 3, 1865, Sarah Jane Sams Letters, South Caroliniana Library, University of South Carolina; *Milledgeville (Ga.) Southern Recorder*, July 2, 1861; Edmondston, "*Journal of a Secesh Lady*," 284.

35. *Atlanta Southern Confederacy*, May 8, 1861; Charleston *Mercury*, May 16, 1861; *Richmond Daily Dispatch*, May 13, 1861.

36. *Fayetteville (N.C.) Observer*, July 1, 1861; *Richmond Daily Dispatch*, May 3, 1861; *Augusta (Ga.) Daily Chronicle and Sentinel*, August 15, 1861; Anna Robinson Andrews to Mrs. Courtney Bird Jones, April 27, 1862, Charles Wesley Andrews Papers, Rubenstein Rare Book and Manuscript Library, Duke University.

37. *Richmond Daily Dispatch*, June 13, 1862; March 29, 1862, Kate S. Sperry Diary, Library of Virginia; Alexander, *Writing and Fighting the Confederate War*, 184; Lesley J. Gordon, "Courting Nationalism: The Wartime Letters of Bobbie Mitchell and Nettie Fondren," in Lesley J. Gordon and John C. Inscoe, eds., *Inside the Confederate Nation: Essays in Honor of Emory M. Thomas* (Baton Rouge: Louisiana State University Press, 2005), 194; Mary Greenhow Lee, *The Civil War Journal of Mary Greenhow Lee of Winchester, Virginia*, ed. Eloise C. Strader (Winchester, Va.: Winchester-Frederick County Historical Society, 2011), 449–50; Eliza Frances Andrews, *The War-Time Journal of a Georgia Girl, 1864–1865*, ed. Spencer Bidwell King Jr. (Macon, Ga.: Ardivan Press, 1960), 148–49. These descriptions are comparable to sixteenth-century British accounts of the "wild Irish." Wayne E. Lee, *Barbarians and Brothers: Anglo-American Warfare, 1500–1865* (New York: Oxford University Press, 2011), 57.

38. Lucy Rebecca Buck, *Shadows on My Heart: The Civil War Diary of Lucy Rebecca Buck of Virginia*, ed. Elizabeth R. Baer (Athens: University of Georgia Press, 1997), 43, 54, 177; Phillips, *Diehard Rebels*, 63; Myers, ed., *Children of Pride*, 1242; Ellen Renshaw House, *A Very Violent Rebel: The Civil War Diary of Ellen Renshaw House*, ed. Daniel E. Sutherland (Knoxville: University of Tennessee Press, 1996), 23; Myra Inman, *Myra Inman: A Diary of the Civil War in East Tennessee*, ed. William R. Snell (Macon, Ga.: Mercer University Press, 2000), 252.

39. September 20, 1863, Kate D. Foster Diary, Rubenstein Rare Book and Manuscript Library, Duke University; April 13, 1865, Mary D. Waring Diary, Alabama Department of Archives and History; *Shreveport (La.) Weekly News*, May 27, 1861.

40. Lee, *Civil War Journal* 44; (Macon) *Georgia Weekly Telegraph*, June 21, 1861; David Jackson Logan, *"A Rising Star of Promise": The Civil War Odyssey of David Jackson Logan: 17th South Carolina Volunteers, 1861–1864*, ed. Samuel N. Thomas Jr. and Jason Silverman (Campbell, Calif.: Savas Publishing, 1998), 144; Lafayette McLaws, *A Soldier's General: The Civil War Letters of Major General Lafayette McLaws*, ed. John C. Oeffinger (Chapel Hill: University of North Carolina Press, 2002), 165; *Charleston Mercury*, October 24, 1861. During the burning and sack of Columbia, South Carolina, some civilians commented on how the soldiers' vulgar language compounded the crime. Megan Kate Nelson has noted how the war broke down barriers to the use of obscenities in various settings. *Ruin Nation: Destruction and the American Civil War* (Athens: University of Georgia Press, 2012), 50–52.

41. John Dooley, *John Dooley's Civil War: An Irish American's Journey in the First Virginia Infantry Regiment*, ed. Robert Emmett Curran (Knoxville: University of Tennessee Press, 2012), 170; Virginia Bedinger to Carrie Bedinger, April 21, 1862, Bedinger-Dandridge Family Papers, Rubenstein Rare Book and Manuscript Library, Duke University; Myers, ed., *Children of Pride*, 1227; Emma LeConte, *When the World Ended: The Diary of Emma LeConte*, ed. Earl Schenck Miers (New York: Oxford University Press, 1957), 44. Confederates hotly denied that southern ladies would ever use coarse language in their confrontations with northern occupiers. *Richmond Daily Dispatch*, May 9, 1862.

42. *Milledgeville (Ga.) Confederate Union*, June 30, 1863; George Fitzhugh, "The Pioneers, Preachers, and People of the Mississippi Valley," *DeBow's Review* 30 (March 1861): 264; Ted Barclay, *Ted Barclay, Liberty Hall Volunteers: Letters from the Stonewall Brigade (1861–1864)* (Natural Bridge Station, Va.: Rockbridge Publishing Company, 1992), 29; *Fayetteville (N.C.) Observer*, May 15, 1862; Wiley, *Life of Johnny Reb*, 309; *Savannah (Ga.) Republican*, May 29, 1863; Edwin H. Fay, *"This Infernal War": The Confederate Letters of Sgt. Edwin H. Fay*, ed. Bell Irvin Wiley (Austin: University of Texas Press, 1958), 342; *Athens (Ga.) Southern Banner*, August 14, 1861; *Richmond Daily Whig*, December 11, 1862.

43. *Richmond Daily Dispatch*, April 7, 1864; Daniel, *Richmond Examiner during the War*, 6; Sue Sparks Keitt, "Sue Sparks Keitt to a Northern Friend, March 4, 1861," ed. Elmer Don Herd Jr., *South Carolina Historical Magazine* 62 (April 1961), 83; *Savannah (Ga.) Republican*, August 7, 1861; *Atlanta Daily Intelligencer*, November 19, 1863; [William Russell Smith], *The Royal Ape: A Dramatic Poem* (Richmond: West and Johnson, 1863); Holmes, *Diary of Miss Emma Holmes*, 241; *Bellville (Tex.) Countryman*, May 2, 1863. For further press commentary on the vulgar Lincoln, see John McKee Barr, *Loathing Lincoln: An American Tradition from the Civil War to the Present* (Baton Rouge: Louisiana State University Press, 2014), 25.

44. For a few of many examples from soldiers, civilians, and poets, see Mills Lane, ed., *"Dear Mother: Don't grieve about me. If I get killed, I'll only be dead." Letters from Georgia Soldiers in the Civil War* (Savannah, Ga.: Beehive Press, 1990), 84, 309–10; *Savannah (Ga.) Republican*, June 18, 1861; *Atlanta Daily Intelligencer*, September 20, 1863; Buck, *Shadows on My Heart*, 43; H. M. Wharton, *War Songs and Poems of the Southern Confederacy* (Philadelphia: American Book and Bible House, 1904), 191; Fayetteville *(N.C.) Observer*, March 24, 1862.

45. *Salisbury (N.C.) Carolina Watchman*, May 13, 1861; Kenneth Walters, *Norfolk Blues: The Civil War Diary of the Norfolk Light Artillery Blues*, ed. Kenneth Wiley (Shippensburg, Pa.: Burd Street

Press, 1997), 38; *Richmond Daily Dispatch*, June 18, 1861; *Atlanta Southern Confederacy*, February 15, 1862; *Fayetteville (N.C.) Observer*, May 2, 1861; *Savannah (Ga.) Republican*, September 8, 1861.

46. Myers, ed., *Children of Pride*, 648; *Athens (Ga.) Southern Banner*, June 19, 1861; *Charleston Mercury*, February 20, 1864; Arthur N. Skinner and James L. Skinner, eds., *The Death of a Confederate: Selections from the Letters of the Archibald Smith Family of Roswell, Georgia, 1864–1956* (Athens: University of Georgia Press, 1996), 83–84; March 6, 1863, Nancy Emerson Diary, Albert and Shirley Small Special Collections Library, University of Virginia.

47. *Edgefield (S.C.) Advertiser*, July 15, 1863; *Athens (Ga.) Southern Watchman*, May 1, 1861; Buck, *Shadow on My Heart*, 42–43; *Savannah (Ga.) Republican*, August 12, 1863; Betsy Fleet and John P. Fuller, eds., *Green Mount: A Virginia Plantation Family during the Civil War: Being the Journal of Benjamin Robert Fleet and Letters of His Family* (Lexington: University of Kentucky Press, 1962), 353–54.

48. *Richmond Daily Dispatch*, May 27, 1861; *Athens (Ga.) Southern Watchman*, June 19, 1861; Eliza Rhea Anderson Fain, *Sanctified Trial: The Diary of Eliza Rhea Anderson Fain, a Confederate Woman in East Tennessee*, ed. John N. Fain (Knoxville: University of Tennessee Press, 2004), 13; *OR*, ser. 1, vol. 3:700; Lane, ed., *"Dear Mother: Don't grieve about me*, 84.

49. Maggie N. Tucker to Mrs. George M. Munford, May 18, 1862, Munford-Ellis Family Papers, Rubenstein Rare Book and Manuscript Library, Duke University; September 1, 1861, Elizabeth Collier Diary, Southern Historical Collection, University of North Carolina; Louis P. Towles, ed., *A World Turned Upside Down: The Palmers of South Santee, 1818–1881* (Columbia: University of South Carolina Press, 1996), 461–62.

3. THE BARBAROUS YANKEES

1. Charles B. Dew, *Apostles of Disunion: Southern Secession Commissioners and the Causes of the Civil War* (Charlottesville: University Press of Virginia, 2001), 52; *War of the Rebellion: A Compilation of the Official Records of the Union and Confederate Armies* [OR], 128 vols. (Washington: Government Printing Office, 1880–1901), ser. 4, vol. 1:9.

2. For useful comments on how historians have dealt with "sensibility," including emotional and irrational elements, see Daniel Wickberg, "What Is the History of Sensibilities? On Cultural Histories, Old and New," *American Historical Review* 112 (June 2007): 662, 664, 675.

3. *Richmond Daily Dispatch*, April 20, 1861; *Gazette Sentinel* (Plaquemine, La.), May 11, 1861; *Salisbury (N.C.) Carolina Watchman*, June 6, 1861; Louis P. Towles, ed., *A World Turned Upside Down: The Palmers of South Santee, 1818–1881* (Columbia: University of South Carolina Press, 1996), 305; *Richmond Enquirer*, July 23, 1861.

4. Michel de Montaigne, *Montaigne: Selected Essays*, ed. Blanchard Bates (New York: Modern Library, 1949), 77; Sam Keen, *Faces of the Enemy: Reflections of the Hostile Imagination* (San Francisco: Harper and Row, 1986), 43–48; John W. Dower, *War without Mercy: Race and Power in the Pacific War* (New York: Pantheon Books, 1986), 33–36.

5. H. M. Wharton, *War Songs and Poems of the Southern Confederacy* (Philadelphia: American Book and Bible House, 1904), 36, 189; Baptist Church, South Carolina, Saluda Baptist Association, *Minutes of the 61st and 62d Anniversaries of the Saluda Baptist Association* (Augusta, Ga.: James Nathan Ellis, 1864), 7–8; Frank Moore, ed., *Songs and Ballads of the Southern People* (New York:

Appleton, 1886), 109–10; *Richmond Daily Dispatch*, April 18, 1862. See the excellent discussion of images of northern barbarism—including poetry, song, and cartoons—in Jason Phillips, *Diehard Rebels: The Confederate Culture of Invincibility* (Athens: University of Georgia Press, 2007), 52–58. One Georgian referred to the Yankees as "Goths and Vandals" even before the war had begun. January 25, 1861, George Anderson Mercer Diary, Southern Historical Collection, University of North Carolina. Or perhaps the enemy's brutality was just unparalleled in human history. *Savannah (Ga.) Republican*, June 11, 1861.

6. *Lynchburg Virginian*, n.d., in *Milledgeville (Ga.) Southern Recorder*, July 21, 1863; *Fayetteville (N.C.) Observer*, September 24, 1863; *Savannah (Ga.) Daily Morning News*, October 6, 1863; *Richmond Daily Dispatch*, May 3, 1861, January 22, 1862.

7. *Charleston Mercury*, August 12, 1861; *Semi-Weekly Raleigh (N.C.) Register*, January 1, 1862; *Fayetteville (N.C.) Observer*, March 23, 1863; Paul Quigley, *Shifting Grounds: Nationalism and the American South, 1848–1865* (New York: Oxford University Press, 2012), 182–83; James C. Bates, *A Texas Cavalry Officer's Civil War: The Diary and Letters of James C. Bates*, ed. Richard Lowe (Baton Rouge: Louisiana State University, 1999), 254; Jefferson Davis, *Jefferson Davis: The Essential Writings*, ed. William J. Cooper Jr. (New York: Modern Library, 2003), 286.

8. David Livingstone Smith, *Less than Human: Why We Demean, Enslave, and Exterminate Others* (New York: St. Martin's Press, 2011), 26–46; Daniel I. Dreher, *A Sermon Delivered by Rev. Daniel I. Dreher, Pastor of St. James Church, Concord, N.C., June 13, 1861* (Salisbury, N.C.: Printed at the Watchman Office, 1861), 13; Robert Garlick Hill Kean, *Inside the Confederate Government: The Diary of Robert Garlick Hill Kean*, ed. Edward Younger (New York: Oxford University Press, 1957), 71.

9. *Vicksburg (Miss.) Citizen*, n.d., in *Milledgeville (Ga.) Confederate Union*, January 27, 1863; *Columbia Daily South Carolinian*, March 6, 1864; Robert Franklin Bunting, *Our Trust is in the God of Battles: The Civil War Letters of Robert Franklin Bunting, Chaplain, Terry's Texas Rangers, C.S.A.*, ed. Thomas W. Cutrer (Knoxville: University of Tennessee Press, 2006), 97; *Milledgeville (Ga.) Southern Recorder*, May 21, 1861; Grace Brown Elmore, *A Heritage of Woe: The Civil War Diary of Grace Brown Elmore, 1861–1868*, ed. Marli F. Weiner (Athens: University of Georgia Press, 1997), 79–80.

10. *Richmond Daily Dispatch*, April 5, 1864; *Milledgeville (Ga.) Southern Federal Union*, November 12, 1861; Eathan Allen Pinnell, *Serving with Honor: The Diary of Captain Eathan Allen Pinnell of the Eighth Missouri Infantry (Confederate)*, ed. Michael E. Banasik (Iowa City, Iowa: Camp Pope Book Shop, 1999), 212.

11. *Milledgeville (Ga.) Southern Recorder*, May 20, 1862; *Milledgeville (Ga.) Southern Federal Union*, February 18, 1862; *Richmond Daily Dispatch*, August 20, 1861.

12. Wayne E. Lee, *Barbarians and Brothers: Anglo-American Warfare, 1500–1865* (New York: Oxford University Press, 2011), 239–40; Robert H. Howison, "History of the War," *Southern Literary Messenger* 36 (September 1862): 520–22; *Atlanta Southern Confederacy*, July 4, 1861; *Salisbury (N.C.) Carolina Watchman*, August 25, 1861; *Lynchburg Daily Virginian*, December 20, 1862; *Richmond Daily Enquirer*, December 22, 1862; Reid Mitchell, *Civil War Soldiers* (New York: Viking, 1988), 26; *Savannah (Ga.) Daily Morning News*, February 3, May 14, 1862.

13. *Lynchburg Daily Virginian*, December 16, 1862; *Richmond Daily Dispatch*, December 23, 1862. Later in the war, General William S. Rosecrans's forces had shelled Chattanooga on a

Confederate fast day while many civilians were attending religious services. Charles D. Roberts to Maggie Roberts, July 8, 1863, Charles Roberts Collection, Special Collections, University of Mississippi.

14. *Richmond Daily Dispatch*, May 27, 1863; *Milledgeville (Ga.) Confederate Union*, September 20, 1864; *Fayetteville (N.C.) Observer*, September 19, 1864, 1 (Macon) *Georgia Weekly Telegraph*, August 1, 1862; Lucy Rebecca Buck, *Shadows on My Heart: The Civil War Diary of Lucy Rebecca Buck of Virginia*, ed. Elizabeth R. Baer (Athens: University of Georgia Press, 1997), 181, 262.

15. For typical examples of anti-Yankee diatribes—including lists of outrages—in a variety of forms and places, see *Charleston Mercury*, October 21, 1862; Henry Champlin Lay, "The Devout Soldier Preached by request to the Powhatan Troop at Emmanuel Church, March 6, 1864," Lay Sermons, Southern Historical Collection, University of North Carolina; *Atlanta Daily Intelligencer*, August 28, 1863; A South Carolinian [pseud.], *The Confederate* (Mobile: S. H. Goetzel, 1863), 89–96; Randall C. Jimerson, *The Private Civil War: Popular Thought during the Sectional Conflict* (Baton Rouge: Louisiana State University Press, 1988), 141–42. Even Yankee women reportedly exhorted their menfolk to desecrate bodies and bring home skulls as souvenirs. *Daily Richmond Examiner*, July 1, 1862; *Richmond Daily Dispatch*, January 18, 1862.

16. *Official Records of the Union and Confederate Navies in the War of the Rebellion* (31 vols.; Washington: Government Printing Office, 1894–1922), ser. 2, vol. 3:991.

17. *Annual Message of Governor Henry Watkins Allen, To the Legislature of Louisiana. January, 1865* ([Shreveport, La.]: Office of the Caddo Gazette, 1865), 12; *Official Report Relative to the Conduct of Federal Troops in Western Louisiana during the Invasions of 1863 and 1864* (Shreveport, La.: News Printing Establishment, 1865), 12–13; Henry Champlin Lay, Fast Day, February 28, 1862, Lay Sermons, Southern Historical Collection, University of North Carolina; Dower, *War without Mercy*, 12; *OR*, ser. 4, vol. 3:131–32.

18. Davis, *Davis: Essential Writings*, 219–20, 336–37; Jefferson Davis, *The Messages and Papers of Jefferson Davis and Confederacy Including Diplomatic Correspondence, 1861–1865*, ed. James D. Richardson, 2 vols. (New York: Chelsea House-Robert Hector, 1966), 1:233, 379–80; Jefferson Davis, *The Papers of Jefferson Davis*, ed. Lynda Lasswell Crist, Mary Seaton Dix, and Kenneth H. Williams,14 vols. (Baton Rouge: Louisiana State University Press, 1971–2015), 8:567. For a somewhat different take on Davis's rhetorical use of northern "barbarity," see the provocative analysis in Paul D. Escott, *After Secession: Jefferson Davis and the Failure of Confederate Nationalism* (Baton Rouge: Louisiana State University Press, 1978), 179–84.

19. Davis, *Davis: Essential Writings*, 336; *OR*, ser. 1, vol. 8:814, vol. 26, pt. 2:114–15, vol. 39, pt. 1:729; *Athens (Ga.) Southern Watchman*, August 7, 1861.

20. Stephen Dodson Ramseur, *The Bravest of the Brave: The Correspondence of Stephen Dodson Ramseur*, ed. George C. Kundahl (Chapel Hill: University of North Carolina Press, 2010), 287; Robert Taylor Scott to his wife, December 31, 1862, Keith Family Papers, Virginia Historical Society, Richmond; Kenneth W. Noe, *Reluctant Rebels: The Confederates Who Joined the Army after 1861* (Chapel Hill: University of North Carolina Press, 2010), 91–92; *Resolutions Adopted by McGowan's Brigade, South Carolina* Volunteers [Richmond, 1865]; Phillips, *Diehard Rebels*, 58–63.

21. Catherine Ann Devereux Edmondston, *"Journal of a Secesh Lady": The Diary of Catherine Ann Devereux Edmondston, 1860–1866*, ed. Beth G. Crabtree and James W. Patton (Raleigh, N.C.:

Division of Archives and History, 1979), 603; Jane S. Tucker to Powhattan Ellis, March 7, 1864, Munford-Ellis Papers, Rubenstein Rare Book and Manuscript Library, Duke University; W. C. Corsan, *Two Months in the Confederate States: An Englishman's Travels Through the South*, ed. Benjamin H. Trask (Baton Rouge: Louisiana State University Press, 1996), 135–37; *Augusta (Ga.) Daily Chronicle and Sentinel*, October 21, 1864; Louis Leon, *Diary of a Tar Heel Confederate Soldier* (Charlotte, N.C.: Stone Publishing, 1913), 17; *Columbia Daily South Carolinian*, April 22, 1864.

22. *Keowee (Pickens Courthouse, S.C.) Courier*, July 13, 1861. For a useful analysis of both northern soldier and southern civilian attitudes toward the destruction of personal property, see Megan Kate Nelson, *Ruin Nation: Destruction and the American Civil War* (Athens: University of Georgia Press, 2012), 81–85.

23. *Charleston Mercury*, June 12, 1863; *Resolutions of the State of Texas, concerning peace, reconstruction, and independence* [Richmond, 1865], 2; *OR*, ser. 1, vol. 51, pt. 2:582, 994; (Macon) *Georgia Weekly Telegraph*, August 8, 1862; Davis, *Messages and Papers*, 1:119–20, 380–81. For a blast against Yankee destructiveness in song, see A. E. Blackmar, *The Southern Marseillaise*, 5th ed. (Augusta, Ga.: Blackmar, 1862).

24. Josiah Gorgas, *The Journals of Josiah Gorgas, 1857–1878*, ed. Sarah Woolfolk Wiggins (Tuscaloosa: University of Alabama Press, 1995), 88; Phillips, *Diehard Rebels*, 62; Ella Washington, "'An Army of Devils': The Diary of Ella Washington," ed. James O. Hall, *Civil War Times Illustrated* 16 (February 1978), 19–20; *OR*, ser. 1, vol. 52, pt. 2:488; William M. McPheeters, *I Acted from Principle: The Civil War Diary of Dr. William M. McPheeters, Confederate Surgeon in the Trans-Mississippi*, ed. Cynthia Dehavan Pitcock and Bill J. Gurley (Fayetteville: University of Arkansas Press, 2002), 153–54; *Milledgeville (Ga.) Southern Recorder*, May 12, 1863; *Richmond Daily Dispatch*, May 10, June 3, 1864; *Columbia (S.C.) Phoenix*, April 18, 1865; Frances Kirby Smith to Edmund Kirby Smith, May 20, 1862, Edmund Kirby Smith Papers, Southern Historical Collection, University of North Carolina.

25. *Richmond Daily Dispatch*, March 21, 1862, November 16, 1863; Mary Jane Chadick, *Incidents of the War: The Civil War Journal of Mary Jane Chadick*, ed. Nancy M. Rohr (Huntsville, Ala.: SilverThreads Publishing, 2005), 85–86; Kate Cumming, *Kate: The Journal of a Confederate Nurse*, ed. Richard Barksdale Harwell (Baton Rouge: Louisiana State University Press, 1959), 82; Allen D. Candler, ed., *The Confederate Records of the State of Georgia*, 5 vols. (Atlanta: C. P. Byrd, 1909–11), 2:619; Moore, ed., *Songs and Ballads of the Southern People*, 166–67. Denunciations of "cowardly" Yankees shifted from citing their behavior on the battlefield to highlighting their ruthless destruction of civilian property. *OR*, ser. 1, vol. 29, pt. 2:835.

26. Towles, ed., *World Turned Upside Down*, 208; *Macon (Ga.) Daily Telegraph*, June 4, 1863; *Natchez (Ms.) Weekly Courier*, May 27, 1863; Edmund Ruffin, *The Diary of Edmund Ruffin*, ed. William K. Scarborough, 3 vols. (Baton Rouge: Louisiana State University Press, 1972–1989), 2:646.

27. October 13, 1862, John Houston Bills Diary, Southern Historical Collection, University of North Carolina; William L. Nugent, *My Dear Nellie: The Civil War Letters of William L. Nugent to Eleanor Smith Nugent*, ed. William M. Cash and Lucy Somerville Howorth (Jackson: University Press of Mississippi, 1977), 138; *Atlanta Southern Confederacy*, January 7, 1863; Isaac Howard to his father, December 25, 1862, Howard Family Papers, Southern Historical Collection, Univer-

sity of North Carolina; Jedediah Hotchkiss to Sara Anne Comfort Hotchkiss, January 21, 1863, Hotchkiss Collection, Library of Congress. By 1864, the *Charleston Mercury* not only accused the Yankees of deeds "in violation of all the rules of civilized or humane warfare" but asserted that they sought to make the Confederacy "a waste, [a] howling wilderness." *Charleston Mercury*, April 13, 1864.

28. *Richmond Daily Dispatch*, January 18, 1862; *Augusta (Ga.) Daily Chronicle and Sentinel*, December 10, 1864; New Orleans *Daily Picayune*, September 7, 1861; *Atlanta Southern Confederacy*, May 22, 1863; *Charleston Mercury*, July 31, December 19, 1862; Jane L. Petigru to Mary L. Baber, November 24, 1861, Baber-Blackshear Papers, Hargrett Rare Book and Manuscript Library, University of Georgia Library, Athens; Daniel R. Hundley, *Prison Echoes of the Great Rebellion* (New York: S. W. Green, 1874), 157–58; Moore, ed., *Songs and Ballads of the Southern People*, 168.

29. *Atlanta Southern Confederacy*, August 8, 1861; *Savannah (Ga.) Daily Morning News*, February 14, 1862; *Milledgeville (Ga.) Confederate Union*, February 10, 1863; *Official Report Relative to the Conduct of Federal Troops in Western Louisiana*, 28.

30. *Southern Christian Advocate* (Charleston), June 19, 1862; John Esten Cooke, *Robert E. Lee* (New York: G. W. Dillingham, 1871), 177; Judith W. McGuire, *Diary of a Southern Refugee during the War by a Lady of Virginia* (New York: E. J. Hale, 1867), 284; Mitchell, *Civil War Soldiers*, 38–39.

31. *OR*, ser. 1, vol. 16, pt. 2:822; *New Orleans Daily Picayune*, April 11, 1862; Jefferson Davis, *Messages and Papers*, 1:381. Of course the clergy pointed out that the southern people were themselves sinners and even preached that Yankee depredations represented condign punishment from God. Stephen Elliott, *Vain is the Help of Man. A Sermon Preached in Christ Church, Savannah, on Thursday, September 15, 1864* (Macon, Ga.: Burke, Boykin, and Company, 1864), 5.

32. *OR*, ser. 1, vol. 51, pt. 2:582–83; *Jackson Weekly Mississippian*, March 5, 1862.

33. *OR*, ser. 1, vol. 27, pt. 3:875; Robert J. Trout, ed., *With Pen and Saber: The Letters and Diaries of J.E.B. Stuart's Staff Officers* (Mechanicsburg, Pa.: Stackpole Books, 1995), 27; *Milledgeville (Ga.) Southern Recorder*, July 12, 1864: John Lee Holt, *I Wrote You Word: The Poignant Letters of Private Holt, John Lee Holt, 1829–1863* (Lynchburg, Va.: H. E. Howard, 1993), 72–73; Francis Marion Parker, *To Drive the Enemy from Southern Soil: The Letters of Col. Francis Marion Parker and the History of the 30th Regiment North Carolina Troops*. Edited by Michael W. Taylor (Dayton, Ohio: Morningside, 1998), 38.

34. *Staunton (Va.) Vindicator*, November 18, 1864; Cumming, *Journal of a Confederate Nurse*, 66.

35. Moore, ed., *Songs and Ballads of the Southern People*, 66; *Milledgeville (Ga.) Southern Recorder*, July 2, 1861; Candler, ed., *Confederate Records of Georgia*, 2:284. For a perceptive treatment of plundering by both sides, see Joan E. Cashin, "Trophies of War: Material Culture in the Civil War Era," *Journal of the Civil War Era* 1 (September 2011): 339–67.

36. *Raleigh (N.C.) Register*, September 28, 1861; Bates, *Texas Cavalry Officer's Civil War*, 154; *Richmond Daily Dispatch*, December 23, 1862; *Mobile (Ala.) Register*, February 1, 1862; (Macon) *Georgia Weekly Telegraph*, May 24, 1861.

37. Ruffin, *Diary of Edmund Ruffin*, 2:341–43; *Mobile (Ala.) Register*, July 8, 1862; *Atlanta Southern Confederacy*, July 19, 1861; *Richmond Daily Dispatch*, September 26, 1862; John K. Gott and John E. Divine, eds., *"My Heart is So Rebellious": The Caldwell Letters, 1861–1865* (Warrenton, Va.: Fauquier National Bank, 1991), 175–76; Washington, "'An Army of Devils'": 24; Ethie M.

Foute Eagleton, "'Stray Thoughts': The Civil War Diary of Ethie M. Foute Eagleton," ed. Elvie Eagleton Skipper and Ruth Gove, *East Tennessee Historical Society's Publications* 40–41 (1968–1969): 134. Ruffin also compared the Yankees to British Colonel Banastre Tarleton's marauders in South Carolina during the American Revolution. Ruffin, *Diary of Edmund Ruffin*, 2:515.

38. *Annual Message of Governor Henry Watkins Allen, To the Legislature of Louisiana. January, 1865* ([Shreveport, La.]: Office of the Caddo Gazette. 1865), 12; Cumming, *Journal of a Confederate Nurse*, 211; *Official Report Relative to the Conduct of Federal Troops in Western Louisiana*, 24; Ruffin, *Diary of Edmund Ruffin*, 3:479; Edmondston, "Journal of a Secesh Lady," 401.

39. *Annual Message of Henry Watkins Allen*, 11–12; Thomas H. Watts, *Inaugural Address of Gov. Thomas H. Watts before the Alabama Legislature, December 1st, 1863* (Montgomery, Ala.: Montgomery Advertiser Book and Job Office, 1863), 15–16. Confederate newspapers reveled in incidents where women bravely confronted northern soldiers trying to make off with their household goods. (Macon) *Georgia Weekly Telegraph*, March 28, 1862; *Richmond Daily Dispatch*, August 20, 1861. Yankee prisoners in Belle Isle prison on the James River reportedly stole from each other. *Charleston Mercury*, August 7, 1862.

40. *Savannah (Ga.) Republican*, August 16, 1862; Richmond *Daily Dispatch*, June 24, 1861, July 14, 1864; *Athens (Ga.) Southern Banner*, August 6, 1862; *Milledgeville (Ga.) Southern Recorder*, July 21, 1863. Some Confederates charged that the Yankees in the border areas or in the old northwest were especially dedicated thieves. Frances Wallace Taylor, Catherine Taylor Matthews, and J. Tracy Power, eds., *The Leverett Letters: Correspondence of a South Carolina Family* (Columbia: University of South Carolina Press, 2000), 390; *Richmond Daily Dispatch*, May 23, 1862.

41. Andre M. Fleche, *The Revolution of 1861: The American Civil War in the Age of Nationalist Conflict* (Chapel Hill: University of North Carolina Press, 2012), 100–1; Edmondston, "Journal of a Secesh Lady," 392; A South Carolinian [pseud.], *The Confederate*, 83.

42. Davis, *Davis: Essential Writings*, 287; *Chattanooga Daily Rebel*, February 1, 1863; Edmund DeWitt Patterson, *Yankee Rebel: The Civil War Journal of Edmund DeWitt Patterson*, ed. John G. Barrett (Knoxville: University of Tennessee Press, 2004), 92; *Richmond Daily Dispatch*, March 21, 1864; John M. Daniel, *The Richmond Examiner during the War* (New York: printed for the author, 1868), 67–68; J. K. Street, *J. K. Street Civil War Letters: 9th Texas Infantry from Paris, Lamar County, Texas*, ed. Julie Williams Coley (Wichita Falls, Tex.: J. Cooley, 2009), 55–56.

43. *Richmond Daily Dispatch*, January 4, July 25, 1862; Wharton, *War Songs and Poems*, 352; Davis, *Papers of Jefferson Davis*, 8:309–10; Davis, *Messages and Papers*, 1:289–90; "Mrs. Henrietta Lee's Letter to General David Hunter on the Burning of Her House," *Southern Historical Society Papers* 8 (1880): 216; Elmore, *Heritage of Woe*, 81–82.

44. Davis, *Messages and Papers*, 1:223–24; *Southern Illustrated News*, October 11, 1862; *Resolutions of the State of Texas*, 3; *Charleston Mercury*, March 18, 1863.

45. Warren Akin, *Letters of Warren Akin: Confederate Congressman*, ed. Bell Irvin Wiley (Athens: University of Georgia Press, 1959), 54; Mitchell, *Civil War Soldiers*, 26–27; Amanda Worthington, *A Delta Diary: Amanda Worthington's Civil War Diary*, ed. Troy Woods (n.p.: Olivewoods Press, 2008), 38; Kate Corbin to Sallie Munford, November 19, 1862, Munford-Ellis Papers, Rubenstein Rare Book and Manuscript Library, Duke University.

46. *Charleston Mercury*, June 6, 1863; Margaret Belser Hollis and Allen H. Stokes, eds., *Twilight on the South Carolina Rice Fields: Letters of the Heyward Family, 1862–1871* (Columbia: University of South Carolina Press, 2010), 175; *Richmond Daily Dispatch*, June 28, 1864; *Annual Message of Governor Henry Watkins Allen*, 18–19; Robert Manson Myers, ed., *The Children of Pride: A True Story of Georgia and the Civil War* (New Haven: Yale University Press, 1972), 666–67; August 1, 1862, Melinda Ray Diary, Civil War Collection, North Carolina Division of Archives and History, Raleigh; *OR*, ser. 1, vol. 4:368. Confederates assumed that all atrocities would eventually bring divine judgment down on their enemies. *Richmond Daily Dispatch*, July 2, 1864.

4. THE INHUMAN WAR, OR THE WAR AGAINST HUMANITY

1. *Milledgeville (Ga.) Southern Federal Union*, May 7, 1861.

2. Judith W. McGuire, *Diary of a Southern Refugee during the War by a Lady of Virginia* (New York: E. J. Hale, 1867), 21–22; Ida Powell Dulany, *In the Shadow of the Enemy: The Civil War Journal of Ida Powell Dulany*, ed. Mary L. Mackall, Stevan F. Meserve, and Anne Mackall Sasscer (Knoxville: University of Tennessee Press, 2009), 80; *Message of the Governor of Virginia and Accompanying Documents* (Richmond: William F. Ritchie, 1863), vi. On Union soldiers targeting pianos, see Christian McWhirter, *Battle Hymns: The Power and Popularity of Music in the Civil War* (Chapel Hill: University of North Carolina Press, 2012), 110.

3. Sarah Morgan, *The Civil War Diary of Sarah Morgan*, ed. Charles East (Athens: University of Georgia Press, 1991), 233–34. At one wealthy family's home near Aiken, South Carolina, Union soldiers forced slaves to tear up the white women's chemises for use as pocket handkerchiefs. Pauline DeCaradeuc Heyward, *A Confederate Lady Comes of Age: The Journal of Pauline DeCaradeuc Heyward, 1863–1888*, ed. Mary D. Robertson (Columbia: University of South Carolina Press, 1992), 67.

4. Lucy Rebecca Buck, *Shadows on My Heart: The Civil War Diary of Lucy Rebecca Buck of Virginia*, ed. Elizabeth R. Baer (Athens: University of Georgia Press, 1997), 177; *Official Report Relative to the Conduct of Federal Troops in Western Louisiana during the Invasions of 1863 and 1864* (Shreveport, La.: News Printing Establishment, 1865), 18; Kate? to Kate McGeachy, March 22, 1865, Catherine Jane Buie Papers, Rubenstein Rare Book and Manuscript Library, Duke University; Catherine Ann Devereux Edmondston, *"Journal of a Secesh Lady": The Diary of Catherine Ann Devereux Edmondston, 1860–1866*, ed. Beth G. Crabtree and James W. Patton (Raleigh, N.C.: Division of Archives and History, 1979), 696. On soldiers, women, and violations of private space, see Megan Kate Nelson, *Ruin Nation: Destruction and the American Civil War* (Athens: University of Georgia Press, 2012), 72–78. For further analysis that emphasizes the relationship between gender and a military campaign, see Lisa Tendrich Frank, "Bedrooms as Battlefields: The Role of Gender Politics in Sherman's March," in LeeAnn Whites and Alecia P. Long, eds., *Occupied Women: Gender, Military Occupation, and the American Civil War* (Baton Rouge: Louisiana State University Press, 2009), 33–48.

5. [Joseph Hodgson], *The Confederate Vivandiere; or, The Battle of Leesburg. A Military Drama in Three Acts* (Montgomery, Ala.: John M. Floyd, 1862); Wirt Cate, ed., *Two Soldiers: The Campaign Diaries of Thomas J. Key, C.S.A. . . . and Robert J. Campbell, U.S.A* (Chapel Hill: University of North

Carolina Press, 1938), 131–32; Jason Phillips, "A Brothers' War? Exploring Confederate Perceptions of the Enemy," in Aaron Sheehan-Dean, ed., *The View from the Ground: Experiences of Civil War Soldiers* (Lexington: University Press of Kentucky, 2007), 78; Emma Holmes, *Diary of Miss Emma Holmes, 1861–1866*, ed. John F. Marszalek (Baton Rouge: Louisiana State University Press, 1979), 263–64.

6. Jefferson Davis, *The Messages and Papers of Jefferson Davis and Confederacy Including Diplomatic Correspondence, 1861–1865*, ed. James D. Richardson, 2 vols. (New York: Chelsea House-Robert Hector, 1966), 1:272, 443. One theory held that failed and frustrated Yankee generals sought revenge against the weak. Union officials arrested women on trumped-up charges when brave Confederate men had eluded their grasp. Left to languish in damp cells with little food, at times sharing accommodations with blacks, and subject to all manner of violations against modesty, these women came to symbolize the true extent of northern brutality. *Augusta (Ga.) Daily Chronicle and Sentinel*, May 17, 1863; *Abingdon Virginian*, January 16, 1863; *Richmond Daily Dispatch*, August 4, 1862, February 23, 1863; *War of the Rebellion: A Compilation of the Official Records of the Union and Confederate Armies* [OR], 128 vols. (Washington: Government Printing Office, 1880–1901), ser. 2, vol. 2:575–76.

7. *Official Report Relative to Conduct of Federal Troops in Western Louisiana*, 34–35, 38; *Fayetteville (N.C.) Observer*, March 17, 1862; Eliza Rhea Anderson Fain, *Sanctified Trial: The Diary of Eliza Rhea Anderson Fain, a Confederate Woman in East Tennessee*, ed. John N. Fain (Knoxville: University of Tennessee Press, 2004), 254–55; *Atlanta Daily Intelligencer*, September 12, 1863. A Georgia newspaper reported that Yankee women had made heroes of Butler and other generals whose conduct had scandalized the civilized world. The editor added that this was hardly surprising in "the land of Free-love ism, where women hold political conventions, the land of spirit rappings and supernal revelations." *Columbus (Ga.) Sun*, n.d., in *Savannah (Ga.) Daily Morning News*, February 28, 1863.

8. Lucy Breckinridge, *Lucy Breckinridge of Grove Hill: The Journal of a Virginia Girl, 1862–1864*, ed. Mary D. Robertson (Kent, Ohio: Kent State University Press, 1979), 186; Arch Frederic Blakey, Ann Smith Lainhart, and Winston Bryant Stephens Jr., eds., *Rose Cottage Chronicles: Civil War Letters of the Bryant-Stephens Families of North Florida* (Gainesville: University of Florida Press, 1998), 310; Edmund Ruffin, *The Diary of Edmund Ruffin*, ed. William K. Scarborough, 3 vols. (Baton Rouge: Louisiana State University Press, 1972–1989), 2:23; *Raleigh (N.C.) Register*, May 7, 1861; Edmondston, "*Journal of a Secesh Lady*," 298.

9. *Milledgeville (Ga.) Southern Federal Union*, June 3, 1862; *OR*, ser. 1, vol. 15:743; Robert Manson Myers, ed., *The Children of Pride: A True Story of Georgia and the Civil War* (New Haven: Yale University Press, 1972), 1127–28; Robert Milton Winter, *Civil War Women: The Diaries of Belle Strickland and Cora Harris Watson, Holly Springs, Mississippi, July 25, 1864–June 22, 1868* (Lafayette, Calif.: Thomas Berryhill Press, 2001), 35–36, 90–91; Cordelia Scales, "The Civil War Letters of Cordelia Scales," ed. Percy L. Rainwater, *Journal of Mississippi History* 1 (July 1939): 179; *Charleston Courier*, n.d., in *Savannah (Ga.) Daily Morning News*, January 24, 1862; *Milledgeville (Ga.) Confederate Union*, June 28, 1864. An account from Mississippi claimed that "two Yankee brutes" had stripped a widow and given her five hundred lashes. *Savannah (Ga.) Daily Morning News*, August 5, 1863.

10. Sam Keen, *Faces of the Enemy: Reflections of the Hostile Imagination* (San Francisco: Harper and Row, 1986), 58–60; *Richmond Daily Dispatch*, August 10, 1861.

11. Allen D. Candler, ed., *The Confederate Records of the State of Georgia*, 5 vols. (Atlanta: C. P. Byrd, 1909–11), 2:620; *Savannah (Ga.) Republican*, July 20, 1863, January 18, 1864; *Resolutions of the State of Texas, concerning peace, reconstruction, and independence* [Richmond, 1865], 3. Both state and Confederate officials sometimes gathered information on individual incidents. Zebulon Vance, *The Papers of Zebulon Baird Vance*, ed. Frontis W. Johnston and Joe A. Mobley, 2 vols. (Raleigh: North Carolina Division of Archives and History, 1963–1995), 1:392; *Richmond Enquirer*, n.d., in *Weekly Raleigh (N.C.) Register*, December 24, 1862.

12. James Mallory, *"Fear God and Walk Humbly": The Agricultural Journal of James Mallory, 1843–1877*, ed. Grady McWhiney, Warner O. Moore Jr., and Robert F. Pace (Tuscaloosa: University of Alabama Press, 1997), 288; *Southern Illustrated News*, June 27, 1863; Buck, *Shadows on My Heart*, 283; Edmondston, "*Journal of a Secesh Lady*," 587, 589–90.

13. *Shreveport (La.) Semi-Weekly News*, July 11, 1862; *Salisbury (N.C) Carolina Watchman*, August 8, 1861. A Virginia newspaper simply reported without elaboration that five "respectable females" had been raped in Hampshire County. *Fredericksburg Herald*, n.d., in *Milledgeville (Ga.) Southern Recorder*, February 25, 1862. A Virginia farmer recorded rumors of rape that he had heard from unnamed sources. Daniel W. Cobb, *Cobb's Ordeal: The Diaries of a Virginia Farmer, 1842–1872*, ed. Daniel W. Crofts (Athens: University of Georgia Press, 1997), 198.

14. *Raleigh (N.C.) Daily Register*, June 5, 1861; *Richmond Daily Enquirer*, November 2, 1862; Salisbury *(N.C.) Carolina Watchman*, November 3, 1862; *Richmond Daily Dispatch*, December 20, 1862; *Charleston Mercury*, June 17, 1864. A woman returning to Virginia from Memphis claimed she had witnessed drunken Union soldiers gang-raping a widow in the street in the middle of the day. Charles W. Turner, ed., *Civil War Letters of Arabella Speairs and William Beverley Pettit of Fluvanna County, Virginia March 1862–March 1865*, 2 vols. (Roanoke: Virginia Lithography and Graphics, 1988), 1:155.

15. Paul Quigley, *Shifting Grounds: Nationalism and the American South, 1848–1865* (New York: Oxford University Press, 2012), 185; Colin Edward Woodward, *Marching Masters: Slavery, Race, and the Confederate Army during the Civil War* (Charlottesville: University of Virginia Press, 2014), 145; St. John Richardson Liddell, *Liddell's Record*, ed. Nathaniel Cheairs Hughes Jr. (Baton Rouge: Louisiana State University Press, 1997), 191; *Edgefield (S.C.) Advertiser*, March 25, October 28, 1863.

16. *OR*, ser. 1, vol. 10, pt. 2:531, vol. 45, pt. 1:760; *Richmond Daily Dispatch*, March 21, 1864; William Fisher Plane, "Letters of William Fisher Plane, C.S.A. to His Wife," ed. S. Joseph Lewis Jr., *Georgia Historical Quarterly* 48 (June 1964): 217; John W. Cotton, *Yours Till Death: Civil War Letters of John W. Cotton*, ed. Lucille Griffith (Tuscaloosa: University of Alabama Press, 1951), 120; Wayne L. Wolf, ed., *Civil War Letters: From Macon to Missionary Ridge: The Civil War Letters of Captain S. C. and Mrs. Nannie Wilkerson* (New York: McGraw-Hill College Custom Series, 1994), 127; William Taylor Stott, *For Duty and Destiny: The Life and Civil War Diary of William Taylor Stott, Hoosier Soldier and Educator*, ed. Lloyd A. Hunter (Indianapolis: Indiana Historical Society Press, 2010), 94.

17. E. Susan Barber and Charles F. Ritter, "'Physical Abuse . . . and Rough Handling': Race, Gender, and Sexual Justice in the Occupied South," in LeeAnn Whites and Alecia P. Long, eds.,

Occupied Women: Gender, Military Occupation, and the American Civil War (Baton Rouge: Louisiana State University Press, 2009), 49–64.

18. *Richmond Daily Dispatch*, April 26, 1862; *Edgefield (S.C.) Advertiser*, June 22, 1864.

19. Thomas R. R. Cobb to his wife, November 22, 1862, Cobb Letters, Hargrett Rare Book and Manuscript Library, University of Georgia, Athens; *Raleigh (N.C.) Semi-Weekly Register*, January 18, 1862; C. Irvine Walker, *Great Things Are Expected of Us: The Letters of Colonel C. Irvine Walker, 10th South Carolina Infantry, C.S.A.*, ed. William Lee White and Charles Denny Runion (Knoxville: University of Tennessee Press, 2009), 135; George Bentley, *"Burning Rails as We Pleased": The Civil War Letters of William Garrigues Bentley, 104th Ohio Volunteer Infantry*, ed. Barbara Bentley Smith and Nine Bentley Baker (Jefferson, N.C.: McFarland, 2004), 106.

20. Keziah Brevard, *A Plantation Mistress on the Eve of the Civil War: The Diary of Keziah Goodwyn Hopkins Brevard, 1860–1861*, ed. John Hammond Moore (Columbia: University of South Carolina Press, 1993), 97; *Milledgeville (Ga.) Southern Federal Union*, April 23, 1861; *Richmond Examiner*, n.d., in *Salisbury (N.C.) Carolina Watchman*, June 22, 1863.

21. John G. Earnest, *All Right Let Them Come: The Civil War Diary of an East Tennessee Confederate*, ed. Charles Swift Northern III (Knoxville: University of Tennessee Press, 2003), 53; *Richmond Daily Dispatch*, January 5, 1864; *Religious Herald* (Richmond), February 13, 1862; Onley Andrus, *The Civil War Letters of Sergeant Onley Andrus*, ed. Fred A. Shannon (Urbana: University of Illinois Press, 1947), 131.

22. *Richmond Daily Dispatch*, January 27, 1862; *Columbia Daily South Carolinian*, May 18, 1864; *Savannah (Ga.) Daily Morning News*, September 11, 1862; *Milledgeville (Ga.) Southern Recorder*, August 23, 1864.

23. *Richmond Daily Dispatch*, August 6, 17, 1863; *Camden (S.C.) Confederate*, August 14, 1863; *Fayetteville (N.C.) Observer*, August 17, 1863; Edmondston, "*Journal of a Secesh Lady*," 452–53; Holmes, *Diary of Emma Holmes*, 296.

24. Candler, ed., *Confederate Records of Georgia*, 2:187–88; *Savannah (Ga.) Daily Morning News*, May 24, 1861; Ellen Renshaw House, *A Very Violent Rebel: The Civil War Diary of Ellen Renshaw House*, ed. Daniel E. Sutherland (Knoxville: University of Tennessee Press, 1996), 157; *Athens (Ga.) Southern Banner*, July 8, 1863.

25. *Official Report Relative to the Conduct of Federal Troops in Western Louisiana*, 43–44; Mary Jane Chadick, *Incidents of the War: The Civil War Journal of Mary Jane Chadick*, ed. Nancy M. Rohr (Huntsville, Ala.: SilverThreads Publishing, 2005), 182; *Richmond Daily Dispatch*, November 4, 1861.

26. Basil Manly, Jr. to ?, July 17, 1863, Manly Family Papers, Southern Baptist Historical Library and Archives, Nashville; *Vicksburg (Miss.) Citizen*, March 2, 1863 in *Savannah (Ga.) Morning News*, March 11, 1863.

27. *OR*, ser. 1, vol. 16:202; *Richmond Daily Dispatch*, September 6, 1861; Dulany, *In the Shadow of the Enemy*, 5; *Richmond Daily Enquirer*, November 5, 1862; Davis, *Messages and Papers*, 1:289. For a provocative and well-documented account that charges both Federal and Confederate officials with both ignoring and contributing to the horrific treatment of prisoners, see Charles W. Sanders Jr., *While in the Hands of the Enemy: Military Prisons of the Civil War* (Baton Rouge: Louisiana State University Press, 2005).

28. August 20, 1864, James Robert McMichael Diary, Special Collections, Davidson College, North Carolina; Edmondston, *"Journal of a Secesh Lady,"* 235; Holmes, *Diary of Emma Holmes*, 383–84; Grace Brown Elmore, *A Heritage of Woe: The Civil War Diary of Grace Brown Elmore, 1861–1868*, ed. Marli F. Weiner (Athens: University of Georgia Press, 1997), 78–79. Confederates claimed to have treated Yankee prisoners humanely—all too humanely, some editors suggested. They recommended putting prisoners to work to save expenses. *New Orleans Daily Picayune*, September 3, 1861; *Milledgeville (Ga.) Southern Recorder*, May 12, 1863; *Charleston Mercury*, August 7, 30, 1861; *Richmond Daily Dispatch*, November 6, 1861.

29. *Daily Richmond Examiner*, May 1, 1863; *OR*, ser. 2, vol. 6:268; *Richmond Daily Dispatch*, February 6, 1862, May 19, 1863, November 28, 1864; *Athens (Ga.) Southern Banner*, August 19, 1863. As for any delay or refusal to exchange prisoners, that simply marked another example of the Federals' murderous policies. Ruffin, *Diary of Edmund Ruffin*, 3:738–39; *Resolutions of the State of Texas*, 2; *Richmond Daily Dispatch*, April 14, 1862.

30. For examples, see *Milledgeville (Ga.) Southern Federal Union*, May 14, 1861; Edward O. Guerrant, *Bluegrass Confederate: The Headquarters Diary of Edward O. Guerrant*, ed. William C. Davis and Meredith L. Swentor (Baton Rouge: Louisiana State University Press, 1999), 271–72.

31. Sue Sparks Keitt, "Sue Sparks Keitt to a Northern Friend, March 4, 1861," ed. Elmer Don Herd Jr., *South Carolina Historical Magazine* 62 (April 1961), 85–86; *Augusta, Ga. Daily Chronicle and Sentinel*, May 3, 1861. One editor, however, maintained that even extermination would be preferable to a "life of degradation and ruin." *Staunton (Va.) Vindicator*, March 29, 1861.

32. May 5, 1861, George Anderson Mercer Diary, Southern Historical Collection, University of North Carolina; *Charleston Mercury*, December 16, 1861; *Savannah (Ga.) Republican*, September 18, 1861; Michael G. Mahon, ed., *Winchester Divided: The Civil War Diaries of Julia Chase and Laura Lee* (Mechanicsburg, Pa.: Stackpole Books, 2002), 51–52; *Southern Illustrated News*, October 11, 1862; *Salisbury (N.C.) Watchman*, November 3, 1862; *Christian Index* (Macon, Ga.), June 15, 1863; Franklin Lafayette Riley, *Grandfather's Journal: Company B, Sixteenth Mississippi Infantry Volunteers, Harris' Brigade, Mahone's Division, Hill's Corps, A.N.V., May 27, 1861–July 15, 1865*, ed. Austin C. Dobbins (Dayton, Ohio: Morningside, 1988), 213; *Athens (Ga.) Southern Watchman*, March 22, 1865; *Edgefield (S.C.) Advertiser*, March 8, 1865. In the aftermath of Gettysburg and Vicksburg, Jefferson Davis issued an appeal to soldiers that the enemy "aims at nothing less than the extermination of yourselves, your wives, and children." This document was printed repeatedly in the Confederate press. Davis, *Messages and Papers*, 1:329.

33. *Milledgeville (Ga.) Southern Recorder*, May 7, 1861; *Mobile (Ala.) Register*, August 27, 1862; *Savannah (Ga.) Daily Morning News*, November 15, 1861; Sam Richards, *Sam Richards's Civil War Diary: A Chronicle of the Atlanta Home Front*, ed. Wendy Hamand Venet (Athens: University of Georgia Press, 2009), 50; *Charleston Mercury*, July 13, 1864; *Edgefield (S.C.) Advertiser*, March 1, 1865. In the spring of 1864, Union General Alexander Hays warned that Confederate authorities were "poisoning the minds of their soldiers" by claiming the Yankees were "determined to kill all prisoners and exterminate the South." Alexander Hays, *Life and Letters of Alexander Hays, Brevet Colonel United States Army, Brigadier General and Brevet Major General United States Volunteers*, ed. George Thornton Fleming (Pittsburgh, 1919), 592.

34. *Augusta (Ga.) Daily Chronicle and Sentinel*, November 20, 1863; *Charleston Mercury*, December 29, 1864; *Atlanta Southern Confederacy*, August 22, 1862.

35. *Richmond Daily Dispatch*, November 5, 1862; Edmondston, "*Journal of a Secesh Lady*," 266; [J. Randolph Tucker], "The Great Issue: Our Relations to It," *Southern Literary Messenger* 32 (March 1861): 177.

36. *Augusta (Ga.) Daily Chronicle and Sentinel*, September 12, 1861; Frank H. Alfriend, "The Great Danger of the Confederacy," *Southern Literary Messenger* 37 (January 1863): 39–43; *Charleston Mercury*, July 29, 1862; *Richmond Daily Dispatch*, October 3, 1862; William L. Nugent, *My Dear Nellie: The Civil War Letters of William L. Nugent to Eleanor Smith Nugent*, ed. William M. Cash and Lucy Somerville Howorth (Jackson: University Press of Mississippi, 1977), 117. For a much more ambivalent statement about the possibilities and results of emancipation, see Walter W. Lenoir to his brother, July 22, 1863, Lenoir Family Papers, Southern Historical Collection, University of North Carolina.

37. A South Carolinian [pseud.], *The Confederate* (Mobile: S. H. Goetzel, 1863), 62–69; *Jackson Weekly Mississippian*, January 7, 1863; *Richmond Daily Whig*, November 22, 1862; Thomas W. MacMahon, *Cause and Contrast: An Essay on the American Crisis* (Richmond: West and Johnson, 1862), 64–65; *Richmond Daily Dispatch*, July 29, 1864; January 8, 1863, Nancy Emerson Diary, Albert and Shirley Small Special Collections Library, University of Virginia; (Atlanta) *Gate-City Guardian*, February 23, 1861.

38. William Henry Holcombe, "The Alternative: A Separate Destiny, or the Africanization of the South," *Southern Literary Messenger* 32 (February 1861): 84; Candler, ed., *Confederate Records of Georgia*, 2:118–25; George Fitzhugh, "Thoughts Suggested by the War—the Past and the Future," *DeBow's Review* 31 (September 1861): 302; George Fitzhugh, "The Revolutions of 1776 and 1861 Contrasted," *Southern Literary Messenger* 37 (November and December 1863): 725; John M. Daniel, *The Richmond Examiner during the War* (New York: printed for the author, 1868), 17–18; Henry Champlin Lay, "The Devout Soldier Preached by request to the Powhatan Troop at Emmanuel Church, March 6th, 1864," Lay Sermons, Southern Historical Collection, University of North Carolina.

39. Stephen Elliott, *God's Presence with the Confederate States: A Sermon Preached in the Christ Church, Savannah, on . . . a Day of Solemn Humiliation, Fasting and Prayer* (Savannah, Ga.: W. Thorn Williams, 1861), 21; Davis, *Messages and Papers*, 1:290. See also [James A. Duncan], *Address to Christians throughout the World* [Richmond, 1863].

40. Blakey, Lainhart, and Stephens, eds., *Rose Cottage Chronicles*, 163; Edmondston, "*Journal of a Secesh Lady*," 115; M. Jane Johansson, ed., *Widows by the Thousand: The Civil War Letters of Theophilus and Harriet Perry, 1862–1864* (Fayetteville: University of Arkansas Press, 2000), 83–84.

41. Shepherd Maugen, Alabama, James Gill, Arkansas, J. H. Day, Texas, Mittie Freeman, Arkansas, *Slave Narratives* CD-ROM (Orem, Utah: MyFamily.com, 2000). At the end of World War II, Japanese schoolchildren seemed similarly disappointed that American troops did not have horns. Haruko Taya Cook and Theodore F. Cook, *Japan at War: An Oral History* (New York: New Press, 1992), 469.

42. John W. Blassingame, ed., *Slave Testimony: Two Centuries of Letters, Speeches, Interviews, and Autobiographies* (Baton Rouge: Louisiana State University Press, 1977), 456; Robert Grand-

champ, ed., *From Providence to Fort Hell: Letters from Company K, Seventh Rhode Island Volunteers* (Westminster, Md.: Heritage Books, 2008), 52; Andrew Boone, North Carolina, Annie Davis, Alabama, Hannah Cresson, North Carolina, *Slave Narratives* CD-ROM (Orem, Utah: MyFamily .com, 2000).

43. Walter Clark, *The Papers of Walter Clark*, ed. Aubrey Lee Brooks and Hugh Talmage Lefler, 2 vols. (Chapel Hill: University of North Carolina Press, 1948), 1:135; Bell Irvin Wiley, *Southern Negroes, 1861–1865* (New Haven: Yale University Press, 1938), 12–14; Warren Akin, *Letters of Warren Akin: Confederate Congressman*, ed. Bell Irvin Wiley (Athens: University of Georgia Press, 1959), 21; *Charleston Mercury*, December 23, 1862; Bettie Alexander to her sister, August 24, 1861, Alexander Papers, Rubenstein Rare Book and Manuscript Library, Duke University; Edward Pierce, "The Contrabands at Fortress Monroe," *Atlantic Monthly* 7 (November, 1861), 638–39; *National Anti-slavery Standard*, September 28, 1861; Allan Pinkerton to George B. McClellan, January 7, 1862, McClellan Papers, Library of Congress; Walter J. Eames to his wife, May 12, 1862, Eames Papers, Murray J. Smith Collection, United States Army Military History Institute, Carlisle, Pennsylvania; May 20, 1862, John Berry Diary, *Civil War Times Illustrated* Collection, United Army Military History Institute, Carlisle, Pennsylvania. Glenn Brasher generously shared some valuable research notes about rumors of the Federals sending emancipated slaves to Cuba.

44. Anna Hasell Thomas, "The Diary of Anna Hasell Thomas (July 1864–May 1865)," *South Carolina Historical Magazine* 74 (July 1973), 137; *OR*, ser. 1, vol. 52, pt. 2:332; *Official Report Relative to Conduct of Federal Troops in Western Louisiana*, 47–48; Candler, ed., *Confederate Records of Georgia*, 2:620.

45. *Official Report Relative to Conduct of Federal Troops in Western Louisiana*, 11, 51–52; Chadick, *Incidents of the War*, 111; Davis, *Messages and Papers*, 1:380.

46. *Savannah (Ga.) Republican*, November 12, 1861; Buck, *Shadows on My Heart*, 186; Edmondston, "*Journal of a Secesh Lady*," 424; *Southern Illustrated News*, June 27, 1863; *Salisbury (N.C.) Carolina Watchman*, March 16, 1863.

47. *Columbia Daily South Carolinian*, February 17, 1863, (Macon) *Georgia Weekly Telegraph*, August 15, 1862; *Savannah (Ga.) Daily Morning News*, June 17, 1861; June 8, 1861, Mary Ezell Diary, in Edward Conigland Papers, Southern Historical Collection, University of North Carolina; Fain, *Sanctified Trial*, 258.

48. Marion Hill Fitzpatrick, *Letters to Amanda: The Civil War Letters of Marion Hill Fitzpatrick, Army of Northern Virginia*, ed. Jeffrey C. Lowe and Sam Hodges (Macon, Ga.: Mercer University Press, 1998), 166; Fain, *Sanctified Trial*, 113; April 26, 1862, Mary C. A. Stribling Diary, Library of Virginia; *Official Report Relative to Conduct of Federal Troops in Western Louisiana*, 47; *Savannah (Ga.) Daily Morning News*, March 23, 1863.

49. January 31, 1861, Susan Cornwall Diary, Southern Historical Collection, University of North Carolina; Henry Champlin Lay, "The Devout Soldier"; *Charleston Mercury*, March 1, 1864; James Henley Thornwell, *Our Danger and Our Duty* (Columbia, S.C.: Southern Guardian Press, 1862), 3. See also Myers, ed., *Children of Pride*, 1244.

50. Edmondston, "*Journal of a Secesh Lady*," 340–41; MacMahon, *Cause and Contrast*, 144; *Jackson Weekly Mississippian*, January 7, 1863; January 1, 1863, Harriet Ellen Moore Diary, Southern

Historical Collection, University of North Carolina. This last misleading statement expresses one of the standard myths about the Emancipation Proclamation, one that echoes among neo-Confederates into our own time.

51. James C. Bates, *A Texas Cavalry Officer's Civil War: The Diary and Letters of James C. Bates*, ed. Richard Lowe (Baton Rouge: Louisiana State University, 1999), 133–34; *OR*, ser. 4, vol. 3:133; *Staunton (Va.) Spectator*, October 7, 1862; *Augusta (Ga.) Daily Chronicle and Sentinel*, February 15, 1863; *Message of the Governor of Florida . . . November 17, 1862* [Tallahassee, 1862], 3. Various wartime songs and poems were replete with the images of violence, blood, and death connected with abolition. H. M. Wharton, *War Songs and Poems of the Southern Confederacy* (Philadelphia: American Book and Bible House, 1904), 55, 102; Frank Moore, ed., *Songs and Ballads of the Southern People* (New York: Appleton, 1886), 167.

52. Holmes, *Diary of Emma Holmes*, 202–3; *Journal of the Congress of the Confederate States of America, 1861–1865*, 7 vols. (Washington: Government Printing Office, 1904), 5:469, 544–47; *Southern Historical Society Papers* 47 (1930), 7–8; *Jacksonville (Ala.) Republican*, April 9, 1863; October 1, 1862, Joseph Addison Waddell Diary, Albert and Shirley Small Special Collections Library, University of Virginia; *Jackson Weekly Mississippian*, January 7, 1863; *Milledgeville (Ga.) Confederate Union*, October 7, 1862; Kate Stone, *Brokenburn: The Journal of Kate Stone, 1861–1868*, ed. John Q. Anderson (Baton Rouge: Louisiana State University Press, 1955), 146. See also [Charles Henry Smith], *Bill Arp's Peace Papers: Columns on War and Reconstruction* (Columbia: University of South Carolina Press, 2009), 27–28.

53. *Southern Illustrated News*, May 23, 1863; Milledgeville *(Ga.) Southern Recorder*, February 23, 1864; House, *A Very Violent Rebel*, 22; *Richmond Daily Dispatch*, August 2, 1864.

54. *Richmond Daily Dispatch*, July 28, 1864; Griffin Frost, *Camp and Prison Journal* (Iowa City, Iowa: Camp Pope Book Shop, 1994), 143–44; April 6, 1862, Kate S. Sperry Diary, Library of Virginia; June 21, July 2, 1862, Ann Wilkinson Penrose Diary, Louisiana and Lower Mississippi Valley Collection, Louisiana State University. For an admission that considerable racial amalgamation had already taken place because white men preyed on black women and then enslaved their own offspring, see Fain, *Sanctified Trial*, 88. For a contrasting attempt to argue that true racial amalgamation was impossible because mulattoes were weak and could not long survive, see [Tucker], "The Great Issue," 163.

55. Forrest G. Wood, *Black Scare: The Racist Response to Emancipation and Reconstruction* (Berkeley: University of California Press, 1968), 53–57; David G. Croly, *Miscegenation: The Theory of the Blending of the Races, Applied to the American White Man and Negro* (New York: H. Dexter, Hamilton, 1864), i, 8–9, 18–19, 40–41, 43. The pamphlet also warmly endorsed the enlistment of black soldiers and the confiscation of Rebel land, even suggesting that black men should rule the southern states. Croly, *Miscegenation*, 45–46, 52, 57.

56. Edmund DeWitt Patterson, *Yankee Rebel: The Civil War Journal of Edmund DeWitt Patterson*, ed. John G. Barrett (Knoxville: University of Tennessee Press, 2004), 172; Edmondston, "*Journal of a Secesh Lady*," 552; *Edgefield (S.C.) Advertiser*, April 21, 1864; Holmes, *Diary of Emma Holmes*, 362; Turner, ed., *Civil War Letters of Speairs and Pettit*, 2:17; *Richmond Daily Dispatch*, March 30–31, 1864. This whole controversy served to remind one Confederate soldier what he was fighting for. Cate, ed., *Two Soldiers*, 70.

57. *Richmond Daily Dispatch*, April 13, 1864; Holcombe, "The Alternative," 85; Jones, ed., *Children of Pride*, 1247; Cornelia Peake McDonald, *A Woman's Civil War: A Diary, with Reminiscences of the War, from March 1862*, ed. Minrose C. Gwin (Madison: University of Wisconsin Press, 1992), 123; Edmondston, "*Journal of a Secesh Lady*," 486.

58. *OR*, ser. 1, vol. 7:801–2; George H. Reese, ed., *Proceedings of the Virginia State Convention of 1861*, 4 vols. (Richmond: Virginia State Library, 1965), 1:66; *Athens (Ga.) Southern Watchman*, March 1, 1865.

59. "M" to Lise Mitchell, February 27, 1863, Mitchell Papers, Special Collections, Tulane University; *Milledgeville (Ga.) Southern Federal Union*, March 18, 1862; Robert Garlick Hill Kean, *Inside the Confederate Government: The Diary of Robert Garlick Hill Kean*, ed. Edward Younger (New York: Oxford University Press, 1957), 92; *Charleston Mercury*, May 3, 1864; William R. Stilwell, *The Stilwell Letters: A Georgian in Longstreet's Corps, Army of Northern Virginia*, ed. Ronald H. Moseley (Macon, Ga.: Mercer University Press, 2002), 109; *Richmond Daily Dispatch*, October 13, 1862; Jane Howison Beale, *The Journal of Jane Howison Beale, Fredericksburg, Virginia, 1850–1862* (Fredericksburg, Va.: Historic Fredericksburg Foundation, 1995), 100; James Rumley, *The Southern Mind under Union Rule: The Diary of James Rumley, Beaufort, North Carolina, 1862–1865*, ed. Judkin Browning (Gainesville: University Press of Florida, 2009), 70–71.

60. Ella Gertrude Clanton Thomas, *The Secret Eye: The Journal of Ella Gertrude Clanton Thomas, 1848–1889*, ed. Virginia Ingraham Burr (Chapel Hill: University of North Carolina Press, 1990), 70–71; Rumley, *Southern Mind under Union Rule*, 71; Davis, *Messages and Papers*, 1:233; *Atlanta Southern Confederacy*, February 13, 1863; *OR*, ser. 1, vol. 13:727.

61. *Salisbury (N.C.) Carolina Watchman*, August 4, 1862; *Richmond Enquirer*, December 18, 1863; William Edward Wiatt, *Confederate Chaplain William Edward Wiatt: An Annotated Diary*, ed. Alex L. Wiatt (Lynchburg, Va.: H. E. Howard, 1994), 142; *Atlanta Southern Confederacy*, June 11, 1863; *Charleston Mercury*, April 29, 1864; Edmondston, "*Journal of a Secesh Lady*," 549; [Richard W. Corbin], *Letters of a Confederate Officer to His Family in Europe, During the Last Year of the War of Secession* (Baltimore: Butternut and Blue, 1993), 66.

62. Blakey, Lainhart, and Stephens, eds., *Rose Cottage Chronicles*, 264; *Augusta (Ga.) Daily Chronicle of Sentinel*, November 20, 1863.

63. Rumley, *Southern Mind under Union Rule*, 82–83; Buck, *Shadows on My Heart*, 61–62; Mahon, ed., *Winchester Divided*, 138–39.

64. Burton Warfield, *Letters to Anna: The Civil War Through the Eyes and Heart of a Soldier*, ed. James R. Knight (Nashville, Tenn.: Cold Tree Press, 2007), 143; Susan M. Kollock, ed., "Letters of the Kollock and Allied Families, 1826–1884," *Georgia Historical Quarterly* 34 (September 1950): 249–50; Edmondston, "*Journal of a Secesh Lady*," 357.

65. Stone, *Brokenburn*, 297–98; McDonald, *A Woman's Civil War*, 138; *Savannah (Ga.) Daily Morning News*, June 16, 1863; *OR*, ser. 1, vol. 40, pt. 2:704–5; Emma LeConte, *When the World Ended: The Diary of Emma LeConte*, ed. Earl Schenck Miers (New York: Oxford University Press, 1957), 80–81.

66. Blakey, Lainhart, and Stephens, eds., *Rose Cottage Chronicles*, 214; *Savannah (Ga.) Republican*, August 7, 1863; Henry Higginbotham to his brother, October 7, 1863, Dore Schary Collection, New York Public Library; *Richmond Enquirer*, December 18, 1863; Patterson, *Yankee Rebel*,

128; William Alexander Graham, *Papers of William Alexander Graham*, ed. Max R. Williams, et al., 8 vols. (Raleigh: North Carolina Office of Archives and History, 1957–), 6:42–43; *Milledgeville (Ga.) Southern Recorder*, May 26, 1863; *Staunton (Va.) Spectator*, June 23, 1863. For Confederates, this whole question of retaliation in response to the enemy's use of African American soldiers was not always as easy a question as some claimed. For example, the Georgia editor quoted in the above paragraph expressed some uncertainty about what exactly to do with former slaves captured in Federal uniforms, believed that northern free blacks had to be exchanged like any other prisoners, and claimed to take some pity on black men who had been "duped" by the Yankees. *Savannah (Ga.) Republican*, August 7, 1863.

67. Josiah Gorgas, *The Journals of Josiah Gorgas, 1857–1878*, ed. Sarah Woolfolk Wiggins (Tuscaloosa: University of Alabama Press, 1995), 120; *OR*, ser. 2, vol. 4:945–46, 954; Ira Berlin, ed., *Freedom: A Documentary History of Emancipation, Series II: The Black Military Experience* (Cambridge: Cambridge University Press, 1982), 570–71; Holmes, *Diary of Emma Holmes*, 281–82; Bates, *Texas Cavalry Officer's Civil War*, 270. For a broad and useful look at Confederate perspectives on black troops, see George S. Burkhardt, *Confederate Rage, Yankee Wrath: No Quarter in the Civil War* (Carbondale: Southern Illinois University Press, 2007), 27–42. For a fuller discussion of retaliation against black troops, see Chapter 5 below.

5. HATRED AND VENGEANCE

1. Eliza Frances Andrews, *The War-Time Journal of a Georgia Girl, 1864–1865*, ed. Spencer Bidwell King Jr. (Macon, Ga.: Ardivan Press, 1960), 67; David Livingstone Smith, *Less than Human: Why We Demean, Enslave, and Exterminate Others* (New York: St. Martin's Press, 2011), 86–102. Ironically, Andrews's father was a strong Unionist. For an important discussion of hatred on both sides, see Caroline E. Janney, *Remembering the Civil War: Reunion and the Limits of Reconciliation* (Chapel Hill: University of North Carolina Press, 2013), 19–34.

2. *Albany (Ga.) Patriot*, August 29, 1861; *Atlanta Southern Confederacy*, May 19, 1863; Kate Cumming, *Kate: The Journal of a Confederate Nurse*, ed. Richard Barksdale Harwell (Baton Rouge: Louisiana State University Press, 1959), 34; John Washington Inzer, *The Diary of a Confederate Soldier: John Washington Inzer, 1834–1928*, ed. Mattie Lou Teague Crow (Huntsville, Ala.: Strode Publishers, 1977), 78.

3. Sarah Morgan, *The Civil War Diary of Sarah Morgan*, ed. Charles East (Athens: University of Georgia Press, 1991), 67; Emilie Riley McKinley, *From the Pen of a She-Rebel: The Civil War Diary of Emilie Riley McKinley*, ed. Gordon A. Cotton (Columbia: University of South Carolina Press, 2001), 47; Cumming, *Kate: Journal of a Confederate Nurse*, 67; Emma LeConte, *When the World Ended: The Diary of Emma LeConte, ed.* Earl Schenck Miers (New York: Oxford University Press, 1957), 41–42; *Charleston Courier, Tri-Weekly*, January 20, 1863; March 16, 18, 1862, Kate S. Sperry Diary, Library of Virginia; March 20, 1862, Alice Ready Diary, Southern Historical Collection, University of North Carolina. Of course, any captured flags (and regimental banners too) became much valued trophies of war. *Southern Illustrated News*, October 4, 1862.

4. Inzer, *Diary of a Confederate Soldier*, 65.

5. Benjamin Morgan Palmer, *A Discourse Before the General Assembly of South Carolina, on December 10, 1863, Appointed by the Legislature as a Day, Fasting, Humiliation, and Prayer* (Columbia, S.C.: Charles P. Pelham, 1864), 18–19; Robert J. and Karin Sternberg, *The Nature of Hate* (Cambridge: Cambridge University Press, 2008), 95–98; *War of the Rebellion: A Compilation of the Official Records of the Union and Confederate Armies* [OR], 128 vols. (Washington: Government Printing Office, 1880–1901), ser. 1, vol. 31, pt. 3:858; *Savannah (Ga.) Republican*, November 23, 1861; James W. Silver, *Confederate Morale and Church Propaganda* (Tuscaloosa, Ala.: Confederate Publishing, 1957), 85–87; G. Ward Hubbs, ed., *Voices from Company D: Diaries by the Greensboro Guards, Fifth Alabama Infantry Regiment, Army of Northern Virginia* (Athens: University of Georgia Press, 2003), 243. By the same token, a writer in the *Southern Illustrated News* claimed that venomous hatred could not harm "the good, the true and the faithful." *Southern Illustrated News*, September 10, 1864.

6. Eliza Rhea Anderson Fain, *Sanctified Trial: The Diary of Eliza Rhea Anderson Fain, a Confederate Woman in East Tennessee*, ed. John N. Fain (Knoxville: University of Tennessee Press, 2004), 8–9, 156; December 1, 1864, Myra Smith Diary, Eunice Stockwell Papers, Mississippi Department of Archives and History, Jackson, Mississippi.

7. May 1, 1862, Mary C. A. Stribling Diary, Library of Virginia, Richmond; May ? to Betty Stuart, June 6, 1863, John B. S. Dimitry Papers, Rubenstein Rare Book and Manuscript Library, Duke University; Robert Taylor Scott to his wife, December 31, 1862, Keith Family Papers, Virginia Historical Society, Richmond.

8. Catherine Ann Devereux Edmondston, *"Journal of a Secesh Lady": The Diary of Catherine Ann Devereux Edmondston, 1860–1866*, ed. Beth G. Crabtree and James W. Patton (Raleigh, N.C.: Division of Archives and History, 1979), 570; Andrews, *Journal of a Georgia Girl*, 148–49. For similar remarks about the divine will in regard to hating Yankees, see Margaret Ann Vogtsberger, ed., *The Dulanys of Welbourne: A Family in Mosby's Confederacy* (Berryville, Va.: Rockbridge Publishing, 1995), 164–65.

9. April 21, 1862, Alice Ready Diary, Southern Historical Collection, University of North Carolina; *Christian Index* (Macon, Ga.), July 29, 1862; Mills Lane, ed., *"Dear Mother: Don't grieve about me. If I get killed, I'll only be dead," Letters from Georgia Soldiers in the Civil War* (Savannah, Ga.: Beehive Press, 1990), 333–34; Bell Irvin Wiley, *The Life of Johnny Reb: The Common Soldiers of the Confederacy* (Indianapolis: Bobbs-Merrill, 1943), 308–9.

10. Walter Herron Taylor, *Lee's Adjutant: The Wartime Letters of Colonel Walter Herron Taylor, 1862–1865*, ed. R. Lockwood Tower (Columbia: University of South Carolina Press, 1995), 137–38; April 1, 1862, Kate S. Sperry Diary, Library of Virginia; Morgan, *Civil War Diary of Sarah Morgan*, 73, 122–23.

11. There was also speculation (and no little wishful thinking) that in the northwestern states, feelings of hatred against genuine New England Yankees would reach a boiling point and even spark another secession movement. *Clark County (Ala.) Journal*, January 20, 1863; *Greensboro (Ala.) Beacon*, January 20, 1863. Thanks to Chris McIlwaine for kindly sharing articles from these and other Alabama newspapers.

12. *Vicksburg Citizen*, n.d., in *Athens (Ga.) Southern Banner*, February 4, 1863; John Samuel Apperson, *Repairing the "March of Mars": The Civil War Diaries of John Samuel Apperson, Hospital*

Steward in the Stonewall Brigade, 1861–1865, ed. John D. Roper (Macon, Ga.: Mercer University Press, 2001), 326–27; *Richmond Daily Enquirer*, December 22, 1862; Sternberg and Sternberg, *Nature of Hate*, 78, 83–95; *Charleston Mercury*, January 29, 1864.

13. James M. McPherson, *What They Fought For, 1861–1865* (Baton Rouge, Louisiana State University Press, 1994), 21. A Union army chaplain claimed that Confederates sought to "intensify the malignancy of the Southern feeling," in part at least, through labeling their enemies, "White-livered scoundrels—Nigger-stealer—fanatical abolitionists—black republicans—robbers—murderers–thieves—plunderers—incendiaries—hypocritical puritans—grovelling Yankees—cowardly cutthroats," and similar "elegancies of billingsgate." Francis Springer, *The Preacher's Tale: The Civil War Journal of Rev. Francis Springer, Chaplain, U.S. Army of the Frontier*, ed. William Furry (Fayetteville: University of Arkansas Press, 2001), 78.

14. Lesley J. Gordon, "Courting Nationalism: The Wartime Letters of Bobbie Mitchell and Nettie Fondren," in Lesley J. Gordon and John C. Inscoe, eds., *Inside the Confederate Nation: Essays in Honor of Emory M. Thomas* (Baton Rouge: Louisiana State University Press, 2005), 195; Ella Gertrude Clanton Thomas, *The Secret Eye: The Journal of Ella Gertrude Clanton Thomas, 1848–1889*, ed. Virginia Ingraham Burr (Chapel Hill: University of North Carolina Press, 1990), 200; Ellen Renshaw House, *A Very Violent Rebel: The Civil War Diary of Ellen Renshaw House*, ed. Daniel E. Sutherland (Knoxville: University of Tennessee Press, 1996), 37; Kenneth W. Noe, *Reluctant Rebels: The Confederate Who Joined the Army after 1861* (Chapel Hill: University of North Carolina Press, 2010), 94–96; *Charleston Mercury*, November 21, 1863; *Milledgeville (Ga.) Southern Recorder*, January 3, 1865.

15. Inzer, *Diary of a Confederate Soldier*, 68; House, *A Very Violent Rebel*, 54–55; Randall C. Jimerson, *The Private Civil War: Popular Thought during the Sectional Conflict* (Baton Rouge: Louisiana State University Press, 1988), 178; Edmondston, "*Journal of a Secesh Lady*," 473; Thomas, *Secret Eye*, 207; Noe, *Reluctant Rebels*, 94; *Charleston Mercury*, February 4, 1862. For hatred as propaganda technique, see Sternberg and Sternberg, *Nature of Hate*, 101–2.

16. Louis P. Towles, ed., *A World Turned Upside Down: The Palmers of South Santee, 1818–1881* (Columbia: University of South Carolina Press, 1996), 317; Nannie Cage to Cornelia Steward, April n.d., 1864, Albert A. Batchelor Papers, Louisiana and Lower Mississippi Valley Collection, Louisiana State University; Wiley, *Life of Johnny Reb*, 309; [William Naylor McDonald], *The Two Rebellions; or, Treason Unmasked. By a Virginian* (Richmond: Smith, Bayley, 1865), 77–78; Betsy Swint Underwood, "War Seen Through a Teenager's Eyes." *Tennessee Historical Quarterly* 20 (June 1961): 181; W. C. Corsan, *Two Months in the Confederate States: An Englishman's Travels Through the South*, ed. Benjamin H. Trask (Baton Rouge: Louisiana State University Press, 1996), 16.

17. *Vicksburg Citizen*, n.d., in *Athens (Ga.) Southern Banner*, February 4, 1863; *Charleston Mercury*, November 16, 1864; John Preston Sheffey, *Soldier of Southwestern Virginia: The Civil War Letters of Captain John Preston Sheffey*, ed. James I. Robertson Jr. (Baton Rouge: Louisiana State University Press, 2004), 15; Paul Quigley, *Shifting Grounds: Nationalism and the American South, 1848–1865* (New York: Oxford University Press, 2012), 172; Lisa Tendrich Frank, "Bedrooms as Battlefields: The Role of Gender Politics in Sherman's March," in LeeAnn Whites and Alecia P. Long, eds., *Occupied Women: Gender, Military Occupation, and the American Civil War* (Baton Rouge: Louisiana State University Press, 2009), 46; March 15, 1862, Kate S. Sperry Diary; Bradley R.

Clampitt, *The Confederate Heartland: Military and Civilian Morale in the Western Confederacy* (Baton Rouge: Louisiana State University Press, 2011), 82–83. A Charleston minister wished that every Yankee "would drop dead" upon touching southern soil but refused to "pursue them beyond the grave." *Countryman* (Turnwold, Ga.), September 29, 1862.

18. September 18, 1862, Sarah Lois Wadley Diary, Southern Historical Collection, University of North Carolina; Morgan, *Civil War Diary of Sarah Morgan*, 65; "Cousin Ella" to Jesse H. H. Person, December 16, 1861, Presley Person Papers, Rubenstein Rare Book and Manuscript Library, Duke University; Edmondston, "*Journal of a Secesh Lady*," 570; Louise Wigfall to her mother, May 29, 1862, Louis T. Wigfall Papers, Library of Congress; April 8, 1862, Alice Ready Diary.

19. *Milledgeville (Ga.) Daily Federal Union*, November 14, 1861; Frances M. Clarke, *War Stories: Suffering and Sacrifice in the Civil War North* (Chicago: University of Chicago Press, 2011), 63; McPherson, *What They Fought For, 1861–1865*, 23–24; Phoebe Yates Pember, *A Southern Woman's Story: Life in Confederate Richmond*, ed. Bell Irvin Wiley (Jackson, Tenn.: McCowat-Mercer Press, 1959), 168; John W. Dower, *War without Mercy: Race and Power in the Pacific War* (New York: Pantheon Books, 1986), 64–66; Paul Fussell, *Wartime: Understanding and Behavior in the Second World War* (New York: Oxford University Press, 1989), 116–18; Taylor and Catharine Peirce, *Dear Catharine, Dear Taylor: The Civil War Letters of a Union Soldier and His Wife*, ed. Richard L. Kiper (Lawrence: University Press of Kansas, 2002), 384–85. There was even some seemingly jocular talk about skinning or scalping Yankees. Felix Grundy Sadler, Texas; General Lee Ballard, Alabama, *Slave Narratives* CD-ROM (Orem, Utah: MyFamily.com, 2000). For a thoughtful discussion of the significance of race, the scientific importance of the human skull, and the Civil War, see Simon Harrison, "Bones in the Rebel Lady's Boudoir: Ethnology, Race and Trophy-Hunting in the American Civil War," *Journal of Material Culture* 15 (2010): 385–401.

20. For northern reports and reactions, including accounts of bodies with severed heads and grave-robbing, see *Report of the Joint Committee on the Conduct of the War* (8 vols.; Wilmington, N.C.: Broadfoot, 1998–2000), 3:456, 458–61, 466–72, 474–77; James B. Thomas, *The Civil War Letters of First Lieutenant James B. Thomas Adjutant, 107th Pennsylvania Volunteers*, ed. Mary Warner Thomas and Richard A. Sauers (Baltimore: Butternut and Blue, 1995), 36–38.

21. *Salisbury (N.C.) Carolina Watchman*, October 14, 1861; Joseph T. Glatthaar, *General Lee's Army: From Victory to Collapse* (New York: Free Press, 2008), 61–62; Isabell Middleton Leland, "Middleton Correspondence, 1861–1865," *South Carolina Historical Magazine* 63 (April 1962), 61–62; William Clark Corson, *My Dear Jennie: A Collection of Love Letters from a Confederate Soldier to His Fiancée During the Period 1861–1865*, ed. Blake W. Corson Jr. (Richmond, Va.: Dietz Press, 1982), 80.

22. *Richmond Daily Dispatch*, May 20, December 24, 1862, June 3, 1864; July 6, 1864, Joseph Addison Waddell Diary, Albert and Shirley Small Special Collections Library, University of Virginia; Ella Washington, "'An Army of Devils': The Diary of Ella Washington," ed. James O. Hall, *Civil War Times Illustrated* 16 (February 1978), 20; Benjamin Morgan Palmer, *A Discourse Before the General Assembly of South Carolina*, 21, 23; August 4, 1862, Fannie Page Hume Diary, Library of Congress; Robert Manson Myers, ed., *The Children of Pride: A True Story of Georgia and the Civil War* (New Haven: Yale University Press, 1972), 922; Moses D. Hoge to Robert Lewis Dabney,

March 17, 1862, Dabney Papers, Union Theological Seminary, Richmond. Confederates added that many Yankees—including church leaders and prominent divines—called for the most bloodcurdling vengeance on southerners. *Southern Illustrated News*, October 25, 1862.

23. *Charleston Mercury*, June 22, 1861; *Salisbury (N.C.) Carolina Watchman*, July 4, 1861; William L. Nugent, *My Dear Nellie: The Civil War Letters of William L. Nugent to Eleanor Smith Nugent*, ed. William M. Cash and Lucy Somerville Howorth (Jackson: University Press of Mississippi, 1977), 74; *Raleigh (N.C.) Weekly Register*, July 16, 1862; *Savannah (Ga.) Republican*, August 11, 1862; *Savannah (Ga.) Daily Morning News*, June 6, 1863; *Richmond Daily Dispatch*, July 5, 1862; *Milledgeville (Ga.) Southern Recorder*, July 21, 1863; *Knoxville Register*, n.d., in *Jackson Daily Mississippian*, May 9, 1863; *Macon Confederate*, n.d., in *Milledgeville (Ga.) Confederate Union*, January 5, 1864; *Staunton (Va.) Vindicator*, October 21, 1864.

24. William Cowper Nelson, *The Hour of Our Nation's Agony: The Civil War Letters of Lt. William Cowper Nelson*, ed. Jennifer W. Ford (Knoxville: University of Tennessee Press, 2007), 118; Jason Phillips, *Diehard Rebels: The Confederate Culture of Invincibility* (Athens: University of Georgia Press, 2007), 61; "Letters from Sumter," *Southern Historical Society Papers* 12 (June 1884): 257; T. H. Galloway, ed., *Dear Old Roswell: Civil War Letters of the King Family of Roswell, Georgia* (Macon, Ga.: Mercer University Press, 2003), 80; December 16, 1862, Osmun Latrobe Diary, Virginia Historical Society, Richmond; *Edgefield (S.C.) Advertiser*, November 9, 1864. Revenge against the enemy also became a theme in popular culture. For examples from a poem and a play, see "Morgan's Men," *Abingdon Virginian*, April 1, 1864; James Dabney McCabe, *The Guerrillas: An Original Domestic Drama, in Three Acts* (Richmond: West and Johnston, 1863), 19.

25. Fain, *Sanctified Trial*, 23; *Athens (Ga.) Southern Watchman*, April 2, 1862; Taylor, *Lee's Adjutant*, 138; Martha Jane Crossley, "A Patriotic Confederate Woman's War Diary, 1862–3," ed. H. E. Sterkx, *Alabama Historical Quarterly* 20 (Winter 1958): 615; Ida Powell Dulany, *In the Shadow of the Enemy: The Civil War Journal of Ida Powell Dulany*, ed. Mary L. Mackall, Stevan F. Meserve, and Anne Mackall Sasscer (Knoxville: University of Tennessee Press, 2009), 87; *Fayetteville (N.C.) Observer*, May 13, 1861; *Religious Herald* (Richmond), June 6, 1861. For a thoughtful discussion of vengeance and retaliation by one Virginia family, see Vogtsberger, ed., *Dulanys of Welbourne*, 164–65, 182–83, 188–89.

26. *Savannah (Ga.) Republican*, June 22, 1863; *Charleston Mercury*, July 18, 1862; *Charleston Courier, Tri-Weekly*, August 9, 1862; *Savannah (Ga.) Daily Morning News*, February 8, 1862; *Camden (S.C.) Confederate*, August 22, 1862; *Milledgeville (Ga.) Southern Federal Union*, May 27, 1862; Burton Warfield, *Letters to Anna: The Civil War Through the Eyes and Heart of a Soldier*, ed. James R. Knight (Nashville, Tenn.: Cold Tree Press, 2007), 59; *Staunton (Va.) Vindicator*, October 21, 1864; Arthur N. Skinner and James L. Skinner, eds., *The Death of a Confederate: Selections from the Letters of the Archibald Smith Family of Roswell, Georgia, 1864–1956* (Athens: University of Georgia Press, 1996), 123–24. There was even talk of matching the Yankees in a war of extermination. *Savannah (Ga.) Republican*, May 12, 1863.

27. *Milledgeville (Ga.) Southern Federal Union*, August 5, 1862; [Richard W. Corbin], *Letters of a Confederate Officer to His Family in Europe, During the Last Year of the War of Secession* (Baltimore: Butternut and Blue, 1993), 38–39; *Columbia Daily South Carolinian*, November 4, 1864; *Richmond Daily Dispatch*, May 10, 1864.

28. E. A. Pollard, *The Rival Administrations: Richmond and Washington in December, 1863* (Richmond: published for the author, 1864), 21, 27–28; *Charleston Mercury*, October 21, December 6, 1862, May 22, 1863; *Richmond Daily Dispatch*, August 6, 1862; *Mobile (Ala.) Daily Tribune*, March 16, 1864; *Knoxville (Tenn.) Register*, August 16, 1862, in *Milledgeville (Ga.) Southern Federal Union*, August 26, 1862; Edmund Ruffin, *The Diary of Edmund Ruffin*, ed. William K. Scarborough, 3 vols. (Baton Rouge: Louisiana State University Press, 1972–1989), 3:27–28.

29. *Richmond Daily Dispatch*, July 12, 1861, June 24, 1863; *Jackson Weekly Mississippian*, August 21, 1861 (Macon) *Georgia Weekly Telegraph*, August 8, 1862; *Charleston Courier, Tri-Weekly*, August 23, 1862; *Charleston Mercury*, November 24, 1862; Edmondston, "Journal of a Secesh Lady," 218; Robert Garlick Hill Kean, *Inside the Confederate Government: The Diary of Robert Garlick Hill Kean*, ed. Edward Younger (New York: Oxford University Press, 1957), 53; *Savannah (Ga.) Daily Morning News*, January 5, 1863; *Athens (Ga.) Southern Watchman*, August 27, 1862; July 30, 1862, Joseph Addison Waddell Diary. By painting themselves as innocent victims of enemy atrocities, Confederates could readily defend bloody retaliation and revenge. Joshua Searle-White, *Psychology of Nationalism* (New York: Palgrave, 2001), 95.

30. *Athens (Ga.) Southern Watchman*, August 27, 1862; *Charleston Mercury*, March 11, 1864; Josiah Gorgas, *The Journals of Josiah Gorgas, 1857–1878*, ed. Sarah Woolfolk Wiggins (Tuscaloosa: University of Alabama Press, 1995), 120; H. M. Wharton, *War Songs and Poems of the Southern Confederacy* (Philadelphia: American Book and Bible House, 1904), 68; *Edgefield (S.C.) Advertiser*, March 8, 1865. For other calls to slay the Yankees without mercy and without a second thought, see McPherson, *What They Fought For*, 24.

31. Clara Solomon, *The Civil War Diary of Clara Solomon: Growing Up in New Orleans, 1861–1862*, ed. Elliott Ashkenazi (Baton Rouge: Louisiana State University Press, 1995), 273; Grace Brown Elmore, *A Heritage of Woe: The Civil War Diary of Grace Brown Elmore, 1861–1868*, ed. Marli F. Weiner (Athens: University of Georgia Press, 1997), 11–12; *Savannah (Ga.) Republican*, August 8, 1862; Robert G. Evans, ed., *The 16th Mississippi Infantry: Civil War Letters and Reminiscences* (Jackson: University Press of Mississippi, 2002), 98; *Southern Historical Society Papers* 47 (1930), 7–8. For a direct threat by a Confederate general to raise the black flag in retaliation for misconduct by Federal troops in the field, see *OR*, ser. 1, vol. 15:550–51.

32. *Savannah (Ga.) Daily Morning News*, November 20, 1861; *Marion (S.C.) Star*, n.d., *Savannah (Ga.) Daily Morning News*, January 18, 1862; *Savannah (Ga.) Republican*, n.d., in *Fayetteville (N.C.) Observer*, August 18, 1862; *Staunton (Va.) Spectator*, June 6, 1863; *Macon (Ga.) Daily Telegraph*, June 13, 1863.

33. Eli Pinson Landers, *In Care of Yellow River: The Complete Civil War Letters of Pvt. Eli Pinson Landers to His Mother*, ed. Elizabeth Whitley Robertson (Gretna, La.: Pelican, 1997), 132; *Charleston Mercury*, February 18, 1864; Mary Anna Jackson, *Life and Letters of General Thomas J. Jackson* (New York: Harper and Brothers, 1892), 309–15; Phillips, *Diehard Rebels*, 65; *Mobile (Ala.) Daily Tribune*, March 16, 1864.

34. *Richmond Daily Dispatch*, August 3, 1861; Ruffin, *Diary of Edmund Ruffin*, 2:158; Myers, ed., *Children of Pride*, 968; Andrews, *Journal of a Georgia Girl*, 30–31; *Augusta (Ga.) Daily Chronicle and Sentinel*, May 23, 1863.

35. Mary Greenhow Lee, *The Civil War Journal of Mary Greenhow Lee of Winchester, Virginia*, ed. Eloise C. Strader (Winchester, Va.: Winchester-Frederick County Historical Society, 2011), 124;

OR, ser. 2, vol. 4, 836–37; *Charleston Mercury*, August 17, 1863; *Augusta (Ga.) Daily Chronicle and Sentinel*, May 23, 1863; Ruffin, *Diary of Edmund Ruffin*, 2:529–30. For a more extended treatment of Confederate discussions about retaliation against prisoners, see Charles W. Sanders Jr., *While in the Hands of the Enemy Military Prisons of the Civil War* (Baton Rouge: Louisiana State University Press, 2005), 129–31, 183–96, 202–3; William J. Cooper, Jr. *Jefferson Davis, American* (New York: Alfred A. Knopf, 2000), 407–8.

36. *Semi-Weekly Raleigh (N.C.) Register*, August 23, 1862; *Richmond Enquirer*, December 18, 1863; Sanders, *While in the Hands of the Enemy*, 146–47; *OR*, ser. 2, vol. 4:954, vol. 5:797; Wildred Buck Yearns, *The Confederate Congress* (Athens: University of Georgia Press, 1960), 164; *Southern Historical Society Papers* 47 (1930): 152–54; Confederate States of America, *The Statutes at Large of the Confederate States of America, Passed at the Third Session of the First Congress, 1863* (Richmond: R. M. Smith, 1863), 167–68. For a general discussion of dehumanizing African American soldiers, see Drew Gilpin Faust, *This Republic of Suffering: Death and the American Civil War* (New York: Alfred A. Knopf, 2008), 44–47.

37. George S. Burkhardt, *Confederate Rage, Yankee Wrath: No Quarter in the Civil War* (Carbondale: Southern Illinois University Press, 2007), 88–90; Samuel B. Barron, *The Lone State Defenders: A Chronicle of the Third Texas Cavalry Regiment in the Civil War* (New York: Neale Publishing, 1908), 183; *OR*, ser. 1, vol. 32, pt. 1:327; Celine Frémaux Garcia, *Celine: Remembering Louisiana, 1850–1871*, ed. Patrick J. Geary (Athens: University of Georgia Press, 1987), 132. See also U. R. Brooks, *Butler and His Cavalry in the War of Secession* (Columbia, S.C.: State Co., 1909), 363–64. For an example of an army commander—in this case Joseph E. Johnston—who did not approve such proceedings, see *OR*, ser. 1, vol. 30, pt. 4:573.

38. Burkhardt, *Confederate Rage, Yankee Wrath*, 109–10. Confederate newspaper reports contained equally damning details. *Fayetteville (N.C.) Observer*, May 19, 1864; *Atlanta Southern Confederacy*, n.d., in *Columbia Daily South Carolinian*, May 5, 1864.

39. "Fort Pillow Massacre," *House Report* 65, 38th Cong., 1st Session (1864), 39, 42, 43. For recent works that largely confirm a good deal of the congressional testimony, see Richard L. Fuchs, *An Unerring Fire: The Massacre at Fort Pillow* (Mechanicsburg, Pa.: Stackpole Books, 2002); Andrew Ward, *River Run Red: The Fort Pillow Massacre in the American Civil War* (New York: Viking, 2005); John Cimprich, *Fort Pillow, a Civil War Massacre and Public Memory* (Baton Rouge: Louisiana State University Press, 2005). For a brief but judicious treatment of the evidence for a massacre, see Albert Castel, "The Fort Pillow Massacre: An Examination of the Evidence," in Gregory J. W. Urwin, ed., *Black Flag Over Dixie: Racial Atrocities and Reprisals in the Civil War* (Carbondale: Southern Illinois University Press, 2004), 89–103.

40. *Milledgeville (Ga.) Confederate Union*, May 3, 1864; Burkhardt, *Confederate Rage, Yankee Wrath*, 135–43; Colin Edward Woodward, *Marching Masters: Slavery, Race, and the Confederate Army during the Civil War* (Charlottesville: University of Virginia Press, 2014), 145; *Charleston Mercury*, May 3, 1864; *Columbia Daily South Carolinian*, April 28, 1864; Jason Phillips, "A Brothers' War? Exploring Confederate Perceptions of the Enemy," in Aaron Sheehan-Dean, ed., *The View from the Ground: Experiences of Civil War Soldiers* (Lexington: University Press of Kentucky, 2007), 81; Henri Garidel, *Exile in Richmond: The Confederate Journal of Henri Garidel*, ed. Michael Bedout Chesson and Leslie Jean Roberts (Charlottesville: University Press of Virginia, 2001), 119; Charles W. Turner, ed.,

Civil War Letters of Arabella Speairs and William Beverley Pettit of Fluvanna County, Virginia March 1862–March 1865, 2 vols. (Roanoke, Va.: Virginia Lithography and Graphics, 1988), 2:25; Edmondston, "*Journal of a Secesh Lady*," 549. For a lengthy defense of Forrest, see *Daily Richmond Examiner*, April 23, 1864.

41. *Richmond Examiner*, April 29, 1864; Burkhardt, *Confederate Rage, Yankee Wrath*, 144–58.

42. Burkhardt, *Confederate Rage, Yankee Wrath*, 159–74; Henry A. Chambers, *Diary of Captain Henry A. Chambers*, ed. T. H. Pearce (Wendell, N.C.: Broadfoot's Bookmark, 1983), 210; Taylor, *Lee's Adjutant*, 179; W. A. Day, *A True History of Company I, 49th Regiment, North Carolina Troops, in the Great Civil War between the North and South* (Newton, N.C.: Enterprise Job Office, 1893), 84; John Cheeves Haskell, *The Haskell Memoirs*, ed. Gilbert E. Govan and James W. Livingood (New York: G. P. Putnam's Sons, 1960), 77; Alva Benjamin Spencer, *My Dear Friend: The Civil War Letters of Alva Benjamin Spencer, 3rd Georgia Regiment, Company C* (Macon, Ga.: Mercer University Press, 2007), 138; Edward Porter Alexander, *Fighting for the Confederacy: The Personal Recollections of General Edward Porter Alexander*, ed. Gary W. Gallagher (Chapel Hill: University of North Carolina Press, 1989), 462, 465; William Cowan McClellan, *Welcome the Hour of Conflict: William Cowan McClellan and the 9th Alabama*, ed. John C. Carter (Tuscaloosa: University of Alabama Press, 2007), 264. For more details, see the outpouring of recent studies, Richard Slotkin, *No Quarter: The Battle of the Crater, 1864* (New York: Random House, 2009); Earl J. Hess, *Into the Crater: The Mine Attack at Petersburg* (Columbia: University of South Carolina Press, 2010); Kevin M. Levin, *Remembering the Battle of the Crater: War as Murder* (Lexington: University Press of Kentucky, 2012). For a rather matter-of-fact defense of killing the surrendering black troops, see William Pegram, "'The Boy Artillerist': Letters of Colonel William Pegram, C.S.A.," ed. James I. Robertson Jr., *Virginia Magazine of History and Biography* 98 (April 1990), 243. A North Carolina private later wished that the black troops guarding (and cursing) Confederate prisoners at Point Lookout had been killed at Fort Pillow. Louis Leon, *Diary of a Tar Heel Confederate Soldier* (Charlotte, N.C.: Stone Publishing, 1913), 61–62.

43. Burkhardt, *Confederate Rage, Yankee Wrath*, 175–201; George Dallas Mosgrove, *Kentucky Cavaliers in Dixie: Reminiscences of a Confederate Cavalryman*, ed. Bell Irvin Wiley (Jackson, Tenn.: McCowat-Mercer Press, 1957), 206–8; Edward O. Guerrant, *Bluegrass Confederate: The Headquarters Diary of Edward O. Guerrant*, ed. William C. Davis and Meredith L. Swentor (Baton Rouge: Louisiana State University Press, 1999), 547. See also Brian D. McKnight, *Confederate Outlaw: Champ Ferguson and the Civil War in Appalachia* (Baton Rouge: Louisiana State University Press, 2011), 146–53.

44. *Richmond Enquirer*, March 14, 1862; *Charleston Courier, Tri-Weekly*, March 22, 1862; *Mobile (Ala.) Register*, March 30, 1862; Savannah *(Ga.) Daily Morning News*, June 27, 1861; Emilie Riley McKinley, *From the Pen of a She-Rebel: The Civil War Diary of Emilie Riley McKinley*, ed. Gordon A. Cotton (Columbia: University of South Carolina Press, 2001), 22; Ruffin, *Diary of Edmund Ruffin*, 3:126, 357; Wharton, *War Songs and Poems of the Southern Confederacy*, 179; Edmondston, "*Journal of a Secesh Lady*," 638. The premier work on the subject is Daniel E. Sutherland's superb *A Savage Conflict: The Decisive Role of Guerrillas in the American Civil War* (Chapel Hill: University of North Carolina Press, 2009).

45. *Richmond Daily Dispatch*, May 21, 1861; J. W. Hosford, "A Florida Soldier in the Army of Northern Virginia: The Hosford Letters," *Florida Historical Quarterly* 46 (January 1968): 258;

Turner, ed., *Civil War Letters of Speairs and Pettit*, 1:155; Nugent, *My Dear Nellie*, 224; Edwin H. Fay, *"This Infernal War": The Confederate Letters of Sgt. Edwin H. Fay*, ed. Bell Irvin Wiley (Austin: University of Texas Press, 1958), 292; Morgan, *Civil War Diary of Sarah Morgan*, 50; *Tuscaloosa (Ala.) Observer*, n.d., in *Chattanooga Daily Rebel*, September 10, 1862; Wiley, *The Life of Johnny Reb*, 16–17; Jedediah Hotchkiss to Sara A. Hotchkiss, May 19, 1863, Hotchkiss Papers, Library of Congress.

46. *Savannah (Ga.) Daily Morning News*, December 20, 1861; Glatthaar, *General Lee's Army*, 151; *Richmond Daily Dispatch*, June 22, 1863; Ruffin, *Diary of Edmund Ruffin*, 3:26–27; Charles Royster, *The Destructive War: William Tecumseh Sherman, Stonewall Jackson, and the Americans* (New York: Alfred A. Knopf, 1991), 37; *Charleston Mercury*, June 23, 1863; Judith W. McGuire, *Diary of a Southern Refugee during the War by a Lady of Virginia* (New York: E. J. Hale, 1867), 226; Edmondston, "*Journal of a Secesh Lady*," 414. Lee's earlier advance into Maryland during the Antietam campaign has also sparked eager anticipation of retaliation for Yankee depredations. "We will carry the War home to them[.] we will Distroy evry cite we come to," wrote one hopeful Georgia private. *Richmond Daily Dispatch*, September 17, 1862; *Chattanooga Daily Rebel*, September 17, 1862; *Southern Historical Society Papers* 46 (1928): 107; William H. Davidson, ed., *War Was the Place: A Centennial Collection of Confederate Soldier Letters* (Old Oakbowery, Chambers County, Ala.: Chattahoochee Valley Historical Society, 1961), 55–56. A little less than a month before the Battle of Gettysburg, a Georgian in the Army of Northern Virginia relished the idea of plundering and destroying Yankee property but promised his mother that he would never rob a woman. H. C. Kendrick to his mother, June 6, 1863, Kendrick Papers, Southern Historical Collection, University of North Carolina. See also press comments quoted in *Savannah (Ga.) Republican*, June 27, 1863.

47. Edmondston, "*Journal of a Secesh Lady*," 537–38; Taylor, *Lee's Adjutant*, 128. For an excellent treatment of Confederate calls for carrying a war of destruction into the northern states, see Royster, *Destructive War*, 34–39.

48. Jefferson Davis, *Speech of the Hon. Jefferson Davis of Mississippi, Delivered in the United State Senate, on the 10th day of January, 1861* (Baltimore: John Murphy, 1861), 11; Royster, *Destructive War*, 35; Elijah P. Petty, *Journey to Pleasant Hill: The Civil War Letters of Captain Elijah P. Petty, Walker's Texas Division, C.S.A.*, ed. Norman D. Brown (San Antonio: University of Texas Institute of Texan Cultures, 1982), 213–14; *Mobile (Ala.) Register*, August 19, 1862. "If we can only get Washington," a cavalry officer wrote hopefully in the late summer of 1864, "and make its destruction as complete as Sodom's, we will have struck our best blow for peace." Vogtsberger, ed., *Dulanys of Welbourne*, 195.

49. Kenneth Walters, *Norfolk Blues: The Civil War Diary of the Norfolk Light Artillery Blues*, ed. Kenneth Wiley (Shippensburg, Pa.: Burd Street Press, 1997), 141; *Richmond Daily Dispatch*, August 5, 1864; *Richmond Enquirer*, August 6, 1864, cited in Megan Kate Nelson, "The Pleasure of Civil War Ruins," in Stephen Berry, ed., *Weirding the War: Stories from the Civil War's Ragged Edges* (Athens: University of Georgia Press, 2011), 40–41; Fain, *Sanctified Trial*, 207–8; Ruffin, *Diary of Edmund Ruffin*, 3:524. A perceptive Virginian admitted that he could not help "entertaining a secret feeling of gratification" over the torching of Chambersburg, but he also considered the whole affair "impolitic" because the "Yankees can burn a hundred of our towns . . . where

we can burn one of theirs." August 4, 1864, Joseph Addison Waddell Diary. For similar ambivalence, see Oscar Hinrichs, *Stonewall's Prussian Mapmaker: The Journals of Captain Oscar Hinrichs*, ed. Richard Brady Williams (Chapel Hill: University of North Carolina Press, 2014), 152–53.

50. *Chattanooga Daily Rebel*, April 28, 1863; Frank Moore, ed., *Songs and Ballads of the Southern People* (New York: Appleton, 1886), 169; Jane Smith to Janie Robinson, April 12, 1865, Miscellaneous Records, Civil War Collection, North Carolina Department of Archives and History, Raleigh.

51. *Charleston Mercury*, June 6, 1863; Frank Moore, ed., *The Rebellion Record: A Diary of American Events*, 11 vols. (New York: Putnam and Van Nostrand, 1861–68), 2 (Diary of Events): 75; December 12, 1862, Fannie Page Hume Diary, Library of Congress; Augustus Pitt Adamson, *Sojourns of a Patriot: The Field and Prison Papers of an Unreconstructed Confederate*, ed. Richard Bender Abel and Fay Adamson Gecik (Murfreesboro, Tenn.: Southern Heritage Press, 1998), 173; McPherson, *What They Fought For*, 22; Ruffin, *Diary of Edmund Ruffin*, 3:664; Steven V. Ash, *Middle Tennessee Society Transformed, 1860–1870* (Baton Rouge: Louisiana State University Press, 1988), 78; *Chattanooga Daily Rebel*, June 3, 1863; *Richmond Daily Dispatch*, August 5, 1864; Dulany, *In the Shadow of the Enemy*, 118. A woman in Richmond hoped to see the United States entangled in a foreign war that would create thousands of refugees and spread ruin across the northern states. John B. Jones, *A Rebel War Clerk's Diary at the Confederate States Capital*, 2 vols. (Philadelphia: J. B. Lippincott, 1866), 2:82.

6. SUBJUGATION

1. To cite but a few examples, the word *subjugation* in various forms appeared at least 217 times in the *Charleston Mercury* and *Richmond Enquirer* and at least 154 times in the *Salisbury (N.C.) Carolina Watchman*. Confederates claimed that northerners clearly spelled out this intention from the start, and this conflict had been forced on innocent southerners. *Savannah (Ga.) Republican*, May 6, 1861. For echoes of this viewpoint at a local meeting in Chatham County, Georgia, see *Savannah (Ga.) Republican*, August 21, 1861.

2. Jason Phillips has noted how the word *subjugation* embodied fears of "confiscation, disfranchisement, imprisonment, and miscegenation." And he could have added several more terms to the list. "A Brothers' War? Exploring Confederate Perceptions of the Enemy," in Aaron Sheehan-Dean, ed., *The View from the Ground: Experiences of Civil War Soldiers* (Lexington: University Press of Kentucky, 2007), 83.

3. Ida Powell Dulany, *In the Shadow of the Enemy: The Civil War Journal of Ida Powell Dulany*, ed. Mary L. Mackall, Stevan F. Meserve, and Anne Mackall Sasscer (Knoxville: University of Tennessee Press, 2009), 65–66; Jonathan Worth, *The Correspondence of Jonathan Worth*, ed. J. G. de Roulhac Hamilton, 2 vols. (Raleigh: Edwards and Broughton, 1909), 1:171; *Atlanta Daily Intelligencer*, September 10, 1863; *Southern Presbyterian*, n.d., in *Atlanta Southern Confederacy*, March 23, 1862; *Savannah (Ga.) Republican*, September 14, 1863; March 2, 1862, Sarah Lois Wadley Diary, Southern Historical Collection, University of North Carolina.

4. *Atlanta Southern Confederacy*, April 11, 1861; *Southern Illustrated News*, October 4, 1862; *Savannah (Ga.) Republican*, September 13, 1861, June 30, 1862; *Milledgeville (Ga.) Southern Recorder*,

July 2, 1861; *Athens (Ga.) Southern Watchman*, December 11, 1861; Samuel A. Burney, *A Southern Soldier's Letters Home: The Civil War Letters of Samuel A. Burney, Cobb's Georgia Legion, Army of Northern Virginia*, ed. Nat S. Turner III (Macon, Ga.: Mercer University Press, 2002), 98; *New Orleans Daily Picayune*, February 11, 1862; *Shreveport (La.) Semi-Weekly News*, March 7, 1862; Edward O. Guerrant, *Bluegrass Confederate: The Headquarters Diary of Edward O. Guerrant*, ed. William C. Davis and Meredith L. Swentor (Baton Rouge: Louisiana State University Press, 1999), 47. After the battle of Sabine Crossroads, a Texas private could hardly believe the horrible toll on the "honest yoemanry" who had been "ruthlessly cut down, by the insolent, and foul hands of so degraded a crew, as the negro equalizing abolitionists of the north. We are fighting for our property and our homes; they, for the flimsy and abstract idea that a negro is equal to an Anglo American." H. C. Medford, "The Diary of H. C. Medford, Confederate Soldier, 1864," ed. Rebecca W. Smith and Marion Mullins. *Southwestern Historical Quarterly* 34 (January 1931): 220.

5. John K. Gott and John E. Divine, eds., *"My Heart is So Rebellious": The Caldwell Letters, 1861–1865* (Warrenton, Va.: Fauquier National Bank, 1991), 99; *Fayetteville (N.C.) Observer*, June 2, 1862; William Dorsey Pender, *The General to His Lady: The Civil War Letters of William Dorsey Pender to Fanny Pender*, ed. William W. Hassler (Chapel Hill: University of North Carolina Press, 1988), 152; *Savannah (Ga.) Republican*, August 20, 1863; January 18, 1862, Joseph Addison Waddell Diary, Albert and Shirley Small Special Collections Library, University of Virginia; Ada W. Bacot, *A Confederate Nurse: The Diary of Ada W. Bacot, 1860–1863*, ed. Jean V. Berlin (Columbia: University of South Carolina Press, 1994), 165; *Athens (Ga.) Southern Watchman*, December 17, 31, 1862; *Charleston Mercury*, December 19, 1862, July 27, 1864; *Weekly Columbus (Ga.) Enquirer*, January 7, 1864; John Blair Dabney, Sermon Preached on March 10, 1865, at Castle Craig, Campbell County, Virginia, Saunders Family Papers, Virginia Historical Society.

6. William States Lee to William Hollinshed Lee, March 29, 1862, Sanders, Lee, and Sargent Families Papers, Special Collections, Mississippi State University, Starkville; *Augusta (Ga.) Daily Chronicle and Sentinel*, December 3, 1862; *War of the Rebellion: A Compilation of the Official Records of the Union and Confederate Armies* [OR], 128 vols. (Washington: Government Printing Office, 1880–1901), ser. 1, vol. 4:368; *Weekly Columbus (Ga.) Enquirer*, June 2, 1863; *Staunton (Va.) Vindicator*, October 28, 1864. For narrower appeals directed to one-time Unionists and women, see New Orleans *Daily True Delta*, August 16, 1861; Kate Cumming, *Kate: The Journal of a Confederate Nurse*, ed. Richard Barksdale Harwell (Baton Rouge: Louisiana State University Press, 1959), 66.

7. James M. Williams, *From That Terrible Field: Civil War Letters of James M. Williams, Twenty-first Alabama Volunteers*, ed. John Kent Folmar (Tuscaloosa: University of Alabama Press, 1981), 92–93; A South Carolinian [pseud.], *The Confederate* (Mobile: S. H. Goetzel, 1863), 7; *Charleston Mercury*, January 6, 1864.

8. Murdoch John McSween, *Confederate Incognito: The Civil War Reports of "Long Grabs," aka Murdoch John McSween, 26th and 35th North Carolina Infantry*, ed. E. B. Munson (Jefferson, N.C.: McFarland, 2013), 98; *Charleston Mercury*, July 17, 1863, November 19, 1864; Grace Brown Elmore, *A Heritage of Woe: The Civil War Diary of Grace Brown Elmore, 1861–1868*, ed. Marli F. Weiner (Athens: University of Georgia Press, 1997), 21–22; *Savannah (Ga.) Daily Morning News*, February 28, 1862; *Atlanta Daily Intelligencer*, August 28, 1863.

9. Walter Clark, *The Papers of Walter Clark*, ed. Aubrey Lee Brooks and Hugh Talmage Lefler, 2 vols. (Chapel Hill: University of North Carolina Press, 1948), 1:140; *Staunton (Va.) Spectator*, August 25, 1863.

10. James Henley Thornwell, *Our Danger and Our Duty* (Columbia, S.C.: Southern Guardian Press, 1862), 3; *Southern Illustrated News*, October 11, 1862; *Richmond Examiner*, n.d., in *Charleston Mercury*, January 12, 1864; *Columbia Daily South Carolinian*, March 1, 1864; Thomas Verner Moore, *God Our Refuge and Strength in this War* (Richmond: W. Hargrave White, 1861), 21; *Richmond Examiner*, n.d., in *Fayetteville (N.C.) Observer*, October 20, 1864; William L. Nugent, *My Dear Nellie: The Civil War Letters of William L. Nugent to Eleanor Smith Nugent*, ed. William M. Cash and Lucy Somerville Howorth (Jackson: University Press of Mississippi, 1977), 129.

11. Allen D. Candler, ed., *The Confederate Records of the State of Georgia*, 5 vols. (Atlanta: C. P. Byrd, 1909–11), 2:486; *Charleston Mercury*, December 9, 1861; *Richmond Daily Dispatch*, June 2, 1862; *Richmond Examiner*, n.d., in *Charleston Mercury*, January 12, 1864; *Salisbury (N.C.) Carolina Watchman*, September 14, 1863; *Secession: Considered as a Right in the States . . . by a Gentleman of Mississippi* (Jackson: South-Western Confederate Printing House, 1863), 44.

12. *OR*, ser. 4, vol. 3:134; Williamson S. Oldham, *Speech of Hon. W. S. Oldham of Texas . . . concerning Peace, Reconstruction and Independence in the Confederate States Senate, January 30, 1865* [Richmond, 1865], 12. Early on there were also predictions that the Federals would execute leading Confederates. *Richmond Daily Dispatch*, March 20, 1862; *Savannah (Ga.) Daily Morning News*, May 6, 1862.

13. *Staunton (Va.) Spectator*, August 20, 1861; Louis P. Towles, ed., *A World Turned Upside Down: The Palmers of South Santee, 1818–1881* (Columbia: University of South Carolina Press, 1996), 447; May 5, 1861, George Anderson Mercer Diary, Southern Historical Collection, University of North Carolina; *OR*, ser. 1, vol. 52, pt. 2:587; *Savannah (Ga.) Daily Morning News*, February 21, 1862; *Milledgeville (Ga.) Southern Recorder*, July 5, 1864; *Milledgeville (Ga.) Southern Federal Union*, April 8, 1862.

14. *Fayetteville (N.C.) Observer*, September 3, 1863; *OR*, ser. 2, vol. 2:789–90; Candler, ed., *Confederate Records of Georgia*, 2:188–89; *Charleston Mercury*, January 30, 1862; Michael W. Taylor, ed., *The Cry is War, War, War: The Civil War Correspondence of Lts. Burwell Thomas Cotton and George Job Huntley, 34th Regiment North Carolina Troops* (Dayton, Ohio: Morningside, 1994), 76; *Salisbury (N.C.) Carolina Watchman*, November 16, 1861; *Augusta (Ga.) Daily Chronicle and Sentinel*, August 6, 1863; *Staunton (Va.) Spectator*, October 13, 1863.

15. Cornelia Peake McDonald, *A Woman's Civil War: A Diary, with Reminiscences of the War, from March 1862*, ed. Minrose C. Gwin (Madison: University of Wisconsin Press, 1992), 31; William Thomas Jackson, *Kiss, Sweet Little Lillah for Me: The Civil War Letters of William Thomas Jackson, Company A, Eighth Alabama Infantry Regiment*, ed. Wayne Wood and Mary Virginia Jackson (Birmingham, Ala.: Ebsco Media, 2000), 53; Warren Akin, *Letters of Warren Akin: Confederate Congressman*, ed. Bell Irvin Wiley (Athens: University of Georgia Press, 1959), 33; Justus M. Silliman, *A New Canaan Private in the Civil War: Letters of Justus M. Silliman 17th Connecticut Volunteers*, ed. Edward Marcus (New Canaan, Conn.: New Canaan Historical Society, 1984), 87; *Salisbury (N.C.) Carolina Watchman*, February 24, 1862; Christopher M. Watford, ed.,

The Civil War in North Carolina: Soldiers' and Civilians' Letters and Diaries, 1861–1865, Volume 2: The Mountains (Jefferson, N.C.: McFarland, 2003), 65–66; H. M. Wharton, *War Songs and Poems of the Southern Confederacy* (Philadelphia: American Book and Bible House, 1904), 191; *Mobile (Ala.) Register*, February 25, 1862. An additional point was that everyone would be enslaved, including Unionists. *OR*, ser. 4, vol. 3:133; *Milledgeville (Ga.) Southern Federal Union*, April 8, 1862.

16. In a fascinating and forceful if somewhat overdrawn new interpretation, James Oakes has argued that the Confederates had a point, because from the outset the Republicans were in fact waging a war against slavery. *Freedom National: The Destruction of Slavery in the United States, 1861–1865* (New York: W. W. Norton, 2013).

17. James C. Bates, *A Texas Cavalry Officer's Civil War: The Diary and Letters of James C. Bates*, ed. Richard Lowe (Baton Rouge: Louisiana State University, 1999), 119–20; J. K. Street, *J. K. Street Civil War Letters: 9th Texas Infantry from Paris, Lamar County, Texas*, ed. Julie Williams Coley (Wichita Falls, Tex.: J. Cooley. 2009), 175; *OR*, ser. 1, vol. 47, pt. 2:1190; *Shreveport (La.) Semi-Weekly News*, December 2, 1861.

18. *OR*, ser. 1, vol. 39, pt. 2:422, ser. 4, vol. 2:961; Charles Royster, *The Destructive War: William Tecumseh Sherman, Stonewall Jackson, and the Americans* (New York: Alfred A. Knopf, 1991), 181; J. J. D. Renfroe, *"The Battle is God's." A Sermon Preached before Wilcox's Brigade, Fast Day, The 21st August, 1863* (Richmond: Macfarlane & Fergusson, 1863), 18; Benjamin H. Hill Jr., *Senator Benjamin H. Hill of Georgia. His Life, Speeches and Writings* (Atlanta: H. C. Hudgins, 1891), 277. For more examples of the predicted suffering of southern white women (including insult, rape, and enslavement) should the Confederacy be subjugated, see *Atlanta Southern Confederacy*, n.d., in *Savannah (Ga.) Daily Morning News*, April 1, 1862; *Mobile Register*, n.d., in *Milledgeville (Ga.) Southern Recorder*, August 18, 1863; (Macon) *Georgia Weekly Telegraph*, May 30, 1862; Anne Sarah Rubin, *A Shattered Nation: The Rise and Fall of the Confederacy, 1861–1868* (Chapel Hill: University of North Carolina Press, 2005), 88.

19. Jefferson Davis, *The Messages and Papers of Jefferson Davis and Confederacy Including Diplomatic Correspondence, 1861–1865*, ed. James D. Richardson, 2 vols. (New York: Chelsea House-Robert Hector, 1966), 1:329; *Charleston Mercury*, May 19, 1862; *Salisbury (N.C.) Carolina Watchman*, September 14, 1863; *Mobile (Ala.) Register*, n.d., in *Milledgeville (Ga.) Southern Recorder*, August 18, 1863; Edmund Ruffin, *The Diary of Edmund Ruffin*, ed. William K. Scarborough, 3 vols. (Baton Rouge: Louisiana State University Press, 1972–1989), 3:799; Street, *J. K. Street Civil War Letters*, 17; Nugent, *My Dear Nellie*, 129.

20. William Beasley to Abner Addison Porter, March 27, 1862, Abner Addison Porter Papers, Presbyterian Historical Society, Montreat, North Carolina; *Richmond Examiner*, n.d., in *Charleston Mercury*, January 16, 1864; *Augusta (Ga.) Daily Chronicle and Sentinel*, May 10, 1861; *Southern Christian Advocate*, n.d., in *Charleston Courier*, May 6, 1862; *Savannah (Ga.) Daily Morning News*, May 14, 1861; *Fayetteville (N.C.) Observer*, March 28, 1864; *Southern Presbyterian* (Columbia, S.C.), July 5, 1862; *Columbia Daily South Carolinian*, April 3, 1864; *Semi-Weekly Raleigh Register*, April 5, 1862; T. Conn Bryan, *Confederate Georgia* (Athens: University of Georgia Press, 1953), 240.

21. For typical précis on the consequences of subjugation, see *Richmond Whig*, n.d., in *Weekly Raleigh (N.C.) Register*, May 14, 1862; *Savannah (Ga.) Daily Morning News*, June 5, 1862; Thomas H. Watts, *Inaugural Address of Gov. Thomas H. Watts before the Alabama Legislature, Decem-*

ber 1st, 1863 (Montgomery, Ala.: Montgomery Advertiser Book and Job Office, 1863), 14–15; William H. Davidson, ed., *War Was the Place: A Centennial Collection of Confederate Soldier Letters* (Old Oakbowery, Chambers County, Ala.: Chattahoochee Valley Historical Society, 1961), 72. At times, conservative northerners expressed similar fears about the prospects of subjugation and military occupation. Worthington Chauncey Ford, ed., *A Cycle of Adams Letters, 1861–1865*, 2 vols. (Boston: Houghton Mifflin, 1920), 1:165.

22. *Savannah (Ga.) Republican*, August 14, 1861; House of Representatives, *Resolutions Adopted by Bratton's Brigade, South Carolina Volunteers, January 30th, 1865* [Richmond, 1865], 2; *Macon (Ga.) Telegraph*, n.d., in *Milledgeville (Ga.) Southern Recorder*, September 15, 1863; *Jackson Mississippian*, n.d., in *Milledgeville (Ga.) Confederate Union*, February 14, 1865; Edgeworth Bird and Sallie Bird, *Granite Farm Letters: The Civil War Correspondence of Edgeworth and Sallie Bird*, ed. John Rozier (Athens: University of Georgia Press, 1988), 145; House of Representatives, *Resolutions adopted by Company "H," "I" and "K" Thirteenth Virginia Infantry, January 28, 1865* [Richmond, 1865], 1; *Eufaula (Ala.) Spirit*, n.d., in *Selma (Ala.) Reporter*, January 19, 1865.

23. Candler, ed., *Confederate Records of Georgia*, 2:470–73; *Charleston Mercury*, September 30, 1864; Henry Wemyss Feilden, *A Confederate Englishman: The Civil War Letters of Henry Wemyss Fielden*, ed. W. Eric Emerson and Karen Stokes (Columbia: University of South Carolina Press, 2013), 70; *Augusta (Ga.) Daily Chronicle and Sentinel*, August 6, 1863; *Macon (Ga.) Telegraph*, n.d., in *Milledgeville (Ga.) Southern Recorder*, September 15, 1863; *Milledgeville (Ga.) Confederate Union*, January 20, 1863; *Shreveport (La.) News*, February 19, 1865; *Fayetteville (N.C.) Observer*, January 30, 1865. Confederates were especially contemptuous of Lincoln's reconstruction proposals. *OR*, ser. 1, vol. 51, pt. 2:809–10; *Richmond Examiner*, n.d., in *Charleston Mercury*, January 12, 1864. Better to be ruled by a foreign power than by the Yankee nation, some fiery southerners maintained. A Georgia editor even preferred seeking the protection of Mexico to facing the prospect of northern domination, or perhaps Confederates would simply go into exile. D. C. Snyder to his wife, January 12, 1865, Snyder Letters, Special Collections, James Madison University; *Milledgeville (Ga.) Confederate Union*, March 3, 1863; Walter R. Lenoir to his brother, September 27, 1863, Lenoir Family Papers, Southern Historical Collection, University of North Carolina.

24. *Richmond Whig*, n.d., in *Raleigh (N.C.) Daily Register*, April 20, 1861; *Milledgeville (Ga.) Southern Recorder*, January 31, 1865; George Bentley, *"Burning Rails as We Pleased": The Civil War Letters of William Garrigues Bentley, 104th Ohio Volunteer Infantry*, ed. Barbara Bentley Smith and Nine Bentley Baker (Jefferson, N.C.: McFarland, 2004), 108; Bates, *A Texas Cavalry Officer's Civil War*, 111; *Athens (Ga.) Southern Banner*, May 6, 1863; *Shreveport (La.) News*, April 4, 1865. For the use of fear as a rhetorical device to rally the southern people, see Paul D. Escott, *After Secession: Jefferson Davis and the Failure of Confederate Nationalism* (Baton Rouge: Louisiana State University Press, 1978), 190–93.

25. *OR*, ser. 1, vol. 47, pt. 2:1190; Josiah B. Patterson, "Irrepressible Optimism of a Georgia Confederate in 1864: A Letter," ed. Martin Abbott, *Georgia Historical Quarterly* 37 (December 1953): 350; James B. Griffin, *A Gentleman and Officer: A Military and Social History of James B. Griffin's Civil War*, ed. Judith N. McArthur and Orville Vernon Burton (New York: Oxford University Press, 1996), 163; Stephen D. Elliott, *Ezra's Dilemma. A Sermon Preached in Christ Church, Savannah, On Friday, August 21st, 1863, Being the Day of Humiliation, Fasting and Prayer* (Savannah, Ga: Power

Press of George N. Nichols. 1863), 25; *OR*, ser. 1, vol. 8:756, vol. 52, pt. 2:587; *Resolutions Passed at a Meeting of the Fourteenth Virginia Infantry* [Richmond, 1865]; *Resolutions Adopted by McGowan's Brigade, South Carolina* Volunteers [Richmond, 1865].

26. Thomas W. Cutrer and T. Michael Parrish, eds., *Brothers in Gray: The Civil War Letters of the Pierson Family* (Baton Rouge: Louisiana State University Press, 1997), 224; Catherine Ann Devereux Edmondston, *"Journal of a Secesh Lady": The Diary of Catherine Ann Devereux Edmondston, 1860–1866*, ed. Beth G. Crabtree and James W. Patton (Raleigh, N.C.: Division of Archives and History, 1979), 658; *Staunton (Va.) Vindicator*, March 24, 1865; Lucy Rebecca Buck, *Shadows on My Heart: The Civil War Diary of Lucy Rebecca Buck of Virginia*, ed. Elizabeth R. Baer (Athens: University of Georgia Press, 1997), 317–38; Marion Hill Fitzpatrick, *Letters to Amanda: The Civil War Letters of Marion Hill Fitzpatrick, Army of Northern Virginia*, ed. Jeffrey C. Lowe and Sam Hodges (Macon, Ga.: Mercer University Press, 1998), 196; *Shreveport (La.) News*, April 4, 1865. For radically different views on the dangers of white enslavement and the necessity for enlisting black troops, see *OR*, ser. 4, vol. 3:915; *Milledgeville (Ga.) Confederate Union*, February 18, 1865.

27. Fred Charles Ilké, *Every War Must End*, 3rd rev. ed. (New York: Columbia University Press, 2005), 95–97; *Jacksonville (Ala.) Republican*, March 20, 1862; *Milledgeville (Ga.) Southern Recorder*, January 30, 1863; *OR*, ser. 4, vol. 3:135; Emma LeConte, *When the World Ended: The Diary of Emma LeConte*, ed. Earl Schenck Miers (New York: Oxford University Press, 1957), 4, 66.

28. *Mobile (Ala.) Register*, February 6, 1862; *Charleston Mercury*, July 31, 1862, December 14, 1864; Cutrer and Parrish, eds., *Brothers in Gray*, 207; C. Irvine Walker, *Great Things Are Expected of Us: The Letters of Colonel C. Irvine Walker, 10th South Carolina Infantry, C.S.A.*, ed. William Lee White and Charles Denny Runion (Knoxville: University of Tennessee Press, 2009), 168; *Richmond Daily Dispatch*, February 14, 1865; *OR*, ser. 1, vol. 47, pt. 2:1190–91.

29. *Milledgeville (Ga.) Southern Federal Union*, May 14, 1861; *Weekly Raleigh (N.C.) Register*, February 26, 1862; Amanda Worthington, *A Delta Diary: Amanda Worthington's Civil War Diary*, ed. Troy Woods (n.p: Olivewoods Press, 2008), 52; *OR*, ser. 4, vol. 2:960–61. Although soldiers occasionally expressed similar sentiments, the war-weary sometimes shunned such appeals from officers seeking to promote reenlistment. John Washington Inzer, *The Diary of a Confederate Soldier: John Washington Inzer, 1834–1928*, ed. Mattie Lou Teague Crow (Huntsville, Ala.: Strode Publishers, 1977), 66; John Booker to Chloe Unity Blair, March 1, 1864, John and James Booker Civil War Letters, Albert and Shirley Small Special Collections Library, University of Virginia.

30. Charles W. Turner, ed., *Civil War Letters of Arabella Speairs and William Beverley Pettit of Fluvanna County, Virginia March 1862–March 1865*, 2 vols. (Roanoke: Virginia Lithography and Graphics, 1988), 1:155; Andrew G. Magrath, Proclamation to "The People of South Carolina," December n.d., 1864, Magrath Letters, South Carolina Department of Archives and History, Columbia, South Carolina.

31. *Edgefield (S.C.) Advertiser*, January 27, 1864; Phillips, "A Brothers' War?" 69–70.

32. *Anderson (S.C.) Intelligencer*, April 20, 1865; Ilkė, *Every War Must End*, 81–83; May 13, 1865, Sarah Lois Wadley Diary.

33. Henry A. Chambers, *Diary of Captain Henry A. Chambers*, ed. T. H. Pearce (Wendell, N.C.: Broadfoot's Bookmark, 1983), 262; Caroline E. Janney, *Remembering the Civil War: Reunion and the*

Limits of Reconciliation (Chapel Hill: University of North Carolina Press, 2013), 54; *Milledgeville (Ga.) Southern Recorder*, June 30, 1863.

34. Lisa Tendrich Frank, "Bedrooms as Battlefields: The Role of Gender Politics in Sherman's March," in LeeAnn Whites and Alecia P. Long, eds., *Occupied Women: Gender, Military Occupation, and the American Civil War* (Baton Rouge: Louisiana State University Press, 2009), 45; William L. Barney, *The Making of a Confederate: Walter Lenoir's Civil War* (New York: Oxford University Press, 2008), 182; Robert Garlick Hill Kean, *Inside the Confederate Government: The Diary of Robert Garlick Hill Kean*, ed. Edward Younger (New York: Oxford University Press, 1957), 182; *Richmond Examiner*, n.d., in *Charleston Mercury*, January 16, 1864.

35. Robert Manson Myers, ed., *The Children of Pride: A True Story of Georgia and the Civil War* (New Haven: Yale University Press, 1972), 1268; James Wren, *From New Bern to Fredericksburg: Captain James Wren Diary*, ed. John Michael Priest (Shippensburg, Pa.: White Mane, 1990), 13; Cumming, *Kate: Journal of a Confederate Nurse*, 228–29; *Columbia (S.C.) Daily Carolinian*, May 19, 1864; Elizabeth Paisley Huckaby and Ethel C. Simpson, eds., *Tulip Evermore: Emma Butler and William Paisley, Their Lives in Letters, 1857–1887* (Fayetteville: University of Arkansas Press, 1985), 28; Ethie M. Foute Eagleton, "'Stray Thoughts': The Civil War Diary of Ethie M. Foute Eagleton," ed. Elvie Eagleton Skipper and Ruth Gove, *East Tennessee Historical Society's Publications* 40–41 (1968–1969): 133–34; February 26, 1865, Nancy McDougall Robinson Diary, Robinson Papers, Mississippi Department of Archives and History, Jackson; Elizabeth Pendleton Hardin, *The Private War of Lizzie Hardin: A Kentucky Confederate Girl's Diary of the Civil War in Kentucky, Virginia, Tennessee, Alabama, and Georgia*, ed. G. Glenn Clift (Frankfort: Kentucky Historical Society, 1963), 233–35; Carolyn L. Harrell, *When the Bells Tolled For Lincoln: Southern Reaction to the Assassination* (Macon, Ga.: Mercer University Press, 1997). The always fiery Louisianan Kate Stone, however, declared "All honor to J. Wilkes Booth." Kate Stone, *Brokenburn: The Journal of Kate Stone, 1861–1868*, ed. John Q. Anderson (Baton Rouge: Louisiana State University Press, 1955), 333. For press comments welcoming the death of the "tyrant" and "despot" Lincoln—especially in Texas, see John McKee Barr, *Loathing Lincoln: An American Tradition from the Civil War to the Present* (Baton Rouge: Louisiana State University Press, 2014), 2, 52.

36. Joshua Lawrence Chamberlain, *The Passing of the Armies* (Dayton, Ohio: Morningside Bookshop, 1981), 267; J. T. Trowbridge, *The South: A Tour of Its Battle-Fields and Ruined Cities, A Journey through the Desolated States, and Talks with the People* (Hartford, Conn.: L. Stebbins, 1866), 577; Ruffin, *Diary of Edmund Ruffin*, 3:946. Even Ruffin's instructions to his son about how his death should be handled concluded with another rant against northerners: "I here repeat, & would willingly proclaim, my unmitigated hatred to Yankee rule—all political, social, & business connection with Yankees, & to the perfidious, malignant, & vile Yankee race" (3:949). For continued expressions of southern hatred for Lincoln after the war, including familiar diatribes about everything from his seemingly barbaric manners to his supposed religious infidelity, see Barr, *Loathing Lincoln*, 77–95.

37. Joan E. Cashin, "Trophies of War: Material Culture in the Civil War Era," *Journal of the Civil War Era* 1 (September 2011): 357–58; Drew Gilpin Faust, *This Republic of Suffering: Death and the American Civil War* (New York: Alfred A. Knopf, 2008), 219, 222–23, 226; Eliza Frances

Andrews, *The War-Time Journal of a Georgia Girl, 1864–1865*, ed. Spencer Bidwell King Jr. (Macon, Ga.: Ardivan Press, 1960), 288.

38. Robert Penn Warren, *The Legacy of the Civil War* (New York: Alfred A. Knopf, 1961), 59–66. Unreliable mails in the aftermath of the war, along with rumors fanned and spread by newspapers, further inflamed opinion and made hyperbolic reports of Yankee intentions appear quite believable. George C. Rable, *But There Was No Peace: The Role of Violence in the Politics of Reconstruction* (Athens: University of Georgia Press, 1984), 3.

39. Hannah Arendt, "Imperialism, Nationalism, Chauvinism," *Review of Politics* 7 (October 1945): 457–58; Mark Grimsley, *The Hard Hand of War: Union Military Policy Toward Southern Civilians, 1861–1865* (Cambridge: Cambridge University Press, 1995), 219.

40. *New Orleans Times*, December 10, 1865.

41. (Macon) *Georgia Weekly Telegraph*, April 16, 1866; *Daily (Little Rock) Arkansas Gazette*, July 29, 1868; "Carey on Reconstruction," *DeBow's Review*, After the War Series 5 (July 1868): 587; *Charleston Courier, Tri-Weekly*, August 8, 1868. The Military Reconstructions Acts and the initial disfranchisement of southern whites all fit into Confederate expectations about the results of their enemies' triumph. *Charleston Courier, Tri-Weekly*, January 14, 1868.

42. *Daily Richmond Examiner*, December 14, 1865; *Atlanta Constitution*, August 12, 1868.

43. (Macon) *Georgia Weekly Telegraph*, April 23, 1866; Rable, *But There Was No Peace*, 4; *Galveston (Tex.) Daily News*, July 5, 1866; *The Southerner* (Tarboro, N.C.), August 11, 1866; *Greenville (S.C.) Mountaineer*, August 2, 1866.

44. *Memphis Daily Avalanche*, January 20, 1866; Jennie Chew Young to Louisa Wharton, January 16, 1866, Edward C. Wharton Papers, Louisiana and Lower Mississippi Valley Collection, Louisiana State University, Baton Rouge; *New Orleans Commercial Bulletin*, April 29, 1868.

45. Robert M. T. Hunter, *The Correspondence of Robert M. T. Hunter, 1826–1876*, ed. Charles Henry Ambler (Washington: American Historical Association, 1918), 353; *New Orleans Times*, June 24, 1865; *Memphis Appeal*, n.d., in *Little Rock (Ark.) Daily Gazette*, April 19, 1866.

46. *Richmond Whig*, September 19, 1865, May 16, 1873; *Raleigh (N.C.) Register*, November 12, 1867; Alexandria *Louisiana Democrat*, July 20, 1870.

47. *Rome (Ga.) Courier*, n.d., in (Macon) *Georgia Weekly Telegraph*, September 13, 1867; Memphis *Public Ledger*, April 25, 1866, February 11, 1871; *Charleston Courier, Tri-Weekly*, March 3, 1868; *Galveston (Tex.) Daily News*, October 31, 1868; *Edgefield (S.C.) Advertiser*, September 9, 1868.

48. *Galveston (Tex.) Weekly News*, December 27, 1865; (Macon) *Georgia Weekly Telegraph*, May 28, 1866; *New Orleans Commercial Bulletin*, July 13, 1868; *New Orleans Bulletin*, n.d., in *Hinds County (Raymond, Miss.) Gazette*, November 8, 1867.

49. *Richmond Whig*, June 26, 1866.

50. *Memphis Public Ledger*, December 17, 1866; *Richmond Whig*, March 27, August 3, November 23, 1866, March 5, 1867; Augusta Jane Evans Wilson, *A Southern Woman of Letters: The Correspondence of Augusta Jane Evans Wilson*, ed. Rebecca Grant Sexton (Columbia: University of South Carolina Press, 2002), 138; *Richmond Daily Dispatch*, August 21, 1866; (Macon) *Georgia Weekly Telegraph*, April 30, 1866; *Mobile Register*, August 13, 1870.

51. Randolph Abbott Shotwell, *The Papers of Randolph Abbott Shotwell*, ed. J. G. de Roulhac Hamilton, 3 vols. (Raleigh: North Carolina Historical Commission, 1929–1936), 2:201–2; *Mem-*

phis *Daily Avalanche*, March 9, 1866; *Staunton (Va.) Spectator*, September 18, 1866; New Orleans *Daily Picayune*, October 3, 1866; (Columbia, S.C.) *Daily Phoenix*, August 30, 1866, January 12, 1868.

52. W. W. Boyce, "State of the Country," *DeBow's Review*, After the War Series 1 (February 1866): 139–40; William W. Hooper to James Buchanan, February 9, 1866, Buchanan Papers, Historical Society of Pennsylvania; (Macon) *Georgia Weekly Telegraph*, April 24, August 21, 1868; *Savannah (Ga.) Daily Morning News*, September 14, 1875.

53. *Raleigh (N.C.) Daily Sentinel*, February 24, July 13, 1869; *Memphis Daily Appeal*, January 13, 1867; Wilson, *A Southern Woman of Letters*, 138; *Augusta (Ga.) Daily Constitutionalist*, June 28, 1868; *Charleston Mercury*, March 16, 1868; Virginia Mason, *The Public Life and Diplomatic Correspondence of James M. Mason* (New York: Neale, 1906), 584; Alexander W. Campbell to William B. Campbell, October 30, 1866, Campbell Family Papers, Rubenstein Rare Book and Manuscript Library, Duke University; *Mobile (Ala.) Register*, September 19, 1869.

54. *Keowee (Pickens Court House, S.C.) Courier*, July 21, 1866; Emily V. Mason, ed., *Southern Poems of the War* (Baltimore: John Murphy, 1867), 385–86; *Dallas (Tex.) Herald*, September 26, 1868; *Mobile Register*, March 29, 1870.

55. New Orleans *Daily Picayune*, April 18, 1868; (Macon) *Georgia Weekly Telegraph*, April 26, 1867, March 6, 1868; Alexandria *Louisiana Democrat*, September 30, 1874; *Little Rock (Ark.) Daily Republican*, July 10, 1872; Hill, *Benjamin H. Hill*, 738. For an argument that southerners had been weak-kneed in their resistance to congressional reconstruction measures, see *Atlanta Constitution*, July 28, 1868.

56. *Memphis Daily Appeal*, September 24, 1867; *Petersburg Index*, February 19, 1868.

57. *Memphis Daily Appeal*, January 5, 1868; *House Miscellaneous Document* 45, 44th Congress, 2nd Session, 1002. This congressional investigation of Mississippi affairs in the mid-1870s contains other similar examples of diatribes against northern civilization.

58. *Montgomery Advertiser*, May 29, 1907, p. 1. Thanks to John Hall for supplying a copy of the article.

59. Walter Brian Cisco, *War Crimes against Southern Civilians* (Gretna, La.: Pelican Publishing, 2007), 16–17. Note also the overwhelmingly positive comments for Cisco's book on Amazon.com.

60. Conversation with the author, October 4, 2011, Birmingham, Alabama; William Faulkner, *Requiem for a Nun* (New York: Vintage Books, 2011), 73.

A Note on Sources

The notes in this volume obviate the need for a full bibliography, but more general comments on sources are in order. In some ways, the material available for a study of how Confederates defined their Yankee enemies is nearly endless, cropping up in everything from cartoons to poems, songs, editorials, letters, and diaries. Of course many southerners for whatever reason had little or nothing to say about the "enemy," while others appeared unable to stop talking about the Yankees.

The approach here has been to look at a wide array of sources. My reading of Civil War–era newspapers dates back to the 1970s, but the digital revolution has greatly expanded the available source base and allowed for complex searches that often proved revealing. Denunciations of the enemy were remarkably consistent, whatever an editor's particular views of the Confederate administration or of the state political situation. As noted in the text, there was some change over time on certain subjects, but a careful reader of the notes will soon see how many standard themes appeared during the antebellum decades, persisted throughout the war, and proved remarkably enduring. For southerners generally, much of their information came from newspapers whose articles became subjects for discussion in families, on street corners, and in army camps. Soldiers' and civilians' comments on newspaper reports and rumors—even when people questioned their reliability—demonstrate the importance of the press as an imperfect but important reflection of wider public sentiments. Indeed, the whole topic of the Civil War–era press deserves much more study.

The *Southern Illustrated News* and *Southern Punch* were hardly masterpieces of graphic art, but both publications offered some significant anti-Yankee illustrations. Periodical and pamphlet literature, including sermons, presented some of the more sophisticated critiques of northern civilization but surely reached a much smaller audience than the newspapers.

Jefferson Davis's messages, proclamations, and speeches represent the most important official source for statements about the enemy. But similar documents produced by state governors are also quite revealing. Some of this material appears, of course, in the *Official Records* along with some significant orders and other documents from Confederate officers. Again it is worth noting that newspapers often reprinted a good deal of this official material.

Previous studies such as Jason Phillips's superb chapter in *Diehard Rebels* have mined soldier comments on the Yankees in both manuscript and published collections. I too have found such sources to be vitally important, especially when linked to statements by politicians, editors, and civilians more generally. The manuscript sources are vast, but there are also a formidable array of published diaries and letter collections, with more appearing all the time. In this regard, carefully edited volumes from university presses were obviously very useful, but so were more haphazardly produced ones from small publishers. In the latter case, some labors of love produced much for the researcher to love.

The explosion of interest in social and women's history over the past several decades has produced a vast outpouring of edited, published sources from southern civilians. There is of course still much unpublished and valuable manuscript material, but we are now blessed with an abundance of printed works. And as with soldier accounts, the publication of civilian sources shows no signs of letting up.

Taken altogether, these primary sources—along with a fair number of secondary works cited in the notes—formed a rich foundation for this study. In fact, so rich that a historian might easily spend a good many years cataloging, studying, and analyzing Confederate statements and comments about their erstwhile foes. For that reason alone, and not to mention all the colorful language that one regularly encounters along the way, I never tired of the research for *Damn Yankees!* even as I recognized that much more work could still be done.

Index